1603

Also by Christopher Lee

NON FICTION
A History of the English-speaking Peoples (Ed.)
Seychelles – Political Castaways
From the Sea End
Nicely Nurdled Sir
War in Space
Through the Covers (Ed.)
The Final Decade
This Sceptred Isle
This Sceptred Isle – the 20th Century
This Sceptred Isle – The Dynasties
Eight Bells and Top Masts

FICTION
The Madrigal
The Bath Detective
The Killing of Sally Keemer
The Killing of Cinderella
The House

1603

A Turning Point in British History

Christopher Lee

review

First published in 2003
by REVIEW

An imprint of Headline Book Publishing

10 9 8 7 6 5 4 3 2

Endpapers: *front* Elizabeth I's funeral procession (Bridgeman Art Library)
back James I's coronation (The Art Archive)

Cataloguing in Publication Data is available from the British Library
ISBN 0 7472 3408 6

Printed and bound in Great Britain by
Mackays of Chatham plc, Chatham, Kent

Typeset in Sabon by Palimpsest Book Production Limited,
Polmont, Stirlingshire

Headline Book Publishing
A division of Hodder Headline
338 Euston Road
London NW1 3BH

www.reviewbooks.co.uk
www.hodderheadline.com

For Charlie

CONTENTS

AUTHOR'S NOTE

DATES ARE NOT ALWAYS WHEN THEY SEEM TO BE. Until 1752 the dating of years in England was not as we understand it today. New Year's Day was 25 March. So, in 1603 it was still the rule to date the year not from 1 January, but from Lady Day: 25 March. Therefore, in Elizabethan dating, January, February and much of March would still be in what we think of as the previous year. We would say that Elizabeth I died on 24 March 1603, whereas Tudor dating would have it as 24 March, the final day of 1602. Thus we have to remember this dating difference – often noted by the words Old Style (or O.S.) or New Style (or N.S.) after ambiguous dates – when drawing together some of the records of the first three months of 1603 because they are generally dated 1602 in England.

In the text where I am quoting from primary sources I have, as far as possible, kept to the original, unless a direct transcription would be confusing to follow. Therefore, to some not used to Elizabethan script, the spellings may seem odd. I have transcribed the original in many places simply to let everyone see how words were used and spelled. I think this is fun as well as historically interesting. We do not change Shakespeare's text, because with a little listening it is clear – unlike, say, an earlier writer such as Chaucer who can be confusing in his form of language. So to read late sixteenth- and early seventeenth-century texts more or less as they were written lets us into the atmosphere of the period whereas a modern English version does not always do so. For example, in Elizabethan English we do not find apostrophes. Thus, *Elizabeth's* is written as *Elizabeths*. Many words end in *ie*, which vowels were later dropped: *Majesty* is written *Majestie*. Others seem to be obvious spelling mistakes, but are not. For example *be* is *bee* and *qu* is sometimes seen in northern orthography where we would expect a *w*. Where we would split into two words, in 1603 one was sufficient: for example, we would write *as well*, but an early seventeenth-century document might read *aswell*. Enthusiasts for Ye Olde Tea Shoppe will feel at home.

By using the original text, we can also spot word and spelling origins. Our modern word *only* is in fact *one-ly*. *Than* could be written as *then*; so on page 188 we find, 'The pestilence is nothing else *then* a rotten . . . fever.' I wonder if we hear the word spoken in an accent that we recognise and, if so, then begin to have an idea of what people sounded like when they spoke. It makes sense when laid out but has no academic importance. After all, if we took it to modern extremes of, say, perceptions of Sloane accents, then we might hear a rock band described as Railing Staines. The principle of reading how people, or some people, spoke is not dissimilar. Also, it gives those who moan about the fashion for using American spellings in England something to think about when they see that an American dictionary would have a lot in common with a Tudor or early Stuart lexicon. For example, *honour* in 'our' English is *honor* in modern American English *and* in Tudor English. We also find differences in transliteration. A West Country dialect would not be written necessarily in a common form with, say, a Court dialect. Certainly it was the case with the letters between James and Elizabeth that we see, for want of better terms, the Scottish and English spellings. This should not be surprising; James was writing in 'Scotch', a dialect that was, in some cases, a different form. A linguistician might tell us if this was the reason that James seemed an accomplished poet in Scottish as well as Latin, but found certain difficulty in writing as competently in English.

There is a further difference in the scripts of these primary sources; we should not neglect mistakes. Because a document is preserved in some modern academic form and environment does not mean that a word might *not* be misspelled. Indeed, a document may have two or even three spellings of the same word. The obvious example would be that *hart* (the animal) appears ten lines down as *harte* and even as *heart* (the organ). A simple uncorrected mistake and nothing more. At the same time, it is true that style was fast changing and fashion compelling. A writer in, say, 1598 may indeed use a variation of the same word by 1603. Just think today how many 'new' words appear in our vocabulary and even spellings – as anyone who has grumbled over *Frying Tonite* signs would confirm. Most of all, towards the end of a long document, the inclination to alter and correct was tempered. Preparing even a Royal Proclamation, never mind a pamphlet, could be a difficult task often without wise and learned copy-editors in sight. Also, clerks were instructed in a style of handwriting and sometimes spelling peculiar to their departments. Considering the gulf between early seventeenth-century printers and modern high-tech newspaper processes complete with spell-checkers and the ability to cut and paste corrections, it may just be that the scribes, editors and printers of 1603 set a standard which many twenty-first-century practitioners have not much bettered.

Many have made this book a pleasure to write. Andrew Parsons presented me with a chronology of and references for major events of the year; the staffs of many libraries and archives throughout the British Isles were always keen to find the smallest item; day after day, working in the Rare Books and Music Reading Room of the British Library confirmed to me what a tremendous bunch of people are behind that long L-shaped desk – ever helpful and cheerful, particularly patient. Jennifer Speake copy-edited the manuscript with enormous tact and learning, and the book is better for her questioning. Celia Kent combined humour, patience and firmness as good editors do. Finally who could do without a Mary Shoesmith? I had the original, who typed, retyped and typed again, and who was so pleased when the computer's spell-check gave up under the weight of Tudor spellings and she could assume complete command and control of the desk-top. With all this enthusiasm, it would be surprising to find any error or wrong interpretation with such a team behind one. If there are mistakes, we all know whom to blame.

1

PANORAMA

This is the story of the year 1603. It is therefore the tale of one of the great step changes in the history of these islands. Noted historians, for example G. R. Elton,* thought 1603 unimportant. Yet the events of any twelve-month period are rarely unimportant, although it is true that there are not that many dates that should stand out in our minds. One certainly is 1066 and the Norman invasion. Another might be 1642, the year which was the beginning of a terribly sad period in our island history, a period which as children we thought a great adventure when, rather like Cowboys and Indians, we chose sides to play Roundheads and Cavaliers. Yet another date might be 1688, the moment when the aristocracy caused the overthrow of the monarch, James II, and replaced him with his son-in-law and daughter, William of Orange and his queen, Mary. From that moment there would be no question that the English monarchy should be Protestant until such time as religion no longer mattered, a point still not fully reached. Others

---

* See G. R. Elton, *England under the Tudors* (Oxford University Press, 1955).

might choose 1805 when the Battle of Trafalgar made certain Britannia could rule the waves for more than a century. Or 1815 and the Battle of Waterloo, which finally did for Napoleon and brought about a sort of peace throughout Europe, especially in these islands, for ninety-nine years. Finally, the modern historian might remind us of 1940, the so-called dark days when the skills and bravery of a few prevented a German invasion of the United Kingdom. Each of these dates might well be remembered. Then why 1603? Could the Eltons be right? I think not. Transition from one dynasty to another should not go unremarked.

Our view of 1603 starts in its late winter when in the bedraggled early hours of 24 March, Elizabeth I turned her face to the wall. Sir Robert Carey, whom she called Robin and cousin, almost before the oils had been returned to their casket, rode north. At his breast he kept a sapphire ring, the sign that James would believe, that the Queen was dead. In three days he had crossed the border and with the pre-arranged authority of that single blue stone summoned James VI to the throne of England and of what James would be the first to call Great Britain. As news of the Queen's death spread, bonfires were lit throughout the land. Beacons of news? Or celebration? Could it be that the people actually cheered the passing of the daughter of Henry VIII and Anne Boleyn? This monarch, with but the body of a woman, surely was mourned. Maybe not so much as we conventionally think. Was it simply, in 1603, time to go? Just as her cold body was abandoned for days 'and mean persons had access to it', so her people easily shook the Elizabethan cloak from their often hungry shoulders. As gentlemen officers of her household snapped their white staffs of office and tossed them down onto her coffin, the bonfires were re-lit for a new monarch as much as to symbolise the passing of a prince incomparable.

It is said that with the passing in 1603 of the last of the Tudors came the end of mediaevalism. Could that really be so? 'Mediaeval' is not a word that would have been used during Elizabeth's reign, or for many years afterwards. It is an invention of the Victorian era –

as so much apparently ancient tradition and expression turns out to be on closer examination. The Victorians (and most people today) imagined that the Middle Ages of English history had ended a hundred years earlier. Yet only dynasties end on time and to date. Periods and influences rarely harmonise with set times and their effects mope among the people long after the historians decide they were done. So the ways of mediaeval England persisted beyond a Tudor and the Constitution longer still.

Now in 1603 the often cataclysmic time of the Stuarts had come. James left Scotland to claim his throne through his great-grandmother, Margaret Tudor, the daughter of Henry VII. His mother, of course, was Mary Queen of Scots, his father Henry Stewart (or Stuart), Lord Darnley – a genetic and chemical mix that could never produce an ordinary offspring. Nor did it. As he drove south into England he preached his gospel. It was not the taut catechism of the Calvinism he had thankfully left behind, but his own gospel of absolute obedience to the fatherly monarch and in particular to him, James VI of Scotland, James I of England. Had not they read His Majesty's *Trew Law of Free Monarchies*? No? They would. It was quickly published in London.* Nevertheless, he and all those who ruled England were to learn that Elizabeth may have commanded the obedience of the people, but James would not – and nor would any sovereign who followed.

A new monarchy is never a dull moment in British history, and 1603 must be known for more than the accession of the Stuarts. It was the year of another epidemic of the often-returning Black Death. Close to 40,000 perished in England, a kingdom of more than four million, 210,000 or so of whom lived in that woeful principality that was London. The capital was about the size of modern Norwich and growing so quickly that James bemoaned that 'soon London would be all England'. More people died in the capital than were

---

* *Trew Law of Free Monarchies* or *The Reciprock and Mutuall Dutie Betwixt a Free king and his Naturall Subjects* (1598; reprinted 1603).

born in it, and London's lasting monument was, appropriately, not a palace, but a fortress – the Tower of London, started by William the Conqueror and in which, in 1603, Sir Walter Ralegh was incarcerated, 'guilty' of high treason (see page 269).

At the very time Ralegh was locked up, John Smith was freed. Smith was an Englishman who had been taken as a slave in the eastern Mediterranean. White slaves were not uncommon long before black slaves were brought to England – after all, feudalism was of recent times in these islands. Smith told his dramatic tale: he had killed his master in the Black Sea and escaped home to England.

Also returning was James Lancaster. Three years earlier Elizabeth had approved the charter to set up the English East India Company. Now, Lancaster returned to the London docks with the Company's first pepper cargo. The new spice route was established.

And just as all England was changing, so too was another and more mysterious society. In 1603, in Japan, began the Tokugawa shogunate. Here was the dynasty that would lead Japan to an, until then, alien era of industry. It would survive beyond the middle years of the nineteenth century. Our images of 'old' Japan begin here in 1603. The first task of the shogunate was to introduce money, to move the peoples of Hokkaido, Honshu and Kyushu from a simple rice economy to a money economy. Incidentally, this was also the year when the kabuki theatre opened.

Across a much shorter stretch of water, the war in Ireland had gone well in 1603. This was the year of the submission of Hugh O'Neill, the Earl of Tyrone. Elizabeth saw this would be possible, just a month before her death. This would be her final triumph. Yet she would die at the moment Tyrone accepted that he should surrender. She would never see Tyrone's submission. He did not know she was dead when he surrendered to her.

In London the Fortune Theatre was now open, although Shakespeare scribbled furiously on the South Bank of the river and in that year was finishing *Othello*, the third of his great tragedies which were performed at the Globe* and probably made that theatre famous. In 1603 James took over the Shakespearean company, the Lord Chamberlain's Company, and it became known as the King's Men.† The more elevated members of the company were appointed Grooms of the Royal Chamber. Dekker presented his masque, *The Magnificent Entertainment*, to James's court – was this the first Royal Command Performance?

And what of ordinary living at the start of this, the seventeenth century? Many were hungry. The population of England had almost doubled in a century but the rate of growth was now accelerating faster than ever, and the farmers and tenants could not cope. Too many mouths to feed. Too many bellies groaned. In 1603 there were no miracles of chemistry and technology that could fertilise and till the land for this growing population. Even though there was a new monarch, even a new dynasty, farmers still farmed and herdsmen still herded as much as they had always done. They could grow not a bushel more. So, 300 per cent inflation. Simple economic rules of supply and demand were alive in the opening years of the seventeenth century across the land and not, as had been, just in specific pockets and parcels. There was plenty of money about, but, as ever, not many people had it.

In 1603 there were two sorts of coinage: angels and crown gold. The angel had been in circulation since the 1400s and got its name because on one side was an engraving of the Archangel Michael, along with a dragon. Three years earlier, in 1600, Elizabeth had ordered her Master of the Mint to produce a gold standard for these coins. Each gold coin would weigh precisely twenty-three carats and three and a half grains. The biggest coin would be an angel which at various times was worth roughly what we would call

---

* The Globe Theatre opened in the spring of 1599.
† *Othello* was probably performed the following year. The seven tragedies were *Julius Caesar, Hamlet, Othello, King Lear, Macbeth, Antony and Cleopatra* and *Coriolanus.*

between thirty-three and fifty pence. There were also half-angels and quarter-angels. There was, too, another coin. This was less pure weight, just twenty-two carats. There would be twenty-shilling pieces (we would have called them pounds), ten-shilling pieces and five-shilling pieces. This currency was called crown gold. A crown, and eventually the half-crown (a silver-based coin), was in circulation until the second half of the twentieth century. It was not until the following year, 1604, that new pieces of gold were coined and that was because James wanted to follow a uniform gold standard with some of the continental European countries. There was, too, a restriction on how much of this gold coinage could be taken out of the country. No one was allowed to 'carry more money about him out of the kingdome then will serve for the expenses of his journie (namely, about twentie poundes sterling)'.

Talk of gold and foreign travel was of not much interest to many people in early seventeenth-century England, Scotland and Wales. Many of the poor were trapped by circumstances and geography. Distance was daunting. There had also been attempts to standardise the measurement of distance. Here was the origin of a country mile. In some places in England miles were longer than in others. A Kentish mile was held to be longer than most. In the Border countries and in Scotland, where a track wandered across small mountains and 'unbeaten waies', a mile at the very least seemed longer and certainly took more time to cover. Continental Europeans had different measurements, as they still do; for example, an English mile would have made approximately one and a half miles' distance in Italy.

However speedily miles could be covered and gold carried, the north/south divide that even the Romans had recognised still existed. In the south there was a fruitful and bountiful land. Beyond the ridges of the Midlands there was a different story to be told among the labourers. The north and west could barely gather a decent harvest. In the southeast there was, just as there had been since the time of the Iron Age tribe of the Cantiaci, great and nourishing abundance. Here was fertile land – and cause for the Levellers, four decades later.*

So in 1603 as in 2003, ambitions and shortages conspired. For example, as the migration to the cities continued so did the ease at which the speculators responded. The Earls of Bedford and Clare developed Covent Garden and Drury Lane to make great sums from seemingly ever-spiralling rents.

And what of the Church? Did it preach against poverty or on its behalf? It preached its own interest. Less than fifty years earlier the Church had been established in law. In law it was beholden to Parliament and therefore the monarch. When, in 1603, a new monarch – whose views spiritual were as aggressive as his views temporal – eyed his bishops, they were confident enough to chant the Bancroft† decree that their spiritual powers were derived *jure divino*. What of the Puritans? 'Brain sick', said the King. But much to the bishops' consternation, James in 1603 agreed to listen to the Puritans' Millenary Petition (see page 235).

A modern concept of the Puritan is too often a person in black suiting with a big white round collar and a severe expression. So-called Puritanism is very difficult to define. Quite often we would find that many in the Church – clergy and followers – had what we would call Puritan beliefs, but would not be classified as Puritans. It would not be inaccurate to suppose that the Protestants, including the ministers throughout James's reign, carried with them much of the baggage of Puritanism.

Thus religious thought at this period, once we set aside a still large number of devout Catholics, is best based on Protestant belief. That, as the Anglican Church is today, was fundamental to the belief that Jesus Christ died to save sinners. Once this Protestant belief is

---

* The Levellers were non-conformist radicals supported by the other ranks of the New Model Army. Their leader was John Lilburne (*c.* 1614–57).
† Richard Bancroft (1544–1610); Elizabeth's Bishop of London (1597) and Archbishop of Canterbury (1604).

widespread (and naturally it pre-dated our period) then the position of the closed orders of friars and monks, while admirable, was irrelevant to daily worship. There was too good ground for those who demonstrated that many ministers of the Church were vulnerable to accusations of poor preaching, unsympathetic parochial guidance and the cause, if not the promotion, of Church schism. The very act of still being against Catholicism was enough to emphasise difference in doctrine and, importantly, explanation of seemingly everyday occurrence, for example, sorcery (see page 245).

Here was wonderful, wicked and spiteful farce and melodrama. The Jesuits? They would have to go. And the forty thousand lay Catholics? James was full of assurances. Not a hair would be harmed, he told their leader, the Earl of Northampton. Yet to Cecil: 'I would be sorry by the sword to diminish their number, but I would also be loth that, to great connivance and oversight given unto them, their numbers should so increase ... as, by continual multiplication, they might at last become masters.' Thus, from the patron of the great King James's Version of the Bible, an encyclical, the sense of which would echo for three centuries and be the root cause of royal downfall and bitter war.

But back to our people of 1603. Here was a time of new industry; even new words to go with it – *factory*, for example.* And just as the holy text was translated to be laid upon and read from all public lecterns (see page 234), the apothecaries gave English tongue to Latin texts, and so enabled people to look after their bodies and cure their simple ills. All this, much to the fright of the physicians, proved grubbily human.

1603 is the year in which these islands set themselves on a journey to regicide. It is the story of the uncommon as well as the common people: Elizabeth, James, Cecil, Catesby, Bancroft, Buckingham, Shakespeare, Whitgift, Egerton, Sackville, Home, Herbert, Coke,

* A *factory* was originally a place for traders with business abroad (factors), but was coming to mean a building in which goods were made.

Knollys. It is, too, the story of the Kentish yeoman, the Cumbrian stockman, the Border baillie, the Highland gillie and the Irish tenant. It is one year in England's history.

2

HOW WE GOT TO 1603

THE YEAR 1603 WAS THE MOMENT WHEN THAT HISTORICAL CALENDAR RECORDED THE END OF THE ELIZABETHAN AGE. The Tudors were dead. Long live the Stuarts. James VI of Scotland would claim the throne of England through his great-grandmother, Margaret, the daughter of Henry VII (reigned 1485–1509).

Therefore, we should really know something of the events which led to this year and in doing so we would find ourselves with a thumbnail sketch of the Tudors. Henry VII became the first Tudor king of England in 1485 after he landed in Wales from Brittany and marched to Leicestershire, where Richard III was killed on 22 August at the Battle of Bosworth Field. The Wars of the Roses* were over, and Tudor rule began once Henry had been crowned in October 1485.

The Tudors were to rule England for close on 117 years.

---

* The term 'Wars of the Roses' was coined by Sir Walter Scott and misleadingly applied to all the English civil wars of the period (1455–85) between the houses of York and Lancaster.

During that time there were only five monarchs: Henry VII himself, followed by Henry VIII (reigned 1509–47), Edward VI (reigned 1547–53), Mary I (reigned 1553–58) and, finally, Elizabeth I (reigned 1558–1603). These were unstable times in England and abroad and it is worth noting a few of their moments so that we can better understand the significance of the transition from Tudor to Stuart that was to come in 1603.

The Tudors came from Welsh stock although Henry VII was the son of Edmund Tudor, Earl of Richmond, and Margaret Beaufort. Edmund had been made an earl by his half-brother, the frankly half-witted Henry VI. Margaret Beaufort was the great-great-granddaughter of Edward III. He had been quite a different kettle of royal fish from Henry VI. Edward III had become king through the power-crazed antics of his mother, the scorned and revengeful Isabella, and her lover Roger de Mortimer. Isabella and Mortimer were responsible for the dreadful execution of Edward II at Berkeley Castle. Edward III eventually got control of his kingdom and had Mortimer executed and his mother isolated. Considering this less than quiet upbringing, it is remarkable that Edward III managed so cleverly to reconcile the differing factions in his country even though he led England, in 1337, into the Hundred Years War. The significance of dwelling on Edward III, apart from his reign of fifty years (1327–77), is that it was he who first claimed title to the French throne and called himself in 1340, 'King of France'. This title, even though it was nonsense, was assumed by his successors, including James I when he became king in 1603.

Let us return to Henry VII. Having slaughtered Richard III's army at Bosworth, he had married Elizabeth of York and so the warring houses of Lancaster and York were apparently reconciled – Henry VII was a Lancastrian. Having noted that, there was always a Yorkist plot ongoing against Henry's reign. Here was the connection also between the first Henry Tudor, King of England, and the first James Stuart, King of England. Henry VII brought about, in 1499, a peace agreement with Scotland. To seal that agreement, he married off his daughter Margaret to James IV of Scotland. That was in 1503. Exactly one hundred years later the great-grandson of Margaret and James IV was the James VI of Scotland who became James I of England. Henry VII arranged another marriage. An earlier truce and treaty, this time with Spain,* was sealed by marrying his elder son, Arthur, to Catherine of Aragon, daughter of Ferdinand and Isabella of Spain. However, Arthur died one year after the wedding, in 1502. In 1509 Henry VII died and because his eldest son had predeceased him, his second son succeeded him as King of England. This was Henry VIII. Catherine had not been abandoned and shortly after Henry became king he married his brother's widow.

Ironically, considering what was to follow, Catherine of Aragon had to have special permission from the Pope to marry Henry. The marriage survived twenty-four years. The great sadness was that only one of their children lived. She was Mary, who later became the rather strident Queen Mary I, known as Bloody Mary because of the number of Protestants executed during her five-year reign – from 1553 to 1558.

To grasp more easily the suspicions of religious groupings in 1603 when there were far more practising Catholics in England than many imagined, it is worth noting that it was Mary I who made clear that a Catholic revival when led by the monarch was very possible. Imagine the consternation when Mary became queen. England had settled to the idea of Protestantism. The Queen was a devout Catholic. Worse still for Protestant suspicions, in 1554 she married Emperor Charles V's son Philip, soon to become Philip II (reigned 1556–98) of Spain. Her marriage to Philip II meant that England was allied with Spain, and that is why England was drawn into the war with France in 1557. The following year, as a result of that war, England was driven from its last colony in continental Europe, Calais. Mary died that year. Philip of course

* Treaty of Medina del Campo, 1489.

13

was not in England, and the animosity between Spain and his wife's country grew.

It was the same Philip who thirty years later launched the Spanish Armada against England. Here were 130 Spanish galleons loaded with more than twenty thousand troops bent on invading England to support a Catholic rebellion against the Protestant Elizabeth I. The similarities between the ambitions of Philip II in 1588 and the collapse of those of Philip III of Spain by 1603 should not be ignored. Both were designed to support uprisings against the English throne. Coincidentally, in both cases the weather played an important part in their failures.

Henry VIII was king from 1509 to 1547. The first part of the reign was inevitably full of war. Rather like his daughter's marriage to Philip of Spain, Henry's marriage to Catherine of Aragon produced an ally in his father-in-law, Ferdinand. It was through him and that alliance that Henry VIII led England into war with France. This was the time of Cardinal Wolsey and the amazing occasion in 1520 known as the Field of the Cloth of Gold. This meeting was in June of that year, between Henry and the King of France, Francis I. It took place at Calais and got its name from the display of opulence, with each trying to outdo the other. For just a year England and France were supposed to be friends. Then Henry VIII switched allegiances and lined up with Emperor Charles V.

War is an expensive pastime for any nation. The Tudors had never been wealthy, and certainly by the late 1520s the state was probably bankrupt. This too was the period when Henry went through the double agonies of not having a male heir and also fancying a younger consort. In 1527 he tried to persuade Pope Clement VII to annul his marriage. The Pope said no, partly influenced by the fact that he was under the sway of Emperor Charles V, who was Catherine of Aragon's nephew. Here was the beginning of the famous stories of Henry VIII breaking with Rome, England becoming a Protestant nation, and Henry a serial husband.

Once more we should understand the feeling about Catholics and the Tudor connection with the England of 1603. It is too easy to say that the Church of England came about because Pope Clement would not do Henry's bidding. That may be the simple explanation. We should, however, not ignore anti-Catholic feeling throughout continental Europe, not only in England. Just as in 1603 when the shogun of Japan would ban Jesuits because he believed they were an arm of the Spanish empire and not just the Christian faith, so many of the English feared continental Roman Catholicism because it was so overtly tied to schemes to overthrow the monarch.

Whatever the reasoning, whether it be politics, religion or straightforward lust, in 1533 Catherine of Aragon became Princess Dowager and retired to live out the rest of her natural life – a bonus in those days. Henry married Anne Boleyn, the second of his wives and the mother of Elizabeth. As we know, Anne was executed in 1536 and Henry married Jane Seymour, by whom he had a son, Edward, who would become Edward VI in 1547 and reign for six years. Jane Seymour died, and in 1540, largely because Henry's secretary of state, Thomas Cromwell, wanted some formal arrangement with the Germans, Henry was persuaded to marry Anne of Cleves. Henry, who had never seen the woman before the marriage in 1540, took one look at her and was appalled at what he saw. They married in January and he divorced her in July, claiming that she was untouched and probably, in his opinion, untouchable. However, Anne did survive and died of natural causes seventeen years later – which was more than could be said for Thomas Cromwell who was executed for treason.

Henry then married Catherine Howard who was, to say the least, flighty. Her head flew off in 1542. His last wife was Catherine Parr, whom he married in 1543. She was a nice lady: twice married and widowed already, she was not that keen on a wedding to Henry VIII – and considering the record who could blame her? She was a quiet woman from the Lake District, a good stepmother, and quietly religious.

Henry VIII was dead by 1547, just four years after his marriage to Catherine Parr. In some ways he was a rumbustious king of fortune.

If his brother had not died, Henry would never have been king and might have become a priest. He was a not inconsiderable theologian in his early years. He was a bad steward, and when his young son succeeded him as Edward VI there was not much in the state coffers; but that was to be a characteristic of Tudor treasuries.

This next Tudor Edward VI was a scholar and only ten years old when he became king. Therefore, there had to be a regency which was, at the start of the reign, controlled by his uncle, Edward Seymour, who was later to become the Duke of Somerset. Regencies are all about power and its exercise. Inevitably this regency became factionalised, and two years after Edward's accession, the Earl of Warwick overthrew Seymour. The most memorable moment of Edward VI's brief reign was in 1549 with the publication of the Book of Common Prayer, a true expression of Protestant devotion and an exquisite document of the English language as well as the sad catalyst of rebellion, including that of Robert Ket in East Anglia. One tragedy of Edward VI's death in 1553 at the age of sixteen was the way in which Warwick (by now entitled Duke of Northumberland) had dominated him to the extent that the princesses, Mary and Elizabeth, were set aside from the succession. Such was Warwick's ambition that he persuaded Edward VI that he should be replaced on his death by Lady Jane Grey who was, of course, Warwick's own daughter-in-law. She was also the granddaughter of Henry VIII's sister, Mary, and there was therefore some dotted line to the succession. She had been married in 1553 to Lord Guildford Dudley, who was Northumberland's fourth son. Northumberland's idea was that if he could push Jane Grey's cause along that dotted line then, rather like the Saxon earl Godwine, who married off his daughter Edith to Edward the Confessor, he, Northumberland, would rule England. On 9 July 1553 Lady Jane Grey was proclaimed queen. She lasted nine days.

Mary Tudor's case was stronger and her supporters more powerful. Northumberland was overthrown and so too was Jane Grey. She might have survived as an innocent in this affair, but we have to remember that Mary was an uncompromising Catholic and Jane

Grey a devout Protestant. It was probably the events around Wyatt's rebellion in the opening weeks of 1554 that cost Jane Grey her life. Sir Thomas Wyatt led a revolt of, it is said, three thousand men from Kent. They were against the proposed marriage of Mary and Philip, and their intention was not to give the throne back to Jane Grey, but to the Princess Elizabeth. The rebellion was put down and Wyatt and dozens of his followers executed. Mary was now convinced that it was Jane Grey (and not Elizabeth) who would always be the icon of Protestant rebellion. She had Lady Jane's head chopped off.

It is not the place in this book to dwell much on the reign of Elizabeth other than to reflect that her background gave her a character as well as an intellect deeper than her recent predecessors, all of whom had one or other quality but never both together. Again, we need to grasp an idea of Elizabeth's background and circumstances if we are to understand the England that she left to her successor.

Elizabeth was formally illegitimate. Parliament declared as much in 1536. She could never have felt secure after her mother's execution. The thoroughness of her classical education in the hands of Roger Ascham, author of the revered work *Toxophilus* (1545), gave her a wit and understanding that were certainly comparable to Jane Grey's. Although she, and not Jane Grey, was the focus of Wyatt's rebellion, her half-sister went no further than putting her under what we would call house arrest, at Woodstock in 1554, after the formality of a brief imprisonment in the Tower. Four years later Elizabeth was declared queen and thus began almost half a century of a state consistently hard up but more or less at peace. The Spanish would never have agreed about this last point, but the English people rarely felt themselves threatened in any extraordinary way, and even the Armada gave the English confidence in their own stability, although few would have thought to light a candle to Thor and so give thanks to the real admiral of that triumph.

Between that momentous day in 1588 and the end of Elizabethan England, the outlines of some of the most exciting tales as well as the most literate ones in English history would be laid down.

When we look to the most influential men in Elizabeth's life, we should look beyond the likes of the Earl of Essex.* The really important people were her Christian viziers, for example Sir Francis Walsingham (1532–90). He was one of her principal secretaries of state and her spy-master. There was one, however, above even Walsingham. He was one of the most remarkable powerbrokers in English history and the first noted member of a remarkable family which would remain a significant influence in the governments of England for four centuries to come. His name was William Cecil. He was born in 1520 and when Elizabeth ascended the throne in 1558 one of her first acts was to make Cecil her principal secretary of state. With his brother-in-law Sir Nicholas Bacon (father of Francis Bacon) Cecil produced the Elizabethan Settlement in 1558 which re-created England as a strictly Protestant state as it had been under Edward VI. Although Bacon fell from favour, Cecil would be at Elizabeth's side for the rest of his life.

In 1603 Cecil's son, Robert, would wheel and deal the politics of the accession of James VI of Scotland and James I of England. So William Cecil manipulated the sixteenth-century politics, far more troubled than those his son would experience, that would lead to what he believed to be the rightful accession of the daughter of Henry VIII and Anne Boleyn. By the day of her coronation in 1558 Elizabeth had come to trust the thirty-eight-year-old Cecil explicitly. As first, or principal, secretary of state, his prime duty was to advise the Queen and administer her and the nation's domestic and foreign policy. No country, no matter how peacefully and quietly governed, could ever do without the crafting of treaties and agreements with other states, nations and alliances. The wrong signature – or even the right one for that matter – could have horrid consequences

* Robert Devereux, first Earl of Essex, for some time Elizabeth's favourite, opposed by many in the pay of William Cecil, defied Elizabeth's orders by returning from Ireland during his campaign against O'Neill, attempted a coup, was convicted of high treason, and was executed.

as military, commercial and religious influence shifted from the Iberian peninsula to the rim of eastern Europe. His perceptions of foreign policy, his instincts for the way power shifts might occur, and his understanding of the growing Puritan cause made him indeed wise counsel. It was Cecil whose influence on the Queen meant that England would come to the aid of the persecuted French Huguenots in the 1560s. It was Cecil who reassured the Dutch Calvinists twenty years later that Elizabeth would, if not exactly champion, then be sympathetic to their plight. She created him Baron Burghley in 1571 and a year later installed him as her Lord Treasurer – a sort of super-Chancellor of the Exchequer. Yet Cecil was not a *laissez-faire* civil servant. His eminence was clear in its black and white rather than grey stature. He reformed the ailing economic system. In his darker moments, it was very likely Cecil who finally persuaded Elizabeth to sign the death warrant of Mary Queen of Scots, in 1587. If there was one continuing difference between mistress and most loyal servant it was the question of marriage. Elizabeth stepped aside from all Cecil's persuasions that she should marry and provide an heir to continue the House of Tudor. Cecil's motives were uncomplicated; an established heir might provoke jealousies, but those ambitions were manageable and were as nothing compared with the instability possible under a monarch without a natural and obvious successor.

So, in 1558 Cecil took the administrative reins of Elizabeth's kingdom. It was the same year that Mary Queen of Scots married the French Dauphin, Francis – a short-lived affair and one which would lead ultimately to Mary's execution. The following year the reforms of Bloody Mary were set aside and Protestantism was formally reinstated as the established religious persuasion of the English, and that astonishingly political prelate, Matthew Parker, became Archbishop of Canterbury. (It was from this archbishop's system of prying into clerical affairs that we get the term Nosy Parker.)

Elizabeth had not come to a steady throne. How could she have done? Two years earlier war with the French had started, yet again, and in the year of her accession England had abandoned Calais to the French. However, in 1559 a peace of sorts was made with the French at Cateau-Cambrésis. It was a convenient peace. The Dauphin, Mary Queen of Scots' husband, had inherited and become Francis II, King of France. He was dead the following year. Mary was living at the French court. In Scotland, while England was making peace with France, the Scots were fighting among themselves over who, among the different Scottish factions, would reform the Church. The reformers had burned down the abbey church of Scone, and it was no coincidence that the uncompromising preacher John Knox had returned.

Knox (c. 1513–72) was a bewildering, single-minded character. He was priested into the Church of Rome in 1542, but four years later he was championing the Protestants. He was also an active rebel and what we might now call an anarchist. He was most certainly involved with the murder of the Archbishop of St Andrews, Cardinal David Beaton. Beaton was one of the leaders of pro-Catholic and French policy-making in Scotland. His literally fatal mistake was having George Wishart, the Scottish Protestant, burned as a heretic. Wishart was a close friend of Knox, who would be implicated, even by association, in the murder of the cardinal. Knox was captured and sent as a galley slave to the French. Little wonder that he despised Catholicism, turned to Protestant teachings, and when he went into exile in Geneva should be influenced by John Calvin.

It was the reformed Calvinist Church that was approved as part of the Treaty of Edinburgh in 1560 which ended the confrontations for the moment in Scotland. The following year saw the return of Mary Queen of Scots, now the Dowager Queen of France, but never able to get on with the woman who really ran the French court, Catherine de Medici. England would make its position very clear regarding Protestantism and in 1562 the French Protestants and the English met at Richmond to sign a treaty of co-operation and friendship. It was the same year that the French wars of religion started.

In 1563 the Church of England published the Thirty-Nine Articles of Religion. The following year the second Treaty of Troyes* brought to an end two years of English skirmishing in France and realistically any hopes the English might have had of holding on to Calais. England was at relative peace. There were few distractions other than the curiosity, in 1566, of pipe-smoking.

It was in this year that tobacco was brought from America for the first time to England. It was also the year that Mary Queen of Scots' personal adviser and secretary, David Rizzio, was murdered – dragged from Mary's chamber and stabbed to death at the instigation of her terrible and jealous husband, Lord Darnley. The following year, 1567, Darnley too was murdered, and Mary married her third husband, the fourth Earl of Bothwell. It was not a happy association. Bothwell was married at the time of Darnley's murder, dumped his wife to marry Mary, and although he was created Duke of Orkney it was not a road to any success. The constitutional set was against Queen Mary and she and her forces were defeated at what was hardly a battle, more an occasion, at Carberry Hill on 15 June 1567. The two sides had lined up, Mary and Bothwell on one and the usually called confederate lords, who were basically against the marriage of Mary and Bothwell, on the other. While both sides discussed the possibility of not having to fight, many of the troops on Mary and Bothwell's side wandered off. Mary was imprisoned. Bothwell, true to his nature, fled. He went to Orkney and from there to Denmark. He was thrown in prison and died there in 1578. After Carberry Hill, Mary was forced to abdicate and the infant Prince James became James VI, King of Scots.

---

* First Treaty of Troyes (May 1420) agreed the marriage of Henry V of England and Catherine Valois, daughter of Charles VI of France, and Henry's right to be heir to the French throne.

In 1568 Mary was allowed to escape and fled to England, where she was imprisoned. An apparently more peaceful exercise was taking place at Douai in France: the establishment of the English college by William Allen (1532–94). At first this may not seem particularly important. It most certainly was. Remember, by now England was fiercely Protestant. Allen was equally fiercely Roman Catholic. There was certainly no place for him in England and he had been in exile since 1565. The college in Douai was established for two reasons: first, it would be the training centre for Englishmen to become Roman Catholic priests; second, it would be the hub of religious propaganda. It was from the college that Cardinal Allen directed the translation of the Bible especially for Roman Catholics, the work known as the Reims-Douai Bible. He also supported Philip II of Spain and understood that if the Spanish Armada had succeeded in 1588 Philip would have appointed him Archbishop of Canterbury. The further importance of this college for our reading is that many of the Catholic tracts appearing around 1603 were written and printed at Douai, although by then Cardinal Allen was dead. The cardinal had trained the first Jesuit mission to England. That was in 1580. Elizabeth had hanged one of those Jesuits, Edmund Campion. Among his Jesuit friends on that mission was Robert Parsons (1547–1610).* Parsons went to live in Spain and became one of the major anti-Protestant agitators and pamphleteers of his time. With the death of Elizabeth and the arrival of James I, Parsons kept the college printing presses hot.

Elizabeth's rival as queen was not welcomed by Protestant England. But not everybody was Protestant. There were certainly many, perhaps a third of the nation, who leant towards Rome. There was a rebellion, albeit a short-lived one, in 1569. It was started because the very silly Duke of Norfolk, Thomas Howard, was particularly upset with the way in which the Cecil family ruled Elizabeth's court. When Howard's opposition (which also had a

* Sometimes known as Robert Persons.

lot to do with the fact that he wanted to marry Mary Queen of Scots) petered out, the rebellion was taken up by the powerful northern dynasties, the Nevilles and the Percys. Their demands were predictable: they wanted the restoration of the Catholic persuasion in England and Mary to be given back her Scottish throne. It is variously estimated that about eight hundred of the rebels were executed. It was all over by 1570, but not before Pope Pius V had excommunicated Elizabeth.

In 1571, with Parliament being called during that spring, the first of the anti-Catholic penal laws was passed. Thomas Howard was still making trouble and in 1572 had his head chopped off.* So did a number of Spaniards. Francis Drake was running riot through many of the Spanish overseas territories.

This period was not entirely given over to bloodshed and plotting. The year 1572, for example, was when the original Society of Antiquaries was founded. Sir Martin Frobisher was busy trying to discover a northwest passage to China; in 1576 he was charting around Baffin Land and Labrador. Elizabeth was even contemplating marriage – or so Cecil thought. Negotiations were taking place between her officials and those who would like to have one of the great French noble houses united with the English monarchy. The would-be consort of Elizabeth was the Duke of Alençon, but we know it came to nothing. Spenser was publishing his *Shepheardes Calender*. In 1580 Drake successfully completed his circumnavigation. Intrigue was nevertheless never far from the palace at Whitehall. Elizabeth's Court would always believe that an event in Spain, France and of course Scotland was of concern to the English throne, if not immediately then maybe one day. The Court rarely ignored the reasons behind, for example, the slicing of a head from a well-placed body. In 1581 Jamie Douglas, the Fourth Earl

---

* Howard, perhaps the richest noble in England, persisted in his suit for Mary Queen of Scots. Letters implicating him in a treasonable act were enough to convict him.

of Morton and regent of Scotland, was executed. And why not? He had been responsible for Rizzio's murder and was involved in that of Darnley.

In 1583 the so-called Throckmorton Plot was revealed with the generous help of the Tower's thumbscrew operator. Briefly, the Roman Catholic Francis Throckmorton (1554–84) had been involved in the planning of a Spanish-supported invasion of England by English exiles led by a Frenchman, the Duke of Guise. Mendoza, the Spanish ambassador, was sent packing and Throckmorton was executed. Within a couple of years another plot was uncovered. This was rather bold and uncompromising, and was put together by Anthony Babington (1561–86). Elizabeth was to be murdered, Mary Stuart was to be released, and yet another plan was drawn for a Spanish invasion. The details were sent by Babington to Mary. Babington and his friends were executed, Mary's complicity established – agonisingly so for Elizabeth – and the following year, 1587, Mary Queen of Scots was beheaded. A year after that, famously now, the Spanish Armada was dispersed in the Channel partly due to good English seamanship and mainly due to appalling weather conditions. It was, too, the same year that Marlowe published his *Doctor Faustus*. In 1590 the first books of Spenser's *Faerie Queene*, in honour of Elizabeth, were published, and across the Irish Sea Trinity College, Dublin was opened. This was a rich period in English literature. Over the next twenty years all Shakespeare's famous plays would appear and many of Ben Jonson's best plays would be performed.

There came, too, an important change in Elizabeth's Court. A new Cecil, Robert, became her secretary of state. It was this man who would secretly coax through the constitutional issues that needed settling so that there could be an orderly transition from Elizabeth to James of Scotland. Before that happened the old Cecil would die in 1598, Essex would fail in Ireland, defy Elizabeth's instructions and return to London, be freed, attempt (in 1601) his pathetic rebellion and be executed. In 1600 the East India Company would be incorporated by royal charter and the Spanish would make one great attempt to invade England by supporting the O'Neill rebellion in Ireland and landing in Kinsale.

That, then, is a sketch of the last of Tudor England as it settled into the winter of 1602 and 1603, tacitly waiting for the death of the second most famous virgin in history.

3

THE LEGACY

THE ELIZABETHAN AGE MAY HAVE BEEN IN FAST-FAILING HEALTH, BUT THIS WOULD NOT MEAN THAT THE DEATH OF THE MONARCH WOULD REMOVE ALL THE FIGURES FROM ITS TABLEAU. True, some had gone. Robert Devereux, Earl of Essex, had been put down in 1601. Yet the sentiment he expressed was not forgotten and probably lived in others. England's artistic heritage remained in good (and the same) hands. Shakespeare was rewriting *Hamlet*. Jonson and Dekker were planning their theatrical extravaganza, *The Magnificent Entertainment*. Hayward was sketching *The Sanctuarie of a troubled soule*.* Norden was busy with *A Pensive Soules Delight*.† Nicholas Breton wagged a finger at the world with his *A*

---

* Sir John Hayward's *The Sanctuarie of a troubled soule* was first published by H. Lownes for C. Burby in London in 1604. There were many editions with slightly varying titles and it was still being published as late as the nineteenth century.
† John Norden followed *A Pensive Mans Practise* (1584), his most famous work, with *A Pensive Soules Delight*.

Mad World My Masters.* Even, or perhaps more importantly, the gloom of poverty and pestilence was reflected in so much sermonising and writing. For example, Thomas Lodge, perhaps more famous for his *Wits Miserie and, The Worlds Madnesse: discovering the Devils Incarnat of this age* (1596), reflected on the darker event of 1603 with his *Treatise of the Plague.*

As the Queen's spirit wilted and her body confessed weakness, the old order looked on, some with passing interest, some with nervousness. Here were the likes of Cecil, Catesby, Bancroft, Buckingham, Shakespeare, Whitgift, Egerton, Sackville, Home, Herbert, Fortescue, Coke and, of course, he who had so much to lose and would, Ralegh. This was a parade of intellectual and political authority tiptoeing through the last and fading moments of Tudor history. No doors were slammed. All opportunities for betterment were left ajar.

For now, though, the Lady lived. Her commands were still obeyed. If indeed she were the last British monarch to command obedience from her people then, in spite of the temperamental occasions of her long reign, the people could at least say that they had been 'godly and quietly govourned'. The indifference of winter in those opening weeks reminds us that this was a spare society. The wealth of the Norfolks, the fineries of the Court, the gathered silks along the stout elm corridors of mansions were distractions for a people vulnerable to withering agriculture and inhospitable ways of living which never, for the so-called commoners, improved. The filmic image of a ruddy-faced England was at the least a detail from a much broader picture.

Diaries and notes are invariably selective. In the late sixteenth and

---

* Nicholas Breton's *A Merrie Dialogue betweixt the Taker and the Mistaker* was published for James Shaw in London in 1603 but is better known by its later title of *A Mad World My Masters.* His style of title was as amusing as his text. In 1602 he had published *Olde Mad-cappes new Gally-mawfrey. Made into a merrie mess of minglemangle out of three idle conceited humours following 1. I will not 2. Oh, the merrie time 3. Out – upon money.*

early seventeenth centuries the numbers who kept records tended to be few and, obviously, educated for or into a certain class of society. Envoys and ambassadors left copious records and reports, but their writings would generally reflect only one element of society: that which had power and influence and therefore interested their masters. Priests and ministers preaching and pamphleteering hardly set themselves out as social workers and observers of parish conditions. They would attack Catholicism or, if they were Puritans, excesses of the Established Church and ineptitude of the ministry. Why not? Patronage meant that a priest in 1603 might easily be a yeoman, a landlord, a draper or a wastrel. Moreover, good priests often had little scholarship. Therefore, the records of the time tend to be predictable. As we shall see, Thomas Dekker the writer would give arranged marriages as well as the iniquities of debt-collecting a good lambasting. Stubbes had already mocked painted ladies in the highest society. Shakespeare might easily reflect whimsical times in sight of Arden. Some travellers should catch our attention. One was Fynes Moryson, an undergraduate and later a fellow of Peterhouse College, Cambridge (the oldest of the Cambridge colleges). He decided that he would read civil law and then, in 1591, at the age of about twenty-five, he set out on a journey which took him through these islands and then across Europe as far as Turkey. He kept a meticulous record of his journey, describing the people and the lands – right down, for example, to a description of each shire and region.

Even Moryson could not give us the detail that we probably want. When, for example, he notes that in around 1603 Scotland does not have inns or public houses whereas England has a lot, this seems hardly credible, considering the reputation of that land of the North Briton. When he pauses in Berwick he leaves us with no impressions of the drinking habits there. But then, Moryson was not writing for us. His record was published in 1617, but it is very much a diary of the turn of the century and some of it centres on the years 1602, 1603 and 1604. If we look at just two entries, one for Scotland and one for England, we can certainly see the contrasts that he notes.

An Itinerary written by Fynes Moryson, gent. Containing his Ten Yeeres travelling through the twelve dominions of Germany, Bohmland, Sweitzerland, Netherland, Denmarke, Poland, Italy, Turky, France, England, Scotland and Ireland. Printed by John Beale dwelling in Aldergate street 1617

Scotland

They eate much red Colewort and Cabbage, but little fresh meate, using to salt their Mutton and Geese, which made me more wonder, that they used to eate Beefe without salting. The Gentlemen reckon their revenewes, not by rents or monie, but by chauldrons of victuals, and keepe many people in their Families, yet living most of Corne and Rootes, not spending any great quantity of Flesh. My self was at a Knights house, who had many servants to attend him, that brought in his meate with their heads covered with blew caps, the Table being more then halfe furnished with great platters of porredge, each having a peece of sodden meate; and when the Table was served, the servants did sit downe with us, but the upper messe in steede of porredge, had a Pullet with some prunes and broth. And I observed no Art of Cookery, or furniture of Houshold stuffe, but rather rude neglect of both though my selfe and my companion, sent from the governour of Barwicke [Berwick] about bordering affaires, were entertained after their best manner. The Scots living then in factions used to keepe many followers and so consumed their revenew of victuals, living in some want of money. They vulgarly eate harth Cakes of Oates, but in Cities have also wheaten bread, which for the most part was bought by Courtiers, Gentlemen and the best sort of Citisens. When I lived at Barwicke the Scots weekely upon the market day, obtained leave in writing of the Governour to buy Pease and Beanes, whereof as also of Wheate, their Merchants at this day send great quantity from London into Scotland.

They drink pure Wines, not with sugar as the English, yet at Feasts they put Comfits in the wine after the French manner . . . I never see nor heare that they have any publike Innes with signes hanging out, but the better sorte of Citisens brew Ale, their usuall drinke (which will distemper a strangers bodie) and the same Citisens will entertaine passengers upon acquaintance or entreaty. Their bedsteads were then like Cubbards in the wall, with doores to be opened and shut at pleasure, so as we climbed up to our beds. They used but one sheete, open at the sides and top, but close at the feete and so doubled.

England

The English are so naturally inclined to pleasure as there is no Countrie wherein the Gentlemen and Lords have so many and large parkes only reserved for their pleasure of hunting, or where all sorts of men a lot [sic] so much ground about their houses for pleasure of Gardens and orchards. The very Grapes, especially towards the south and west are of pleasant taste and I have said that in some counties as in Glostershire, they made wine of old, which no doubt many parts would yeeld at this day but that the inhabitants forebeare to plant vines aswell because they are served plentifully and at a good rate with French wines, as for that the hills most fit to beare Grapes, yeeld more commoditie by feeding of Sheepe and Cattell . . . England abounds in Cattell of all kinds and particularly hath very great Oxen, the flesh whereof is so tender, as no meate is more desired. The Cowes are also great with large udders, yielding plenty of Whitemeats, no part in the Worlde yeelding greater variety, nor better of that kind . . . for the point of drinking, the English at a Feast will drinke two or three healths in rememberance of specially friends, or respected or honoured persons . . . in generall the greater and better part of the English hold all excesse blameworthy and drunkenesse a reproachfull vice. Clownes and vulgar men only use large drinking of Beere or Ale, how much soever it is esteemed excellent drink even among strangers, but Gentlemen garrawse [carouse] only in wine, with which many mix sugar, which I never observed in any other place or Kingdom . . . and because the taste of the English is delighted with sweetenesse, the wines in Tavernes (for I speake not of Merchants or Gentlemens Cellars) delight in sweeteenesse hath made the use of Corands of Corinth so frequent in all places, and with all persons in England, as the very Greekes that sell them, wonder what we do with such quantities thereof, and not know how we should spend them, except we use them for dying, or to feede Hogges.

Moryson paints a picture of a crude society. The imagined sight of Scottish gentry with bowls of porridge on their tables, even on special occasions, leaves little reason to wonder why James and his Court were so eager to hurry south where the reputation was for a much finer and more comfortable way of life. We know from Moryson that across the Continent of Europe almost no nation had a higher reputation for enjoyment than the English. Even taking into account stories of arranged marriages and their treatment as drudges, it does seem that English womanhood by and large had the best of it and certainly more freedoms than, say, their Spanish continental cousins. Yet this was no merrie England. In certain parts of the country people died no more painfully than they lived. In certain cities the death rate was higher than the birth rate. Our breath may be caught by the numbers of people who died from disease, especially the plague, but it was no less true that in 1603 many in England were starving to death. We also have a view that other than those who lived in London, the vast majority of people were yokels. This again is an image best left for the jigsaw puzzle. About half the country was involved in farming. There were three groups, or four if you include the great landowners within the aristocracy. The three categories of working farmer were gentlemen, yeomen and husbandmen.

Obviously the size of a farm did not necessarily indicate its importance. The significance of the holding was whether it was good, bad or indifferent land. As a rough indicator, a gentleman farmed some three hundred acres and might have had such a standing that he would have been granted his coat of arms. A yeoman might farm up to two hundred acres depending on which area of the country he lived in. The husbandman might farm anything between ten and eighty acres. These descriptions – gentlemen, yeomen and husbandmen – were used as social distinctions, and who and who was not a gentleman or a yeoman or a husbandman was important. For example, even though a yeoman was not such a big farmer, if he were a rich one he would not necessarily have much less local social status than a gentleman. There were, too, tenants who had their lands by right and custom, and they were called customary tenants. In 1603 their status changed because England now had a Scottish king. How could this be? Until 1603 they had been protected against unreasonable costs of entry rights into their contracts – a sort of farming key money. In 1603 they could no longer claim this right because, now the Scots and English were ruled by the same king, there was no longer an obligation to provide militia service on the Borders with the Scots. Until 1603 tenants could be called out in the same way as the Saxon *fyrd* had been in earlier centuries. Now, thanks to the new harmony of the joint nations (although full union with Scotland was still more than a century away), their tenancies were less protected. At the lowest end of the scale, of tilling, were those who had their own cottages. A 1598 Act of Parliament said that cottages should be allowed four acres. The generosity of the legislation was not reflected in the deed of its enactment. By 1603 not many more than six hundred had their four acres. Most were lucky to have one.

Although perhaps only half the country was involved in farming, many other industries relied upon it for raw materials and also for workforce. A farmhand might easily work on the land and in a cottage industry or even a building in which all the people were making the same thing. They were, as we would say, manufacturing, and it is from about this time that the word 'factory' came into use in the way in which we understand it today. Now, in 1603, leatherworkers, for example, were gathered together under one roof. With the arrival of James I and his determination to end the war with Spain, the cloth industry found new markets abroad. There were also finer clothmakers arriving in England, who could teach the English weavers to make more than heavy broadcloths. Protestants escaping persecution on the Continent had settled in centres such as Norwich. With them came the skills to produce finer materials. The other industries that were developing, although not spectacularly in 1603, included coalmining – exclusively open cast. With the huge demand for coal, particularly in London, there followed a sturdy market for the shipbuilding industry which was building on the Tyne as many shallow-draughted colliers as it could. Both the shipbuilding and the coal industries were to accelerate rapidly towards the end of the century. About 17,000 tons of iron were produced in 1603, although it was not too profitable an industry, largely because it was cheaper to import iron from Sweden.

Another image that does not always stand close examination is that of tiny villages and hamlets where a labourer would live man and boy and never think to move beyond the parish boundary. Work done by the Cambridge Group for the History of Population and Social Structure in 1981 suggests that there was more mobility of population than might be imagined. Parish records which show new family names or missing old names suggest that people moved from one village to another on a regular basis. Given the high unemployment on the land, it was hardly surprising in terms of looking for work, but perhaps surprising when we consider the cost of moving about, with poor transport, little money for expenses, and limited parish support.

It is also true that young people left home much earlier than we might imagine. In this period the average household was between four and five people. Teenagers left home probably earlier than they do in the twenty-first century. The reasons, again, are obvious. They left home to work. The men also married later – although some girls as young as eight or nine were forced into arranged marriages. In 1603 the average male probably did not marry until his late twenties. A large percentage never married. The Cambridge group noticed in parish records that, for example, in the parish of Ealing 25 per cent of women over forty appeared to be unmarried. We do not know if they were widows. In 1603 the life expectancy was thirty-two. Almost a third of the population of 4.2 million was under the age of fifteen. Men married late; women did not. A woman might well be pregnant when she married, but in this period marriage was often seen as dating from the day of betrothal. Therefore, illegitimate births were low.

Even by the start of the Stuart Age there remained a mediaeval aspect of betrothal and marriage. Arranged marriages were quite common and for the most part acceptable among often anxious, forlorn and hard-up people. The moralist and probably the victims could not tolerate the idea of selling off daughters – which is how we today would see this practice. We should not, however, feel alone in our indignation. Writing at the time, Thomas Dekker railed against the practice, particularly in his long pamphlet, *The Seven Deadly Sinnes of London.*

The Seven Deadly Sinnes of London: Drawne in Seven Severall coaches through the seven severall gates of the Cittie, bringing the plague with them,
Printed by EA for Nathaniel Butter and are to be solde at his shop neere Saint Austens Gate 1606

Crueltie is a large tree and you all stand under it: you are cruell in compelling your children (for wealth) to goe into loathed beds, for thereby you make them bond slaves. What ploughman is so foolish to youke young heffars and old bullocks together. Yet such is your husbandry. In fitting your coaches with horses you are very curious to have them (so neere as you can) both of a colour, both of a height, of an age, of proportion; and will you bee carelese in coupling your children? He into whose bosome three score winters have thrust their frozen fingers, if he bee rich (though his breath be rancker than a muck-hill, his bodye more drye than mummi, and his minde more lame than ignorance itselfe) shall have offered unto him (but it is offered as a sacrifice) the tender bossome of a virgin upon whose fore-head was never written sixteene yeares: if she refuses this living death (for less than a death it cannot be unto her) she is threatened to be left an outcast, cursd for disobedience, raild at daily and revilde howerlye: to save her selfe from which basenes she desprately runnes into a bondage and goes to church to be married as if she went to be buried. But what glorie atcheive you in these conquests? You doe wrong to time, inforcing May to embrace December: you dishonour age in bringing it into scorne for insufficiency, into loathing for dotage, into all means laughyter for jealousie. You make your daughters looke wrinckled with forrowes before they be olde, and your sonnes by riot to be beggars midst of their youth. Hence comes it that murders are often contrived, and as often acted: our countrie is woful in fresh examples. Hence comes it that the courtier gives you an open scoffe, the clowne a secret mock, the citisen that dwelles in your thresholde a leery thrump. Hence it is that if you goe by water in the calmest day, you are driven by some fatall storme into the unlucky and dangerous haven between Greenwich and London.

When we consider that the legal age for a boy was fourteen and for a girl twelve, we can see why the opportunities for age disparities in marriage were widespread, even though many did not formally wed until their twenties. Equally, what we would call children were married off. None was surprised that Shakespeare's Juliet was thirteen – a full year over her majority. Even marriages among the very young, which were hardly approved of, might comply with the law. To be married would take nothing more than vows in a church porch and a declaration that the couple – perhaps hardly teenagers – were living as man and wife or had simply slept with each other. The bride, or fiancée as we might say, would be given a ring for her right hand. In public, the declaration of vows and the passing of virginity would be made outside the doors of the church when presents were exchanged. This was the marriage ceremony. The blessing of the marriage was the ceremony inside the church. The priest, such as he was, would kiss the groom who would pass this kiss to the bride – the origin of 'you may now kiss the bride' in modern services. (This is why the bride is not told 'you may now kiss the groom'.) The priest would bless them, their presents and the tokens of their wedding breakfast. Usually the wedding breakfast took place in the groom's house. Even among the modestly wealthy a wedding feast might last three days. Entertainers would be brought in. One source might even be from what were later called almshouses or even from the asylum where the inmates would be brought to the ceremony to perform as curious, unknowing animals. The whole throng would escort or even carry the bride and groom to the bedroom. By this time the wedding guests might have become revellers with many emptied flagons to their credit. Some contemporary accounts tell of drunken goings-on in the nuptial chamber with dancing and nakedness and with the 'poore bryd' dancing with all who wished it while the whole occasion descended into, at the very least, a romp. Only supper would attract the wedding guests away from the couple. But after supper the diners would regard it as their duty to return to the corridor outside the bedroom and with imaginative suggestions and advice egg on the newly-weds.

The Puritans and the Established Church had deep differences of opinion on marriage and divorce. The Puritans of course did not care for the way the Church dominated any liturgy and this included the marriage service. We can see from the Millenary Petition how the Puritans wanted to get rid of much ceremony, and so it should be no surprise that they wanted marriage to take place outside the Church establishment. Indeed, these beliefs were so strongly held that they were carried to the colonies in America, and the early marriages there in the new England were civil arrangements. If we should be surprised by the lack of a Christian stamp on marriage, we might consider that even in the twenty-first century in some places, for example France, a civil service is the legally binding marriage. The ceremony in a church follows.

These differences extended to divorce. Curiously, although the Established Church had, for political as well as doctrinal considerations, distanced itself from Rome, it did not really differ very much. (Even today there are absolute similarities between the Roman missal and the Anglican prayer books.) The Puritans on the other hand, quite contrary to our modern conceptions and use of the term, would allow divorce, whereas the Anglican Church did everything to oppose it. The Puritans would say that adultery was ground for divorce and they took no notice of the law which said that would-be divorcees had to attend a church court. It was also true that most officials at these formal courts (there were five of them in England) could be bought with a bit of silver. The courts became so discredited that in 1603 laws were drafted that would allow divorce to be sanctioned by a minister or even a local magistrate. The biggest contention between the two was that the Established Church officially would not let divorced couples remarry. But this was no honestly structured society and those who would remarry often did.

There was among both groups a belief that arranged marriages might stand a good chance of survival. Parents would bring together sons and daughters for all the right reasons. The selection of brides and grooms was very much in keeping with the parents' decision to choose a trade or profession for a son. The male often accepted this simply because there was not much else that he could do. The female did so because that was her lot. This was a society that still blamed a woman for usurping the dignity and honesty of Adam. It was a common 'joke' that the two best days of a woman's life were her wedding day and the day she died. It was Bishop Aylmer* who thought women 'foolish and wanton, flibbergibs, careless, evil tongued, gossips' and 'in every way doltified with the dregs of the devil's dungill [dung-hill]'. Considering he was Lady Jane Grey's tutor, that is quite a declaration. When Spenser wrote his *Shepheardes Calender*, he thought so little of Aylmer that he created the character Morrell to poke fun at this 'proude and ambitious pastoure'.

From this we should not get the idea that women were wholly on the wrong end of fortune at the beginning of the seventeenth century. Compared with many other countries they had a very free and sporting life. Comparisons were made at the time and there was hardly a woman who would have liked to be a Spanish or French housewife. It was certainly true that there were those on the Continent, including one Dutch diarist, Van Meteren, who noted that 'England is called the paradise of married women'. Philip Stubbes, that most strait-laced of late sixteenth-century pamphleteers, wrote uncompromisingly of the excesses of the period. As for the gaudiness and self-delight of women, one of Stubbes's last pamphlets before he died made clear where they stood in his list of the ways of an increasingly vile world.

The Anatomie of Abuses
Very godly, to read of all true Christians, every where: but most chiefly, to be regarded in England
Matthew 3 ver 2
Repent, for the kingdome of God is at hande

---

* John Aylmer (1521–94), Archdeacon of Stowe, was persecuted under Bloody Mary's Catholic enthusiasms and after his return from exile became, in 1577, Bishop of London.

Printed at London by Richard Jones, 1595

The women of Ailgna [England] use to colour their faces with
certaine Oyles, Liquors . . . whereby they think of their beautie
is greatly decored [embellished]: but who seeth not that their
soules are thereby deformed and they brought deeper into the
displeasure and indignation of the Almightie, at whose voice
the earth doth tremble . . . Do they think thus to adulterate
the Lorde . . . and be without ofence . . . do they not know
that he is . . . a jealous God and can not abide any alteration
of his woorkes, otherwise than he hath made them . . . and doe
these women thinke to escape the judgement of God who hath
fashioned them to his glory . . . doe they suppose they can make
themselves fayrer than God that made us all. These must needes
bee their intentions or els thee would never goe about to colour
their faces.

Stubbes spent pages ranting against the painting of faces and about
the indignation of God who has made us all as he wanted us to
be. But this diatribe against the fashion of the day went higher
than the eyebrows. There 'followeth the trimming and tricking of
their heades in laying out their haire . . . which of force must be
curled, frilled and crisped, laid out (a world to see) on wreathes
and borders, from one eare to an other. And least it should fall
down, it is under propped with forks wiers and I can not tell
what.'

Hair would be dyed, often blonde – even then it was considered
that gentlemen preferred them – or wigs were worn. Elizabeth I,
towards the end, dressed every day in a red wig.

The 'oyles' Stubbes complains of were not the only face paints of
the day. Cheeks were reddened by a somewhat dangerous mixture of
lead in a carbon base, mixed with bear's fat. Crude crayons and face
powder made from crushed and ground alabasters were common
enough on any pedlar's tray. More practical decorations were the

nosegays and pomanders to protect against the stench of uncleansed towns and slowly flowing drains.

Cosmetics, which were coarse and ran easily in a hot summer or a dank autumn, were not considered luxury decorations. A lady who decked herself with silk and jewel finery might be fined a full £10 for every month she so dressed unless, of course, her husband made himself ready to answer the Queen's call to war. Elizabeth, until her death, kept a woman who knitted her silk stockings. Thomas Nash(e) had long grumbled about fashionable ladies.

> Their heads, with their top and top-gallant lawn baby-caps, and snow-resembled silver curlings, they make a plain puppet stage of. Their breasts they embusk up on high, and their round roseate buds immodestly lay forth to show at their hands there is fruit to be hoped. In their curious antic-woven garments, they imitate and mock the worms and adders that must eat them. They shew the swellings of their mind, in the swellings and plumpings out of their apparel. Gorgeous ladies of the court, never were I admitted so near any of you, as to see how you torture old Time with sponging, pinning, and pouncing; but they say his sickle you have burst in twain, to make your periwigs more elevated arches of.*

Although there were large areas of unemployment, the towns continued to support increasingly wealthy artisans and craftsmen. They certainly were able to take home a living wage – an expression of the period. A glance at some of those wages suggests demand and levels of craftsmanship which we would recognise today. The difference, for example, between a bricklayer's pay and that of a plumber is not

* Thomas Nash(e) (1567–1601), dramatist and miscellaneous writer. This extract is from his *Anatomie of Absurditie: Contayning . . . a confutation of the slender imputed prayses to femmine perfection, etc.* J. Charlwood for T. Hackett (London, 1590).

unlike that seen in the twenty-first century. It is difficult to compare a shilling during that first year of James's reign with a 5p coin in Elizabeth II's, even though we might think of the 5p replacing the shilling on decimalisation in 1971. The computation simply does not work. We should just accept the 1603 currency as a unit and that the craftsman could expect to afford the same social position in his town or village as his descendant might have in, say, the 1930s. (Post-World War Two Britain produced anomalies of living styles and opportunities that make comparisons after 1945 almost impossible.)

If we look at a nineteenth-century study of 1603 prices and wages by James E. Thorold Rogers, we see a carpenter in that year, paid by the day, would expect to get between 1s and 1s 2d.* His average weekly pay would be 7s 3d. A mason would have 6s a week. A bricklayer would be better paid – 6s 8d a week. A tiler would get 6s. The best-paid craftsman was the plumber. Now, given the state of domestic arrangements and facilities in 1603, we might wonder why a plumber was so important. The word comes from the Old French *plummier* and the modern French for the metal lead, *plomb*. So our 1603 plumber was a lead-worker, probably in towns, working with fashioned pipework, troughs, gutters, coffins and even shrouds. It was, in some families, still fashionable to have lead from the open mines that had been worked since Roman times in the Mendip Hills moulded to 'mummify' corpses in lead shrouds. For all his skills, the plumber would be paid certainly 10s a week. (It is tempting to wonder if a plumber called in 1603 might not turn up until 1604.) As might be expected, a drudge, or cleaning woman in a house, would be the lowest-paid worker – perhaps 2s 6d a week at the most. On the land, farmworkers were poorly paid or not at all, because they worked their land for what they could sell or eat. A hedger and ditcher might be paid short of 5s for a long week.

* James E. Thorold Rogers, *Agriculture and Prices in England*, vol. V (1583–1702) (Clarendon Press, Oxford, 1887).

If we look at these wages and compare them with a few food items, we can make a rough stab at the cost of living for a tradesman's family. A carpenter, a mason, a bricklayer and a sawyer (usually working in pairs on the long tree-felling saws) would take home about 1s a day. A capon would cost 2s; a goose 1s 8d; a pullet 1s 6d. Chickens were cheap, not more than 4d each. Pigeons could be bought at 2s a dozen; eggs for 2s 4½d a hundred. Butter was 3s 8¾d for a dozen pounds (although many would make their own), and cream could be had at 1s 6d a gallon. It may have been some consolation that good ordinary claret could be had for 2s a dozen bottles.

Two days' wages for capon and more than a day's for a goose. Wheat and meal on the rise, unless you lived in East Anglia: the prices at Theydon were the cheapest in the country, but mostly went to the colleges who owned the land and livings. Let them eat cream. In 1603 there was nothing new in this.

Some Oxford and Cambridge college records (reliable sources for food prices) suggest that in 1603 the people were living on the proceeds of a good harvest the previous year, but were predicting a bad year ahead – suggesting that the 1603 harvests were indifferent or poor. Indeed, by the next Lady Day rents, prices for wheat and other cereals had risen considerably. Prices in 1603 were low, but records show they would, just a generation earlier, have been considered very high indeed.*

The colleges, institutions and schools kept careful records and accounts of what was paid either in kind through rents or by the bursars for the kitchens and stables. Those prices and diets would reflect what was available in the region rather than any national figure. So, for example, in Oxford beasts were fed beans because they were easily had, and in Cambridge, for the same reason, the stables would be supplied with peas; so too would the piggeries, it being considered that the sweetest pork came from an animal fattened on unshelled peas.

* Ibid.

Further anomalies in prices and quantity came about because, for example, Oxford University through charter and law had powers over brewers and bakers who had to supply the colleges. Cambridge, Eton and Winchester, on the other hand, had no such charters and so they were forced to be self-sufficient. Also, payment of corn, etc. came on rent days. Oxford bursars had one rent day a year and therefore changed rents on that day. Cambridge bursars, perhaps more self-sufficiently businesslike and Puritan-based, had at least two rent days a year; King's College, Cambridge had ten, and so could make ten rent rises. Winchester and Eton had the same policies: the former made seven changes and the latter six changes to rent demands every year. This meant that if a tenant's rent was, say, £5 a time, then he would have to pay according to the price of, say, £5 of corn. In 1603 Eton was rating 34s 8d for a load of corn, Oxford 29s 1¾d and Cambridge – where cornfields were plentiful – 22s 6½d.

In the sixteenth century it was common enough for major towns to give out food tokens. A 1547 Act of Parliament introduced what was called a poor rate to help those in great distress. In 1572 this was amended so that parishes could collect money for a parish poor rate, and just five years before our year, 1603, an Act of Parliament ordered that the parish should look after the destitute. This act lasted until 1834. From it we get the term 'on the parish'. Robert Gray in 1609 was writing that agriculture was doing its best, but it was not good enough and 'it hath not milk sufficient'.

A product of this poverty was the huge vagrant population. Many roamed the whole country seeking work occasionally and easy pickings mostly. Others, such as the gang led by Black James in Sussex, terrorised whole counties. From them came the nursery rhymes and inn songs. Lines such as 'hark, hark the dogs do bark, and the beggars are coming to town' reflected a social malaise rarely seen in the popular image of Elizabethan England. So terrible were the consequences of vagrancy that in 1603 passports were introduced with the idea that a vagrant could travel across counties to his or her home village or town without being apprehended by the law. While we should not see England as the only state in Europe suffering from violence and vagrancy (twenty-first-century puzzles concerning refugees were, proportionally, as difficult four hundred years ago), it is certainly true that there was a very dangerous, certainly violent element among the down-and-out English abroad as well as at home. The levels of violence and dangers were enough for the Privy Council itself to issue a decree against the dangerous vagabonds. Tough-on-crime was not yet a political slogan, but there is no doubt that Sir Robert Cecil and his fellow privy councillors had decided that 'incorrigible or dangerous Rogues' should be deported.

> Forasmuch as it hath appeared unto us aswell by our owne viewes in our travailes in this present progresse of his Majestie, as also by good and credible information from divers and sundrie partes of the Realme, that Rogues grow againe and increase to bee incorrigible and dangerous not onely to his Majesties loving subjects abroad, but also to his Majestie and his honourable houshold and attendants in and about his Court, which growing partly through the remissenes of some Justices of the Peace, and other Officers of the Countrey, and partly for there hath beene no Suite made for assigning some place beyond the Seas, to which such incorrigible or dangerous Rogues might be banished, according the Statute in that behalfe made: We therefore of his Majesties privie Council, whose names are hereunto subscribed, finding it of necessitie to reforme great abuses, and to have the due execution of so good and necessarie a Law, doe according to the power limitted unto us by the same Statute, hereby Assigne and thinke it fit and expedient, that the places and partes beyond the Seas to which any such incorrigible or dangerous Rogues shall be banished and conveyed according to the said Statute, shall bee these Countries, and places following, viz. The New-found Land, the East and West Indies, France, Germanie, Spaine, and the Low-countries, or any of them.

T. Buckhurst	Lenox	Nottingham
Suffolke	Devonshire	Mar
Ro. Cecil	E. Wotton	Jo. Stanhop

It is interesting to note the range of places to which miscreants could be banished – from the wild Canadian territories to the Caribbean to continental Europe. Dorset became a 'holding place' for hapless deportees scheduled for Newfoundland fishing ports. Not all vagrants, vagabonds and incorrigibles were deported or jailed. Some swung for their pains. In 1603 the most famous vagabond was the highwayman Gamaliel Ratsey. He had fought with valour in Ireland and when the war finished in Kinsale, he returned to England. In the romantic phraseology used by apologists for ne'er-do-wells in the 1940s, he 'found it hard to settle down'. In fact, he was hard up, a good fighter, daring and not inclined to work for a living. He had a large black hunter on which to make his escape and wore a hideous mask which, by most accounts, worked its magic by terrifying his victims as well as disguising his face. Some – including Shakespeare – would boast that they had been held up across the eastern counties by the infamous Gamaliel Ratsey. There was something of the thespian in Ratsey, who would insist on ladies dancing, lawyers making closing speeches in their own defence, actors performing a scene, and priests chanting before he robbed them. In 1603 he achieved the sort of celebrity given in the next century to Dick Turpin, an altogether more violent highwayman who was hanged for murder at York in 1739. Ratsey's reputation would not protect him for ever, and on 26 March 1605 he was hanged at Bedford.

Poor harvests, poor society – a notion as old as any scripture. In the London of 1603, the plague gripped every street and alley. In the towns beyond, there was good work for the shroud-maker and the burial clerks.

The winter months of 1602 and 1603 passed cruelly for many of Elizabeth's people. This was not a land of double-glazed and draught-free living. The north wind that dumped its sleet across these islands left more than a shiver through the people. Agriculture would always survive an English winter if husbandry were sensible and well founded. Yet there is little evidence that the yeoman had much changed his management of stock in centuries. Nor was there the sophistication of wintered root crops. What was in the barn was what the nation had to make do with. Perhaps the jolly milkmaid (see page 59) would be right for summer cuddling and late Victorian jigsaw puzzles, but as 1603 grew through its first few days it revealed a cold, bleak picture of muddied fields.

The population ignored the neat lines of the actuary. The numbers of people in London grew, not because they overcame disease and the frailties of childbirth, but as a result of a remorseless stream of immigrants. It was common, for example, for Londoners to die quickly of consumption, for the streets to be littered with piles of animal dung, for sewers to be open and clogged, for sulphurous fires of workshops to taint each nostril and lung in a yellow mist.

The inventors, the preachers, the elucidators of socially stricken conscience were in their elements. Just as the parsons and pamphleteers spread their words to a diseased and fearful public for a penny a sheet, so there were those like 'the Man from the Ministry' in the 1940s who saw it a matter of duty to inform and encourage. All had a cure, an exhortation and often an admonishment for the poverty they saw about them. Here were the original notions that cleanliness was next to godliness. Soap and water and bathing were not common habits. The monarch might dab at cheekbones with sponge and rose-watered fingertips. Not much more. The poor had few rose-water toilets. Poverty was everywhere, and pamphleteers had true as well as quack remedies.

One of these fine people was Hugh Platt Esq. He was a persistent pamphleteer with a patent solution to, or at the very least a way of alleviating, the ills of poverty. Platt's introduction to his pamphlet on coal tells us something of hardship and its sensitivities in 1603. The harvests had been poor; there was famine in the land and much disease; the scatterers of quicklime on mass graves did not rest. More than 37,000 out of London's 210,000 were buried. Platt was known for his pamphlets on what we would call famine relief, although few remedies ever came to much. He now thought of a way to improve the lot of the poor, recognising that few would ever have an opportunity to climb from their desperate state.

> H. Platt Esquier
> A new, cheape and delicate Fire of Cole-balls, wherein Seacole is by the mixture of other combustible bodies, both sweetened and multiplied
> Imprinted at London by Peter Short dwelling at the signe of the Starre on Bredstreet-hill, 1603

Being everie way willing though no waie able, out of my manie and manifold travels to bring foorth some substantial and commodious intention for the avoiding of idleness, and relieving the present misery, which the fortunes of warres, together with the want of profitable labors hath brought upon us: I could not (on the sodaine) bethinke my selfe of a better discoverie, then how to imploy the poore and maimed persons of this land, who (having their hands only) might be sufficiently able to worke up these sweet and profitable fireballes, for the benefit and pleasure of the rich. And as I have alreadie in my booke of Remedies against famine, freely and plainly delivered, sundrie new and cheap kinds both of meate and drinke to bee used in a dearth of victuall; so if now in the scarcitie of fewel I may alsoe prove so happy as to bring forth a cheape and saving fire to warme and cherish their cold and frozen limmes with the recompense of their labors, I shall bee greatlie encouraged to devote and consecrate the fruits of some of my intermissiue houres upon these and such like charitable and godly uses.

Platt begins by entreating all those (magistrates) who monitor the landing of sea-coal to make sure that the quality is the best and that at the very least the coal is the sort that will knit and cake 'and so make hot and durable fire'. This, to Platt at least, was so important that he wanted every master of every ship to heat up coals and show they were of the highest standard before they were allowed to unload. If they were not? Then the cargo should be returned or confiscated. He also warned against corrupt magistrates who might let duff coal ashore. How was one to know a good from a poor coal?

> [I]f the same being held over a candle, or rather over a flaming fire, do melt, & as it were drop or frie; for this is an argument of his fattie and sulphurious nature, which ministreth store of foode for the fire; but if the flame grow hard and drie over the flame, it is a signe of a leane and hungrie cole, and such as will not cake or knit in the burning; of which kind are the Sunderland coles, whereof the poores wharfe in London can give a sufficient testimonie; which has lien one winter already without anie great decrease, saving that some parcell thereof hath rather beene translated to another place to make the bulke seeme lesse then sold and distributed among the poore for whom that charitable provision was first meant. Here xviii.pence or five grotes in the price of a chaldron* was ill saved.

The coal testers looked for a not too heavy knob. The lighter the coal, the less likely it had impurities to make burning slow or over-sulphurous. The trick was to always keep a sample, at least a peck,† of the finest coal dust. And where did Platt think the best coal came from? 'Durham, Blaidon, Stillow, Redhew and Bourne; the rest being ten or eleven more are of a worser kind and the worst of all are those of Sunderland.' This coaling trade, according to Platt,

---

* A measure used for coal; either 32 or 36 bushels.
† Dry weight equivalent of two gallons, a quarter of a bushel.

was full of crooks who would mix bad coal with good. Moreover, the cut-price coal merchants were at work, and this meant that credit was offered and taken and misery too easily followed.

> And if usurie bee so dangerous a trade as both the word of God and al the ministers thereof do daily publish and proclaime unto us, the same for the most part being drawne from men of good estate and credit (for the usurer will seldom trust any other) what shall wee thinke of a double and treble usurie, nay of a doubling the principall it selfe (whereof there hath beene a miserable & wretched experience of late memorie within this honourable citie of London) & that wrung out even from the backs and bellies of the poorest sort of people.

Having identified the best coal, having warned of the dirty deeds of money-lenders, and made a few comments on the best sort of sack, Platt moves on to how the poor were to make sea-coal balls – the sixteenth- and early seventeenth-century version of anthracite nuts. The answer, or at least the first part of the answer, lay in the soil. During the winter and after a couple of heavy frosts, the task was to gather the finest of the soil made crumbly, or friable, by the frost. Half a peck, left to soak in a small pail of water, was probably sufficient to make a paste that would hold together a bushel of sea-coal dust. The dusting of raw coal was simplicity itself. Here was a recipe of making do and making most that was not greatly dissimilar to that which appeared in leaflet form 340 years later during World War Two; even the language and style had not much changed, which is hardly surprising when we consider that until the 1960s officialese owed much to the grammar of the Book of Common Prayer and seventeenth-century proclamation. Here, then, in the original style, is the recipe for good sea-coal balls, using a little pap of loam that the 'cook' had prepared earlier – that is, during the winter.

> [T]ake a bushel of the best seacole, which being strewed upon

a stonie or paved floore, you must breake or bruise with a hammer, mallet, or some other apt toole or instrument, or otherwise you may sufficiently powder them under your feete, which I have founde the readiest and cheapest way of all other. This is entended of the greater sort of coles; but if your coles be of the smaller kind, then are they sufficiently prepared for this worke to your hand.

Spread these coles abroad some handfull thicke, or there-abouts, equally upon the floore, then sprinkle some of your thinne pap all over the heape: then turne them with a shovell or a spade, and spread againe as before, throwing more of your lomy liquor upon them. Continue this course till you have made the whole masse or lumpe of your coles soft enough to be wrought up into balles, between your hands, according to the manner and making of snowbals: then place them one by one, so as they touch not each other til they be thoroughly drie, which will be in a few dayes. Then may you pile or lay them up in heaps in any convenient place where they may bee defended from raine, which if it were to fall in any great quantitie upon them, they would be in danger to be disolved againe.

These precise instructions for the hand-moulding of coal dust made grubby but small fortunes. After all, a penny-halfpenny was rich-ness when all a man could bring home was a farthing, which he had been doing since the coin, a quarter of one penny, had been introduced in the late thirteenth century during the reign of Edward I.

In 1603 there were no miracles – some may think tragedies – of chemistry and technology that could satisfactorily fertilise and till this land for its growing population. True, the lands-men dunged their acres and the coastal farmers had for centuries understood the properties of seaweed. But their efforts had not much changed since the beneficial effect of crop rotation was first discovered. As it would until the nineteenth century, the feeding of the people would rely on the cunning as well as the sloth of the countrymen. Britain would eventually become self-sufficient and would remain so until the 1880s. In parts, England was badly managed. It was and would be ever thus. There was a movement towards understanding better estate management and the sensitivities of the farmworkers who could, if handled efficiently and considerately, make all the difference to an estate's profitability. However obvious this may now seem, it should not obscure the point that in the early seventeenth century estate management was rarely an accomplishment of many landowners, gentlemen and yeomen.

Thomas Wilson, a failure in so many aspects of his life, yet a colourful recorder of the shape and form of Britain at this period, noted that times were changing because society in general had altered. Wilson was born in or about 1560, the youngest son of a country squire or gentleman. Being the youngest son did not give him much of a start, his brothers having had many of the advantages of their father's estate. Wilson was sent to Cambridge where he was a reasonable student, although he left without remarkable distinction. He had little money, yet certainly sound patronage, including that of William Cecil. He became an intellectual and political artificer, trying his hand at most things from journalist to quasi-academic to junior diplomat, but proving to be master of none. Yet Wilson did prove to be a very able keeper of records in Whitehall and was highly thought of during his time. Lord Buckhurst, the Treasurer, sent him, with Robert Cecil's blessing, as a spy to Italy. More importantly, he was sent into the Tower to gain the confidence of Ralegh in the hope that the great man would give Wilson self-incriminating information. Wilson was not much of a spy, and failed. Yet today we should be thankful to him for his description of England. True, it is written from a single perspective, but then so are most diaries and commentaries – even today, when we kid ourselves with rigorous standards of intellectual honesty. The original documents are defective inasmuch as one manuscript is a transliteration from Thomas's Elizabethan English (and not always trustworthy) and another is incomplete.* But between them we have snatches of the early seventeenth century otherwise missing.

It cannot be denied but the Comon people are very rich, albeit they be much decayed from the States they were wont to have, for the gentlemen, which were wont to addict themselves to the warres and nowe for the most part growen to become good husbandes and knowe well how to improve their lands . . . the yeomanry of England is decayed and become servants to the gentlemen, which were wont to be the Glory of the Country . . . I knowe many Yeomen in divers Provinces in England which are able to despend betwixt 3 or 5 hundred pound yeerly by theire Lands and Leases and some twise and some thrise as much; but my yonge masters the sonnes of such, not contented with their states of their fathers to be counted yeoman . . . But must ski into his velvett breches and silken dublett and getting to be admitted into some Inn of Court of Chancery, must ever after thinke skorne to be called any other than gentleman . . .

Notwithstanding this that the great yeomany is decayed, yett by this meanes the Cominality is encreased, 20 nowe perhaps with theire labor and diligence living well and welthily of that land wich our great yeomen held before, who did no other good but maintayne beefe and brewes for such idle persones as would come and eate it, a fyne daughter or 2 to be maried after with 1000 pounds to some Covetouse Mongrell. Of these yeomen of the richest sort . . . are accounted to be about 10,000 in Contry Villages besides Cittisens.

* *State of England 1600*, from the *Camden Miscellany*, vol. xvi; *The State of England Anno Dom. 1600* by Thomas Wilson, State Papers Domestic PRO (ed. F.J. Fisher). The following extract is taken from the latter.

Wilson thought there were to be found about 80,000 freeholders and the rest were Copyholders and Cottagers.

A land surveyor of the time, not a very common profession, was John Norden. He felt that English agriculture was in poor fettle and, believing that there was too little understanding of estate management, took the opportunity of a new monarch (new monarchs seemingly like all new management and inspire opportunists to considerable activity) to write at some length to Robert Cecil about the subject. In the twenty-first century, a letter to *The Times* might have done just as well. Norden wrote five 'books' to Cecil. They were a few pages each, but we should remember the comparative novelty of an ordinary person's access to the printed word.

The first book is a justification of the profession of surveyor. (No estate should have been without one.) The second instructs the lord how to deal with his tenants. The third book is about surveying and record-keeping. The fourth and fifth books are on how best to farm. Dull in the early seventeenth century? Not at all. Here were the principles of surveying a farm, knowing how best to farm, getting the best and the truth out of tenants, and thereby producing the right taxes and the right means of compassion for the poor. The good master would hope to reap more than corn. Extracts show Norden's enthusiasm, and the whole work came complete (as most tracts did) with a biblical text: 'A discreet servant shall have rule over an unthrifty sonne, and he shall divide the heritage among the brethren' (Prov. 17.2).*

The Surveyors Dialogue
John Norden
Divided into five Bookes: Very profitable for all men to peruse, that have to do with the revenues of Land, or the manurance,

* Note that the text references would have been to translations of the Bible earlier than the King James Version.

use, or occupation thereof, both Lords and Tenants as also and especially for such as indevor to be seene in the faculty of surveying of Mannors, Lands, Tenements &c.*

Norden's 'covering letter' printed at the start of his work most certainly has a moral message; it is also good sense and reflects a time when there was enormous hardship and the poverties of England were only just beyond the porches of even the most powerful – including Cecil.

[I]s it not the least regard, that men of whatsoever title or place, should have of the lawfull and just meanes of the preservation and increase of their earthly revenues. And that especially, by justly achieving, and rightly using Dominion and lordship which principally grow (omitting public office and authority) by Honors, Mannors, Lands, and Tenants: for, according to the largenesse of revenues, are the means to enable the Honorable to shelter the vertuous distressed, and to cherish such, as by desert may challenge regard: And according to their will and power therein, is the vulgar reputation of their Magnificence. But (my good Lord) as mine indevor in this rude Dialogue, tendeth but, as it were to plow: So I omit to wade into the impassable censure of Honor and Dignitie wishing it ever deserved reverence. And as touching Land-revenues, when with many are (but especially the Honorable are, or ought to be principally) endowed, I presume onely in this simple Treatise to discourse so farre (according to my slender capacitie and weake experience) as concerneth the ordinary necessary meanes of the maintenance & increase of Land revenues. And because the true and exact Surveying of Land, is the principall, I have herein indevoured more of Desire than of Power (for the use and benefite of all sorts of men, having to deale with land

* British Library shelfmark c.113.b.16.

both Lords and Tenants) to shew the necessitie, and simple method thereof, Most humbly intreating your Lordship (the fruites of whose, and of your honorable Fathers favours, I have many ways tasted) to vouchsafe me your Honorable parden for presuming and your like patience in accepting at my hands, this little mite . . .

At my poore house at Hendon,
Your Lordships ever to be commanded
Jo. Norden

None of this means that Elizabeth was handing on an impoverished society. True, poverty in some forms was apparent and widespread; but wealth was not hidden. That may seem an obvious statement inasmuch that for the poor to be always with us there have to be rich – also always with us. Society itself (that too often carelessly defined grouping that means people in general) really lived up to a cliché of rich tapestries of cultures and ambitions. The education system, for example, was surprisingly good. Most large villages would have a petty school where a child could be taught to read and write. In 1603 a third of the male population had a very basic ability to read and write. Most villages would have a schoolmaster of sorts, and grammar schools were being built every year. Between 1603 and 1649, 142 new grammar schools were built. However, this is not to suggest a remarkable age of education and learning: books could only be owned by men who owned property; women were discouraged from reading; literacy in any extensive form was really confined to the higher classes.

In 1603 more than a thousand young men went to Oxford and Cambridge. So it was not until the twentieth century that the same percentage of the population was receiving a university education.*

* Lawrence Stone, 'The Educational Revolution in England 1560–1640', *Past and present*, 28, 1966, pp 54–64. See also references in Lawrence Stone, *The causes of the English Revolution, 1529–1642* (Routledge and Kegan Paul, 1972).

There was a third university, the Inns of Court, which provided the lawyers, but was also where young men were sent to learn a little law in order to manage the family estates. And many of the estates needed good legal minds to preserve them. In 1603 there was considerable debate about the laws of inheritance. Sir Francis Bacon wrote that the laws of inheritance were often confusing and obscure and thus landowners were often worried about the process of passing on the family estate. This applied across the landowning spectrum. It is perhaps surprisingly difficult to separate the two terms 'aristocracy' and 'gentry'. At certain levels distinctions between the so-called upper classes melted. Thomas Wilson, writing in 1600, recorded one marquess, nineteen earls, two viscounts, thirty-nine barons, five hundred knights and sixteen thousand gentlemen. If we take our definition of a gentleman as someone with an estate of, say, three hundred acres, we should add to it a further definition: 'gentleman' was a recognisable title for someone who did not have to labour.

There we have the basic structure of an England (and Wales) with a population of 4.2 million. Between 90 and 92 per cent of the population lived outside the towns. Most towns which we today consider cities were, in 1603, little more than what we would now call large villages. Even places such as Southampton, Worcester, Coventry, Colchester and York had populations of not much more than five thousand. The two big cities were Norwich and Bristol, with perhaps fifteen thousand people in each. By far the biggest city was London: in 1603 more than 200,000 were living there. As with any capital, it was a place of disease and poverty as well as riches. The Court lived on the west side of the city around Westminster and therefore the gentry and aristocracy, to use the terms generally, also built their houses there. There was a certain wisdom and convenience in living west of London's centre. One theory was that the prevailing wind from the west meant that those at Westminster and just beyond were spared the stench of London and the fumes of the smouldering 'seacole' fires (see page 48). The capital was a magnet for everyone with a craving for influence, whether political, social or commercial. Yet what of the hearts of oak? What of those chocolate-box images of the early seventeenth century?

The satirist John Stephens (fl. 1615) in his *Satyrical Essayes, Characters and Others* (1615), reflecting on the first decade of the century, had a considerable opinion of a countryside in which some 90 per cent either lived or visited. Even the big towns were small then, and, for example, in London what is now Regent's Park was countryside in 1603. Stephens thought a farmer a good man who had religion enough to say, 'God Bless Her [Elizabeth] or His [James] Majesty.' His farmer would also be religious enough to request publicly that God send peace and fair weather. Yet the farmer was not generally in 1603 a deeply religious man. He was, as he always had been and always would be, more inclined to hire reapers and ploughmen for a pittance, and to give even less to the maintenance of a parson.

The early seventeenth-century farmer could read and write and could, by necessity, tend a gashed leg in either human or cow. (There were no vets in 1603.) He was, in the great and continuing tradition of farmers, a splendid moaner. As a yeoman he was allowed to own only a small amount of land. He would complain about the restriction. He would, too, complain that he never had enough money to buy any more anyway. His ambition was to be out of debt and to provide a better life for his eldest son. He stuck with the prejudice of his Queen and so hated all Spaniards, although he probably had not met one, and believed quite strongly that his hatred and bigotry declared him a very loyal subject.

Sir Thomas Overbury* comes somewhere between Gervase Markham (see page 61) and John Stephens with his character sketches of the English countryside. Overbury's position in Tudor history has far more to do with the nature of his death than his undoubted

---

* The *Characters* by Overbury (1581–1613) and 'other learned Gentlemen his Friendes' appeared from 1614 in a number of rapidly enlarging editions.

literary reputation. His name has always been associated with the incident in 1613, known as the Overbury Murder, that followed when Robert Carr, very much the favourite of James I, decided he would marry the divorced Countess of Essex, Frances Howard. Lady Essex hated Overbury, who had strongly advised Carr against the match. James I had created Carr Viscount Rochester and in 1613 Earl of Somerset. Overbury was influential at Court, but he relied very much on the patronage of Carr. However, this did not mean that he did not also have the King's ear. Carr and Lady Essex tried to force him out of the country. He refused to go on a trumped-up diplomatic mission, and on a charge of disloyalty he was sent to the Tower. It is said that Lady Essex, as ruthless as any determined character in history, had Overbury fed each day with small amounts of poison until he succumbed. Overbury's death was not the end of the matter. Somerset did marry Lady Essex. Her agents in the Tower were convicted of Overbury's murder and hanged. Indeed, the Somersets themselves were found guilty, but pardoned. They were now disgraced and spent the rest of their lives without any influence and in what is called social obscurity.

Overbury may be remembered for the circumstances of his death, but he is also applauded as a literary figure. He was a student of the works of the Greek philosopher and pupil of Aristotle, Theophrastus (c. 372–286 BC), who wrote a series of character sketches describing human failings and joys. They attracted many English imitators, including Overbury in his collection of *Characters*. He may not have written them all, but they appeared beneath his by-line, including 'The fayre and happy Milk Maid' – that 'queen of curds and cream' of Shakespeare's *The Winter's Tale*.

A fair and happy milkmaid is a country wench, that is so far from making herself beautiful by art, that one look of hers is able to put all face-physic out of countenance. She knows a fair look is but a dumb orator to commend virtue, therefore minds it not. All her excellencies stand in her so silently, as if they had stolen upon her without her knowledge. The lining of her apparel (which is herself) is far better than outsides of tissue; for though she be not arrayed in the spoil of the silkworm, she is decked in innocency, a far better wearing. She doth not, with lying long abed, spoil both her complexion and conditions. Nature hath taught her too immoderate sleep is rust to the soul. She rises therefore with chanticleer, her dame's cock, and at night makes the lamb her curfew. In milking a cow, and straining the teats through her fingers, it seems that so sweet a milk-press makes the milk the whiter or sweeter; for never came almond glove or aromatic ointment on her palm to taint it. The golden ears of corn fall and kiss her feet when she reaps them, as if they wished to be bound and led prisoners by the same hand that felled them. Her breath is her own, which scents all the year long of June, like a new-made hay-cock. She makes her hand hard with labour, and her heart soft with pity: and when winter evenings fall early (sitting at her merry wheel) she sings a defiance to the giddy wheel of fortune . . . Lastly, her dreams are so chaste, that she dare tell them; only a Friday's dream is all her superstition: that she conceals for fear of anger. Thus lives she, and all her care is she may die in the spring-time, to have store of flowers stuck upon her winding sheet.

Sixteenth- and seventeenth-century England hunted as enthusiastically as any other country in the world. When he travelled from Scotland to London to claim the throne, James appeared to spend much of his time breaking off for hare-coursing and hart-chasing. In fact on one occasion, so enthusiastic was the new monarch that he suffered terrible injury and was confined to the indignity and the discomfort of a carriage for some of the journey to the capital. Mostly, the prey would be roasted and devoured. There was, too, prey in abundance in these green and pleasant islands. It is not, therefore, surprising that we see references to hunting in all manner of landscape painting and portraiture of the period, in

lyric and verse, and in court diaries. There were some who became
remembered simply for their writings about field sports. One such
author was Gervase Markham (1568–1637). Markham was a soldier
who, like many of his military calling, spent much of his time in the
Netherlands. He gave up being shot at and turned to his pen. He
then wrote about war, but more particularly about horses, that
beast being closest to the soul of the early seventeenth-century
officer; hence titles such as *Cavelarice, or The English Horseman,
The Faithfull Farrier* and *A Discourse of Horsemanshippe*. It was
Markham who first brought the famous Arab stallions to England.
He had first heard of the horses in Paris and admired them, as well
he might, for the English fashion was for fast, sturdy horses – as
opposed to bold and big-chested hunters. To get some idea of the
keenness on hunting at this period, therefore, Markham is worth
reading on this subject.

I think it not amiss to begin and give that recreation precedency
of place, which in mine opinion (however it may be esteemed
partial) doth many degrees go before and precede all other, as
being most royal for the stateliness thereof, most artificial for
the wisdom and cunning thereof, and most manly and warlike
for the use and endurance thereof. And this I hold to be the
hunting of wild beasts in general: of which, as the chases are
many, so will I speak of them particularly in their proper places.
But before I proceed any farther I will tell you what hunting
is, and from the true definition thereof make your way more
easy and plain into the hidden art of the same. Hunting is
then a curious search or conquest of one beast over another,
pursued by a natural instinct of enmity, and accomplished by
the diversities and distinction of smells only, wherein Nature
equally dividing her cunning giveth both to the offender and
offended strange knowledge both of offence and safety. In this
recreation is to be seen the wonderful power of God in his
creatures, and how far rage and policy can prevail against

innocence and wisdom. But to proceed to my main purpose, you shall understand that as the chases are many which we daily hunt, as that of the stag, the buck, the roe, the hare, the fox, the badger, the otter, the boar, the goat and suchlike, so the pursuers or conquerors of these chases (speaking of hunting only) are but one kind of creatures, namely hounds.*

Shakespeare often made reference to hunting and loved sporting metaphors. So it is not surprising to find in *As You Like It*, performed in 1603 three or four years after its original production, giving us:

> Come, shall we go and kill us venison?
> And yet it irks me, the poor dappled fools,
> Being native burghers of this desert city,
> Should in their own confines with forked heads
> Have their round hanches gor'd.†

In the midst of the quarrels of Oberon and Titania and the mischief-making of Puck, Duke Theseus observes,

> My hounds are bred out of the Spartan kind,
> So flew'd, so sanded; and their heads are hung
> With ears that sweep away the morning dew;
> Crook-knee'd, and dew-lapp'd like Thessalian bulls;
> Slow in pursuit, but match'd in mouth like bells,
> Each under each.††

Let us not believe that the countryman of 1603 amused himself only by chasing fur-coated creatures for fun or the pot or both, or by searching for partridge. As Shakespeare tells us in *The Comedy of*

---

* Gervase Markham, *Countrey Contentments* (1611).
† *As You Like It*, II.i.
†† *A Midsummer Night's Dream*, IV.i.

Errors, the rough-and-tumble sport of that year – soccer – would have been recognised in this century.

> Am I so round with you as you with me,
> That like a football you do spurn me thus?
> You spurn me hence, and he will spurn me hither:
> If I last in this service, you must case me in leather.*

Philip Stubbes had already written a huge denunciation of the game, though it might be remembered that Stubbes was an unrepentant Puritan who saw most things frivolous as perilously close to simple wickedness. He believed that football was a murdering practice rather than a felony, sport or pastime. There were no well-tended soccer pitches lime-lined and properly refereed according to official rules. The game would have been more recognisable in the roughest and tumblest backstreet areas of nineteenth-century Britain than in the executive-boxed stadia of the early twenty-first century. Stubbes's description is one of a startling contact sport: 'sometimes their necks are broken, sometimes their backs, sometimes their legs, sometime their arms, sometime one part thrust out of joint, sometime another, sometime their noses gush out with blood, sometime their eyes start out, and sometimes hurt in one place, sometimes in another'.† It seems that no rules were good rules. The so-called dead legging, when the knee is used to give a sharp jab to the outer thigh, was a common trick to slow someone on the ball. If that did not work, then why not try a sharp elbow to the heart? It did seem that Tudor football was nothing less than a man's sport, and how much shirt-exchanging and shaking of hands went on is unclear. If we are to believe our Puritan Stubbes, not much: 'hereof groweth envy, malice, rancour, choler, hatred, displeasure, enmity and what not else: and sometimes fighting, brawling, contention,

---

* *The Comedy of Errors*, II.i.
† Philip Stubbes, *The Anatomie of Abuses* (1583).

quarrel picking, murder, homicide and great effusion of blood, as experience daily teacheth'.

The term 'dying seconds of the game' takes on new meaning when studying Stubbes. The last of the Elizabethans certainly didn't lounge around in some English idyll waiting to become Stuarts. Even the bowls alley was a lane for cursings and senseless wrangling. As a sport, bowling was easy to enjoy. Its style and purpose were not much altered until the introduction in the twentieth century of mechanised bowling halls. The pastime of 1603 survives throughout the British Isles in the twenty-first century; as the Victorian Du Maurier observed, 'life ain't all beer and skittles and more's the pity; but what's the odds so long as you're happy?'*

Considering the miseries of 1603 – appalling weather, the death of the Queen, and of course yet another dreadful plague (or the return of the old one) – the people most certainly needed diversions. In any society, successful, although not necessarily long-lasting, pastimes need two ingredients: they must be available to the majority of people either as participants or spectators and they must display, however gently, continuous competition. In our period perhaps the most popular pastime was cockfighting.

George Wilson, the vicar of Wretham in Norfolk, even preached 'The Commendation of Cocke & Cocke-fighting wherein is shewd that cocke-fighting was before the coming of Christ'. Richard Willis (who was born in the same year as Shakespeare, 1564) remembered with some pride his son's birds at Stanwick. One was a young cock of a stout and large breed with very large jollops hanging either side of his beak. The jollops and the cockscomb were often snipped off. The keen owners of fighting cocks would allow the opponent no advantage, certainly not that of hanging jollops. After all, like a modern boxer done for in the sixth round but refusing to drop to the canvas, an ageing and exhausted fighting bird would cling to the champion's fleshy flaps rather than stumble and be pecked to death.

* George Louis Palmella Busson Du Maurier, *Trilby* (1894).

At Stanwick, Willis observed, 'the young cock turning again and they falling to a new fight, very sharp and eager on both sides, at last the old cock finding his old hold of the young cock's jollops taken from him was fane to cry creak, and to run away as fast from the young cock . . . and ever after the young cock was master of the field'.*

There were bloodier occasions and pits in England. Fighting bears and dogs were commonplace. Their trainers and owners were as famous as any sporting hero of the twenty-first century. The reputations of men like Harry Hunks, Tom of Lincoln, George Stone and the Mighty Sackerson commanded respect wherever their deeds were retold. This was everyday entertainment, and the theatre manager Philip Henslowe, with his actor stepson-in-law Edward Alleyn (who married Henslowe's stepdaughter Joan Woodward), put on shows of baiting as well as plays at his Bankside theatre. Blood sports were followed by the whole nation, whatever their station. Even, or perhaps especially, the King loved cockfighting (one of his first appointments was that of Royal Cock Master), bear-baiting, and fights between lions and dogs.

In 1603 the Tower of London kept a fighting menagerie including lions. The keepers liked to boast that in England there were beasts as courageous as the lion, and they kept at least one pack of bull mastiffs. The kennels were over at Southwark and if the mastiffs did not actually bay across the Thames for lions' blood, their keepers and grooms certainly barked their reputation. The King did not quite believe these claims. He wanted to see the dogs take on a lion.

Whereupon the king caused *Edward Allen*,† late servant to the Lord Admirall, now sworne the Princes man, and Master of the Beare-Garden, to fetch secretly three of the fellest dogs in the Garden, which being done, the king, Queen and Prince, with foure or five Lords, went to the Lions Tower, and caused the

* Richard Willis, *Mount Tabor* (1639).
† Otherwise Edward Alleyne.

lustiest Lion to be separated from his mate, and put into the Lyons den one dog alone, who presently flew to the face of the Lion, but the Lyon suddenly shooke him off, and graspt him fast by the neck, drawing the Dog up staires and downe staires. The king now perceiving the Lyon greatly to excaede the Dogge in strength, but nothing in Noble heart and courage, caused another Dogge to bee put into the Denne, who prooved as hotte and lustie as his fellow, and tooke the Lyon by the Face, but the Lyon began to deale with him as with the former, whereupon the king commanded the third dog to be put in before the second dog was spoyled, which third dogge more fierce and fell then eyther of the former, and in despight either of clawes or strength, tooke the Lyon by the lippe, but the Lyon so tore the dog by the eyes, head, and face, that he lost his hold, and then the Lyon tooke the Dogs necke in his mouth, drawing him up and downe as hee did the former, but being wearied, could not bite so deadly as at the first, now whilest the last dog was thus hand to hand with the Lyon in the upper roome, the other two Dogs were fighting together in the lower roome, whereupon the king caused the Lyon to be driven downe, thinking the Lyon would have parted them, but when hee saw he must needes come by them he leapt cleane over them both, and contrary to the Kings expectation, the Lyon fled into an inward den, and would not by any means endure the presence of the dogs, albeit the last dog pursued eagerly, but could not find the way to the Lyon. You shall understand the last two dogs whilest the Lyon held them both under his pawes, did bite the Lyon by the belly, whereat the Lyon roared so extreamely, that the earth shooke withall; and the next Lyon rampt and roared as if hee would have made rescue. The Lyon hath not any peculiar or proper kind of fight, as hath the Dog, Beare, or Bull, but only a ravenous kind of surprising for prey. The two first dogs dyed within few dayes, but the last Dog was well recovered of all his hurts, and the yong Prince commaunded his servant *Ed. Allen* to bring the dog to him to Saint James, where the Prince charged the sayd *Allen* to keepe him, and make much of him, saying, hee that had fought with the king of beasts, should never after fight with any inferiour creature.*

That winter England needed more than lions, mastiffs, spiteful cockfighting and rough footballing to give it a bit of cheer. Elizabeth's court, like any, was a royal hatchery of style and wit. Though we often think of the dandy as something from Regency England born of a vision of Beau Brummell, the Prince Regent's rakish but most definitely fashionable friend, Elizabeth's court was no less adorned with fops and baublers.† There is a wonderful example in 1603 of the most delicately dressed gallant in *Father Hubburds Tales*, written, we think, by Thomas Middleton. Father Hubburd was a ploughman, though educated enough, thanks to Middleton, to leave us a diary account of the farmworkers' amazement at the sight of the return of their gentleman farmer all dolled up from London in its latest styles.

[E]nters our young landlord, so metamorphosed into the shape of a French puppet, that at the first we started, and thought one of the baboons had marched in in mans apparel. His head was dressed up in white feathers like a shuttlecock, which agreed so well with his brain, being nothing but cork, that two of the biggest of the guard might very easily have tossed him with battle dores, and made good sport with him . . . his doublet was of a strange cut; and to shew the fury of his humour, the collar of it rose up so high and sharp as if it would have cut his throat by daylight. His wings, according to the fashion now, were as little and diminutive as a Puritans rough, which shewed he neer meant to fly out of England, nor to do any

---

* Edmund Howes, *Annales* (London, 1631), p. 824.
† George Brummell, born 1778 and died penniless at Caen in 1840.

exploit beyond sea, but live and die about London, though he begged in Finsbury. His breeches, a wonder to see, were full and deep as the middle of winter, or the roadway between London and Winchester, and so large and wide withall, that I think within a twelve month he might verie well put all his lands in them . . . his cloak of three pounds a yard, lined clean through with purple velvet, which did so dazzle our coarse eyes that we thought we should have been purblind ever after, what with the prodigal aspect of that and his glorious rapier and hangers all bossed with pillars of gold, fairer in show than the pillars in Pauls or the tombs at Westminster . . . casting mine eyes lower I beheld a curious pair of boots of king Philips [i.e. Spanish] leather in such artificial wrinkles, sets and plaits, as if they had been starched lately and came new from the laundress, such was my ignorance . . . with the fashion, and I dare swear my fellows and neighbours here are all as ignorant as myself . . . lastly he walked the chamber with such a pestilent gingle that his spurs over squeaked the lawyer and made him reach his voice three notes above his fee . . . thus was our young landlord accoutred in such a strange and prodigal shape that it amounted to above two years rent in apparel.

Fashion for the people, even Middleton's young landlord, usually consisted of cast-offs. There were two levels of fashion. The first was that of the Queen's and, later, James's Court. It was as if we had in the early seventeenth century some sense of Parisian haute couture, but for courtiers' wear only, which would later be bootlegged for the prêt-à-porter high streets. As soon as a new Court style appeared, then the old – maybe only weeks old – would be quickly abandoned. Here was the origin of the second tier of fashion. The landlord dandy was far from the court when he was at Finsbury and even more so at Winchester. He would hardly be admired at a royal levee even though he would be a figure of considerable astonishment down on the farm – and certainly in James VI's Scottish salon. In fact so sensitive was Elizabeth's Court that if a glimpse of legitimate fashion was had beyond St James's, then it would be discarded immediately by courtiers. By the time the landlord had returned with his hangers as thick with pearls as the white measles upon hog's flesh, he was woefully out of fashion. But as Breton had observed, it really was a mad world. Hope, but little sanity among his masters, was all that was in sight.

KING IN WAITING

IN THE OPENING MONTHS OF 1603 THE NATION UNDERSTOOD, SOME OF IT TACITLY, THAT IT WAS TO EMBARK ON A NEW DYNASTIC ADVENTURE. Yet a change in monarchy does not mean a dramatic change in society. We may talk and write about the end of the Tudors and the beginnings of the Stuarts, but the farmer and the herdsman did not leap from their beds one March morning sensing dramatic change and therefore do things differently. The simplest economic law of supply and demand reigned. Prices climbed in some parts of the food supply chain by 300 per cent. This is a general picture, and inevitably there were contradictions in the wealthy southeast as there had been when Caesar came and as there would be in the twenty-first century. The north and west, with their poorer lands, vulnerable to more extremes of climate, as well as to less deft management, could barely gather consecutive decent harvests. In the southeast there was, just as there has been since the Cantiaci, good and nourishing abundance.

We might add to this dank scenario at the start of the year a sense of expectation and impatience among the people. It was long known that the Queen was ailing. The glorious days of the defeated Armada had long passed. The cloud that hovered over Elizabeth's heart after the betrayal by Essex was reflected through the country. There is not much difference between the twenty-first century and the early seventeenth in the nation's interests and hopes for and against the subjects of its gossip. It is appropriate for the people who invented the net curtain and such a complex class system (the two go together) to be so nosy about the doings of others, especially the rich and powerful. But even the Court was stilled and drab as it waited for the end of Elizabeth's reign.

By contrast, the Scottish Court excitedly awaited a profound change in its fortunes. For now, in 1603, the often cataclysmic time of the Stuarts had come. We should never underestimate the importance of the accession of James VI of Scotland to the throne of England. Here was the first Scottish king to rule over both countries. For the first time a monarch would be styled, albeit at his own insistence, King of Great Britain.

Just as the people in the shires did not change their way of life because of a new monarch, the Constitution of England did not alter, nor was it corrupted. We talk of the last of the Tudors and the first of the Stuart monarchs. But there was no constitutional upheaval as there was, say, in 1688 when James II was chased from the throne by his daughter Mary and son-in-law William of Orange. It was certainly true that James I's son Charles precipitated the most enormous constitutional change, but that was not until 1640 and the meeting of the Long Parliament which began in November of that year. By then the whole concept of obedience to the monarch that Elizabeth enjoyed had dissipated.

In 1603 England was safe with its Elizabethan Constitution, although it had arrived at one of the historical post houses on the way to regicide and civil war. Yet even with the coronation of James I we should not think that the terrible events which followed were inevitable. James I was sometimes considered boorish and unwise, in spite of his intellectual talents. Yet there is no firm evidence to blame him for the collapse of the fretwork of unwritten constitutional mechanisms. All that would come later through Charles, who at the time of the coronation was but three years old and not then heir to the throne.

The greater concern of his courtiers, apart from their personal positions (which of course may have been their greatest concerns), was that James's smooth transition from Scotland to England, masterminded by Robert Cecil, should survive the traditional animosities between the two countries. Equally, considering the years and reputations that had been spent thinking about the Tudor successions to the throne, the fact that James and Anne had two sons who might succeed him was a blessed constitutional relief to the likes of Cecil.

Who should succeed Elizabeth had been the subject of enjoyable gossip and speculation, that most agreeable of pastimes. It was not confined to the likes of Cecil. In 1600 Thomas Wilson (see page 52) joined in and told us what people were surmising.

The nerest in bliud is James the Sixth, king of Scotland, as yet heire of the eldest sister of king Henry 8, Father to this Queene. The 2d is yoing damsell* of 18 yeares who cometh of the same lyne and by some thought more capable then he, for that she is English borne (the want thereof, if our Lawyers opinions be corant is the cause of his exclusion). She is thoght to be the lykelyest next the king of Scotland if she cann be proved to be daughter to a bastard, as they alledg her father was. The 3d is the eldest sonne of the Earle of Herteford, called the Lord Beauchampe, whose mother Katheryne was daughter to the Duke of Suffolke, sonne of Mary the 2d daughter of Henry 7. The 4th is his brother Henry Seymor . . . who thinketh he is the nerest because his brother . . . was begotten & borne before wedlock,

---

* Lady Arabella Stuart (1575–1615) whose sad life was blighted by this claim and ended in the Tower. See Ralegh trial, page 276.

but the truth is they will bothe be found bastards and double bastards . . . the 5th is the Earle of Derby . . . but by reason before aledged all the lyne must need be bastards . . . the 6th is the Earle of Huntington, who fynding all these the offspring of Henry 7 (cutt of eyther) by foranage, lawe or bastardy, cometh in with a tittle before Henry 7 from George, Duke of Clarence, brother to Edward the 4 of the house of Yorke, 240 yeares since; and so meanes to revive the tittle of ye house of Yorke, and so the variance betwixt the 2 houses of Lancaster and Yorke, which hath cost 20 hundred thousand mens lyves and 30 yeare Civill Warr. But his grandfather, the Lord Montague, was attayned of treason and putt to death by Henry 8, and so his heyers cutt off . . . 7 is the Earle of Westmorland whoe lyveth nowe with the Spaniard . . . the Earle of Northumberland is the 8th who fetched itt yett further of, from Mary the 2d daughter to Henry, Earl of Lancaster, sonne of Edmund Crouchback . . . the 9 . . . is the king of Portugals poore sonne . . . the 10 is the Duke of Parma, whose mother was Mary, eldest daughter of Edward, brother to Emmanuell king of Portugal . . . the 11th is the king of Spayne whose clayme is double; the first and eldest from Katherine, daughter of John of Gant [Gaunt] who was married to Henry 3, king of Castille of whom Charles the 5 and he is lineally descendet . . . the 12th is the Infante of Spayne, now married to the Archduke Albertus . . . there is a father fryer called Robt. Parsons in Spayne, who hath lately made a booke whereby, they say, he proves her to be the next undoubted heyre to the king of England . . . thus you see this Crowne is not like to fall to the ground for want of heads that claime to weare it.

So, in spite of a dozen claimants, there was little doubt that James would be monarch, whatever some thought of him, and certainly many were uncharitable in their opinions. James's character, whether or not that of the wisest fool in Christendom (according to Henry IV of France), is generally recorded in such a disparaging manner that any damage to the smooth running of the Constitution is too often laid at his door. James was something of an intellectual. He was well read. He had great mental as well as physical stamina. Given the chance, he would hunt from dawn to dusk for reason as well as for deer.

We must therefore examine this monarch's origins. After all, in 1603 James, with many bold statements of what people should think of him as a king and how he should be (note: not *might* be) treated as a monarch, may have caused many dissatisfactions and sneerings, but little damage to his political programme for a Great Britain. When those like Lady Anne Clifford described in scathing terms the state of James's Scottishness and court, then we should remember that very often people do not like change, especially among the aristocracy and even more especially if they feel their positions are threatened. This was particularly so in 1603 when, naturally, new faces appeared at Court, with many of them bearing more scars of revolution and plotting than designs of gracious and sophisticated living. With such a mixture of old and new orders it was only natural that a variety of views would be made known directly to the monarch. Consequently, with their formality, they survived, even though rejected. The Millenary Petition is an example of a strong view held by influential people; it was deflected but its message was not forgotten and influenced relations between Church and state long after the 1604 Hampton Court Conference which it helped to inspire (see page 240).

In 1603 James had more immediate concerns with what he thought would be greater policy. For example, he had inherited a throne somewhat drained of its resources through the war with Spain. This had to be stopped. To do so meant more than a pact or treaty with the Spanish king. It meant, for example, pulling the teeth of one of the most successful trades in late Elizabethan England – piracy (see page 321).

James was preparing the way for what he hoped was to be a

peaceful reign. Within twelve months of becoming king he was telling his first Parliament of the blessings 'which God hath, jointlie with my persone, sent unto you his outwarde peace . . . for by peace abroad with their neighboures the townes flourish, the merchants become riche, the trade doth increase and the people of all sortes of the land enjoye free libertie to exercise themselves in their severall locations without peril or disturbance'. It was of course all very well for the King to call for peace. That was not so easy among his people, merchants and pirates who had long profited from war and therefore the right to plunder, as well as the instinct to guard against and if necessary fight Catholic ambitions. Again we remind ourselves, when James became king it was only fifteen years since the Armada. The better-known history of Elizabethan England shows that the country survived on self-interest. It was no different in 1603.

So even with the apparently religious nature of the demands of the Puritans, there was a great deal of self-interest, and not only from the parish priests. After all, it was not the priests who owned the parishes and the glebe lands. There were more than 9000 church livings in England alone. Almost 4000 of them were 'owned' not by the Church but by private individuals, landowners and aristocracy. So when taxes, tithes and rents were raised on church livings, more than 40 per cent of the profits were going to the laity. Clearly self-interest could be seen as a motive for reform or resistance to reform. The Puritan reformers, of course, who were at the front of the objections, were in James's mind verging on zealous indignation. Given his character, his religious upbringing and his ability to spot a schemer (his formative years had been spent almost entirely with such people), it was always more likely that the guile of a Cecil would succeed where beckoning and accusing fingers failed. Again, it is not surprising that James, probably a little testy with the whole religious business, never went much beyond his initiatives at the Hampton Court Conference and was quite content once Richard Bancroft had been translated to the see of Canterbury shortly before Christmas the following year. He allowed Bancroft to 'sort out and settle' the case for uniformity even when it meant stripping ministers of their livings – although only 90 of the 9244 clergy lost their jobs. James's contentment with the running of the Church in the northern part of his new kingdom was complete when Tobie Matthew became Archbishop of York in 1606.

James's reign was also the point from which we might plot the decline in constitutional obedience to the British monarchy by the people. In the constitutional memoir of that monarchy we might at first glance read the enormous difference between Elizabeth – perhaps the most famous sovereign to rule these islands – and James VI of Scotland and I of England, who probably rates among the lesser-known rulers. Too often he is dismissed as ugly-mannered, self-opinionated and homosexual.

Yet Elizabeth and James had one particular bit of their history in common: they both came from uncertain times. Elizabeth was the child of Anne Boleyn whose imperfect life had an unhappy ending. The young Elizabeth could so easily have perished before reaching the throne. James's mother stormed through the wretched early days of her own reign and met a violent end. And like Elizabeth, James too had a less than stable youth, including being kidnapped, and might never have reached his inheritance. We could argue that this was about par for the constitutional course of many monarchs. Certainly the way to regicide had not been abandoned, although next time it was trodden it would leave a terrible unease and stain in British history and never again occur.

James VI of Scotland was born shortly after breakfast on Wednesday, 19 June 1566 in Edinburgh Castle. He was Mary Queen of Scots' only son. After lunch her husband, Lord Darnley, came to Mary's bed to see not his wife but the child. Darnley was, not unreasonably, suspicious and was eager to search the face of the infant for any alien characteristics. Mary confronted her husband's suspicion with her famous words, 'My Lord, here I protest to God, as I shall answer to Him at the great day of judgement, this is your son and no other man's son.'* This pronouncement by Mary did little to silence the suspicions that Darnley was not the father. The magic of that marriage had long been exposed as an illusion, and it was not to last. Mary must have felt considerable triumph at the birth of James. She was convinced that one day he would be monarch of both countries. She was perhaps rather pleased to have done what Elizabeth had failed to do – produce an heir.

Mary had been in Scotland but five years and was aged just twenty-four. She had arrived as the widow of Francis II of France, and she had met with no pretence of love and tolerance from and by her mother-in-law, the celebrated yet feared Catherine de Medici. The Scotland to which she had returned was predominantly Protestant. John Knox stormed, with his sermons declaring that a Roman Catholic mass was more dangerous than an armed invasion, and castigated Mary for being a Catholic. The Protestant cause could only succeed if Knox had the support of much, although not all, of the Scottish nobility. He had. Thus Mary was soon to discover that she did not rule Scotland. The Protestant nobles and the Kirk regarded themselves as guardians of that nation. Consequently, the nobles ruled and Mary quietly and privately followed the Roman order of service. More than that, she was overwhelmed by the authority of Elizabeth. The English monarch, fearful of Mary's motives, ambitions and religiosity, refused her permission to marry as she would, suggested whom she might wed, and most of all would not even consider recognising Mary's legitimate entitlement to succeed to the English throne.

As we know, Mary Queen of Scots was not faint-hearted. She would not, if at all possible, do as she was bid, especially by Elizabeth. So in 1565 she married her cousin, Henry Stewart, Lord Darnley, descended from Henry VIII's sister, Margaret Tudor. He was born in England and nominally a Protestant, but in truth a Catholic. In theory, then, Mary was the temporal governor of

* Lord Herries, *Historical Memoirs of the Reign of Mary, Queen of Scots and of King James the Sext* [Sixth], Abbotsford Club, no. 6 (Edinburgh, 1836).

the Catholics in both countries. The marriage was not successful, although she thought him a lusty enough fellow of nineteen when they first met. In reality Darnley was a lout, and a drunken one at that. She turned for confidences to David Rizzio, her Italian secretary, and, worse still, to the ruthless Earl of Bothwell. In 1566, when Mary was pregnant with James, Darnley could contain his jealousy of Rizzio no longer, stormed the Queen's rooms at Holyrood House, and stabbed Rizzio to death across the threshold. This was a terrible conspiracy which had involved William Ruthven,* the first Earl of Gowrie, whose family would be damned by James. Darnley, do not forget, was king consort although we always refer to him simply as Darnley. The whole incident put both King and Queen at great peril. They managed to escape to Dunbar. As a consequence of Rizzio's murder and the events that had led to it, Mary Queen of Scots, although restored to her nominal power, had come to detest Darnley.

Elizabeth and her ministers did not think much of these events north of the border. Sir Henry Killigrew, who had been sent by Elizabeth to enquire into the goings-on, was the first of her court to see the less than sweet baby James. Mary was keen that he should take a strong impression back to the childless Elizabeth. Just five days after James's birth Killigrew was writing to his Queen that the baby displayed 'head, feet, and hands, all to my judgment well proportioned and like to prove a goodly prince'. There is no sure indication that this filled the heart of Elizabeth with joy.

Meanwhile the politics of religion reigned. The general assembly of the Kirk respectfully requested that James should be baptised a Protestant. A charade was enacted when John Spottiswoode of the Kirk, in private with Mary, held James in his arms, muttered a short blessing, the baby gurgled, and this was taken as sufficient 'amen'

* William Ruthven (c. 1541–84). His second son, John, became the third Earl of Gowrie, was involved in the so-called Gowrie conspiracy and was killed in Perth in 1600 during an apparent attempt to capture James.

for the liturgy to be satisfied. A more formal occasion took place six months later, in December 1566, in the chapel at Stirling Castle. This was a pompous occasion, with the Earl of Bedford representing Elizabeth, who sent a gold font for the child. Mindful of the politics as well as Mary's dowager position, France also was represented, by the Count of Brienne. Indeed it was the French ambassador who carried Prince James to the chapel between lines of noblemen. None would have been on easy terms with Spottiswoode. These nobles were Catholics. The president of the service was the Archbishop of St Andrews, a Catholic. He baptised in the style of the Roman Church, with the Scottish Protestants, including the nobles and the Earl of Bedford, remaining outside the chapel. Formal names and titles were proclaimed – Charles James, Prince and Stewart of Scotland, Duke of Rothesay, Earl of Carrick, Lord of the Isles and Baron of Renfrew. It was an occasion of much festivity. Missing was the child's father, Darnley, who two months later was murdered at Kirk o'Field in Edinburgh. His murderer was Mary's lover, the Earl of Bothwell. Few regretted the death of this individual, but the consequences, both religious and political, were beyond doubt: Mary and Bothwell were doomed.

The young Prince was given into the care of the Earl of Mar at Stirling Castle. In April Mary saw the ten-month-old future King of Scotland and England for the last time. The following month, May 1567, she and Bothwell married. Immediately they plotted to kidnap James, and the Protestant lords determined this should not happen. In June the Queen's soldiers confronted the Protestant lords at Carberry Hill. Bothwell, true to character, abandoned Mary and fled Scotland. There had been no fighting. There had been no need for it. Mary was confined to Lochleven Castle and before the summer was out had abdicated, leaving the Earl of Moray to act as regent. And on 29 July 1567 at the little parish church of Stirling, Charles James was crowned King of Scots. Knox was triumphant. There was no need for hellfire and brimstone. He preached mightily at that coronation of the need for the true faith and the lords took oaths on behalf of the new monarch that he too would be Defender of the Faith, the Protestant faith.

Therefore, it is very probable that James VI of Scotland and I of England could never recall a time when he was not King. He would not for the moment have his palace at Holyrood House, although later he would issue brotherly proclamations to the people of England from there. He would stay at Stirling under the protection of the Earl and Countess of Mar. The Mar family would continue in that role until the King's majority.* Most important at this stage and to our story of the man who would be King of England was the young Prince's education.

James was given into the academic hands of Peter Young, a scholar from Geneva. It was, however, the second tutor who was to dominate James's education and discipline. This man was George Buchanan, the Scottish historian and poet. He was the strictest disciplinarian ever to enter the royal life.

George Buchanan was an odd choice as tutor. He was in his sixties, whereas Peter Young was youthful and gentle. Buchanan was short-tempered, stern and intolerant of any slight, and so would seek vengeance for any he felt. He also loathed Mary Queen of Scots. He made clear to James that his mother should be hated. He also regarded his position so strongly that if he chose to punish the young King then he would do so – and violently if he thought it best, which he usually did. On one occasion, having thrashed the infant James – and apparently quite thoroughly – the Countess of Mar told Buchanan that he had stepped beyond his position. Buchanan regarded her with contempt and said that if she wanted to kiss the boy's backside that was fine by him, but he would continue to thrash it when he thought necessary. We should not underestimate the effects on James of the years under Buchanan.

Equally, Buchanan did beat much learning and even knowledge

---

* When the Earl died in 1572, Sir Alexander Erskine, Mar's brother, became James's guardian.

into the Scottish King. Buchanan was a brute, but he was too an accomplished scholar. When James became King of England in 1603 there were those who much respected his Latin and Greek, and James, recovered from the sting of his punishments, if not the scars, always sang the academic praises of Buchanan, almost as if he were proud to have survived the old man's strict regime. Peter Young must not be forgotten. It does not take a behavioural psychologist of the Good Cop/Bad Cop school to anticipate that James sheltered in Peter Young's gentleness and therefore learned much from his other tutor, who apparently did not offend Buchanan with his quieter approach to education. It was probably Young who built James's library during those early schooldays. He certainly salvaged more than a hundred books from Mary's collection at Holyrood House.

Mary's leaning had been towards romance, which in the late 1500s was the equivalent of a collection of eighteenth- and nineteenth-century novels. She had read the mediaeval romances in addition to Italian and French poets. Buchanan and Young (especially the latter) built the boy's library from Greek and Latin classical works. Most of them were in the original ancient languages (remember, Latin was widely used at that time), but sometimes they were French and Italian translations. It is little wonder that James was more than simply well read and tutored. He found it easier as a child to work and think in Latin, Greek and, particularly, French. So it should not be surprising that when James fancied his skill as a poet, his better work was written in French as well as 'Scotch' and very little successfully in English.

By the time he was eight years old he was considered a scholar by many of his adult companions. He was taught to pray before breakfast and read from the New Testament in Greek. After breakfast he read first-century BC authors Cicero and Livy in the original. His afternoons might be spent on rhetoric, mathematics and astronomy. By the time he was sixteen in 1582 James could recite the histories of every known nation-state outside these islands. He was also receiving from Young, who had studied under Théodore de Bèze in

Geneva, tutoring in Calvinistic theology.* He became attracted to, so presumably influenced by, Calvinism, with all its arguments for scepticism, pronouncement and reasoning. The journey from premise to Calvinist truth had a simplicity, rigidity and intellectual cleanliness which appealed to James. Equally, with all the clarity of youth and the logic of a rigorous classical education, he was unattracted by the mysticism surrounding the Roman Catholic faith.

There was no father and no mother at hand to be proud of the little scholar. There was no one, not even the Mars, there to dispute Buchanan's notion that the King should be the most learned man in the country, his country. As much as he might have been in the affections of the Countess and the rest of the family, James as a boy had nothing that could be regarded as a natural upbringing.

He showed some interest in hawking and falconry and there is some evidence that he took a little exercise as a golfer.† Buchanan saw no clear reason why his charge should be either sporty or particularly well mannered. In fact Buchanan was altogether a curious tutor for a prince and king. He told James that titles and formal address were nonsensical and that James should not set too much store by them. (It would be interesting to know what lasting influence this had on James and how much it tempered his reaction to the Millenary Petition, which was certainly against clerical pomp.) We do not know if Buchanan did this as some kind consolation for James's physical difficulties. He was ungainly, awkwardly mannered and hardly handsome – not at all an image of the strapping and lusty Darnley, his father. Whatever the reason, Buchanan's influence stood the test of James's reign in Scotland and England. James's was a slovenly image and he passed to his son, Charles (born 1600), a warning against over-royal behaviour, apparently to

* Théodore de Bèze (or Beza) was celebrated for his New Testament translation which appeared in Geneva in 1590 and which James had studied.
† By then golf had been a sport for over a century. The word (from the Dutch *kolf*, club) certainly dates from 1457.

no great effect. Maybe another influence of Buchanan, a committed bachelor, was James's regard for women. He appears to have thought little of them.*

This is not the place for a biography of King James, but his childhood is of some importance if we are to understand the sort of person who became King of England in March 1603. For example, it wasn't until June 1579, when he was thirteen, that James was given much freedom from his studies. That autumn a great pageant was created for his first and triumphal entry into Edinburgh. A tableau of mythological characters and those of the Scottish royal family tree greeted him through every sequence of his festival arrival. Houses draped with tapestries and banners set a wonderful cheering and cheerful background. This was hardly the bare-boned existence Buchanan maintained for his student. Others understood the need for Scotland to have a king on display, particularly as there was ever an uncertainty about the authority and motives of the regency. There was no suggestion that James ignored the celebrations nor failed to delight in them. For all this, his childhood must have been lonely. Apart from his few friends, including the personable young Earl of Mar and a couple of other schoolfriends, among them William Murray and Walter Stewart, he was kept away from poor influences. His mother wanted him sent to France. No one in Scotland was fooled by her wishes: Mary wanted him to be brought up a Catholic, to be safe from Queen Elizabeth's influences and grasp, and perhaps even one day to lead the revolution that would restore her to the throne. James was kept in Scotland.

In 1579 James met his father's cousin, Esmé Stuart, who arrived from France in September. He had been sent to win over the affection of James and thus influence him in the direction of France, the ambitions of his mother and, of course, Catholicism. His motives were not obvious. For example, Esmé Stuart claimed to be a Protestant convert. He was also an opportunist and so could not help

* T. F. Henderson, *James I and VI* (Paris, 1904).

but work out for himself that he was better off with James's affections than with those of Mary. He also had a bright and engaging personality, a truly handsome distraction for James from his classical studies. James loved Esmé Stuart.

Stuart was no ordinary envoy. He was Seigneur d'Aubigny and soon Earl of Lennox and, thanks to the King, holder of the abbey of Arbroath and constable of Dumbarton Castle. The two factions that tried to hold sway over the King within the regency saw Stuart, by now known as Lennox, as the focal point of their ambitions or hatred. One side, led by the then regent, the Earl of Morton, disliked Lennox intensely. Morton's enemies, the Highlanders, the Earls of Atholl and Argyll, lined up with Lennox. Now the young King feared all about him and believed he was to be kidnapped and given to Queen Elizabeth. One of his problems was that he was broke, by royal standards. He may have been surrounded by courtiers, but he trusted few of them and could not afford to keep a reliable bodyguard. Elizabeth kept her distance and, for the moment, also her anxieties. James was rather like – constitutionally at least – an earlier English king, Edward II, whose courtiers had demanded that he choose between the kingdom and his lover, Piers Gaveston. Now the young James was warned that he should choose between Lennox and the protection and affection of the Queen of England. King James VI could not bear to be parted from Lennox's counsel.

With such a background of severe tutoring by Buchanan and explicit schooling in the midst of the intrigues of Morton, Argyll and Lennox, the barely teenage King grew up rapidly. He took refuge in rough sports, not gentle pastimes. He was surrounded, or surrounded himself, with ribaldry, infidelity and crude hedonism. Was this debauchery? Perhaps. Yet the Bible was still read at mealtimes. His Protestantism remained firm although the Church was convinced that he might turn to the Pope at any moment. But by the time he was fifteen or sixteen James was beginning to set aside the wisdoms of Buchanan. He was now beginning to set out in his own mind the beliefs of monarchy that were to be made famous shortly before his accession to the English throne. Even in his teenage years, James was being convinced of his Divine Right and, more importantly, responsibility, and not simply his constitutional right to rule. Imagine then the confusion in the minds of the clergy who perceived that their monarch saw the Scottish Reformation as a trend away from the Divine Right of kings. Was there Lennox's influence here? Certainly Huguenots were regarded in France as revolutionaries. And what did he think of John Knox, still fiercely preaching that no king could be above the Church, whatever powers and rights he claimed from his beliefs? Here was the basis of two kingdoms: the civil power of the monarch to run the country; the spiritual power of the Church, that is the Kirk, to be responsible for the moral and theological guidance of the nation. This meant that the spiritual power was from God and that there should be no temporal governor. Thus the monarch could not be chief governor of the Church on earth. Should the monarch choose to protect that Church then all was well, but that monarch should have no Divine Right over the Church. Therefore, the clergy ruled. Consequently the state had less authority than the Church. The young James was inclined to his own mind, and only Lennox might influence it. Whenever he might be criticised, James easily denounced his critics as undermining not him personally but the monarchy itself. Thus the critics had no right.

In 1581 Mary – still very much regarding Lennox as her envoy – made it clear to James that her abdication had been forced upon her and that therefore she was still queen and, although he could call himself king, he was really to rule in both their names. For good measure she expected her son to give up Protestantism and return to Rome. If he had any doubts about this proposition, Mary reminded him that the only way to absolute power on the Scottish throne and eventually on that of England was with the support of the Roman Catholic allies. The Jesuit William Crichton was sent to bring together a so-called Jesuit plot for James's, if necessary, forcible conversion to Catholicism. In this, there was great support from Philip of Spain who saw very good reason to have a Catholic king of Scotland, not for any religious motive, but simply as an ally against England. This was just five or six years before the Armada. Lennox might be imagined quite keen on using the Spanish – and of course their money, of which there was very little in Scotland – to bring about the Catholic ascendancy. The Jesuits fouled the enterprise, probably because they were too zealous. Philip withdrew and left Mary, and therefore Lennox, high and dry.

It could not be long before Lennox's enemies attacked him. But he was no slouch in these matters himself and it became a race to see which side could destroy the other first. The good Protestants, as they might have been called, included the Earl of Angus, Gowrie and Mar, the King's former schoolfriend, on one side; Lennox was on the other. In August 1582, during a hunting expedition, young James was 'invited' into Ruthven Castle, which was owned by Gowrie. He had been kidnapped, and we shall see that in one of his earliest proclamations in 1603 James demanded the apprehension of the Ruthvens, reminding the nation they were related to the ruthless Gowrie (see page 152). Lennox was told to get out of Scotland and James never saw him again.

King James never forgave the Ruthven lords, nor did he forgive this victory of the Protestant Kirk. No wonder he wished to put it behind him once he arrived in England. Lennox had not gone immediately from Scotland and had taken some sort of refuge at Dumbarton. There was talk of him rescuing the King and therefore his own fortune. The Ruthvens made it clear that if he tried such an adventure then the King's life, or probably death, would be in his hands, if not on his conscience. Lennox returned whence he had come, to France, and lived but a short time after that.

Elizabeth watched the goings-on with mixed feelings. She was obviously well pleased with the defeat of Lennox, but equally she would not want her own people to examine too closely the example of a nation forcing their monarch to do their bidding. And there was still the question of Mary Queen of Scots. Could this be an opportunity for Elizabeth to negotiate with Mary an alliance between the two states? A so-called 'association' was dangerous in James's eyes. Moreover, he could not see how her Catholic persuasion would allow her to rule in Scotland or have an alliance with England. Furthermore, he knew that unless there should be an heir born to Elizabeth that he, James, would one day rule both kingdoms. So why would he want his mother in everyone's good books? He would not. Much better to strike up good relations with Elizabeth on his own account. With James so inclined, it was also easier for Elizabeth to abandon any negotiations with Mary and to pay promises or more to James. Meanwhile he was still held by the Ruthvens.

In June 1583, after much muddling and incompetence on everyone's part, James was rescued. He was now in the debt and under the influence of the Earl of Arran. Whether he had been better off with the Ruthvens is a point for debate elsewhere. Arran ruled Scotland. Consequently it was a violent kingdom: Gowrie was executed and in the spring of 1584 the rest of the Ruthvens escaped to England. The differences between the factions were so great that many, including church ministers who were not on Arran's side, had to take refuge in England.

There remained the vexed matter of the Presbyterian Church which Arran and James appeared bent on destroying. In May 1584 the King was declared head of the Church – it proved to be a tenuous assumption. Walsingham was sent by Elizabeth to find out what was going on. He lectured James, who threw a variety of mood changes and resorted to the standard reply of all despots: it would be best to allow him to choose his advisers, just as it would be best for him, James, not to interfere with Elizabeth's choice of those who should run her country. Walsingham was rather grand. He treated James as an irritatingly ignorant youth and told him that he had no judgement or experience in these matters and that he might remember that absolutism when not supported by wisdom, or at the very least guile, would probably result in a fall from power.

It was all very well for James VI to cloak himself in indignation, but the surer truth was that Scotland was badly governed and in a seemingly constant state of insurrection. Nor was there any sign of a friend, apart from a reassuring letter from the Duke of Guise, which in a quieter moment James might have understood would never have been written without an ulterior motive.

No wonder James read too much into the smallest hope and then came to believe that his so-called allies, the Pope, the French, the Spanish and even his mother could not get him out of his constitutional and personal difficulties. He was forced to try to arrange better relations with Elizabeth, who, for her part, thought it best to do no more, in the summer of 1584, than to discuss the possibility of an agreement for Mary Queen of Scots' freedom under certain guarantees, one of which had to be that James would stop his mother causing trouble. For all his difficulty James was not, as Walsingham had told him, stupid. He may have been crudely mannered, but his mind had been well fashioned.

By spring 1585 James had sufficiently distanced himself from Mary's idea of the association. Mary was furious and threatened to disinherit him. From what? James had had enough and from that point he did not even bother to write to his mother again. Was this a future king of England with no compassion? No. This was a young man of extraordinary upbringing bereft of any family life whose first taste of any affection had been with Lennox. And even that had not been what it seemed.

By the second half of 1585 Arran had been deposed as a power, although his new ministers effectively held the King prisoner. They allowed him very little constitutional freedom. Yet he would not give way so easily on points of religion and his own belief in the Divine Right to rule. Nor could his feelings and reactions be ignored when more and more evidence filtered to the royal apartments of the very real possibility that Mary Queen of Scots might be killed. For the English, this was no small matter. There was now an agreement with Scotland. Might James revoke that agreement if his mother were executed? James, who was poorly represented in Elizabeth's court, made a personal plea that Elizabeth should be mindful of not simply Scottish reaction, but of those in other countries should his mother die. James never made a direct threat to Elizabeth. He was really in no position to do so. His mother was beheaded on 9 February 1587. James made no suggestion that he would retaliate. Why not? Perhaps he had, even indirectly, been party to her dramatic departure. There was now no question of the association. There was but one monarch of the Scots and no pretender.

James had, however, to go through the rigmarole of protest. Elizabeth had wronged him, so she should pay. Moreover, he may have been playing a complex game, but there were those whose raw reactions could not be ignored. Whether or not they had supported Mary, the Scots had lost a queen to the most terrible of enemies. Many wanted and demanded vengeance. It is said that James did little to stop the raids on England that followed, though in fact there was nothing he could do. He went through the motions, partly to reassure the Scottish nobles and peers, of writing to the French asking them to help him avenge Mary's death. The French wrote back but said very little, which did not disturb him – the correspondence had all the ritual of an unpaid and written-off tailor's account.

Anyway, most attention was now on the Spanish, who were planning the Armada. And if the Spanish got England it would not be long before they got Scotland. James's own Scottish Catholic nobility were in on this plot and they were planning to bring Spanish soldiers to Scotland. However, there is hardly any evidence to suggest that Philip of Spain would have been capable of stretching his army, logistics and influence that far from London. He would never physically have been able to hold England, let alone Scotland. Although James seemed in constant fear for his position, the Catholic plotting might have been seen as to his advantage. If Elizabeth saw him threatened and knew that he opposed that threat, however weak he might be, she would be well disposed to him. It is not clear how much real comfort Elizabeth took in James's offer of his soldiers and 'all that he commanded against you strangers'. The weather saved everyone further anxieties in 1588, the Armada dispersed and with it the threat of invasion.

We are still fifteen years away from 1603, and if James were to consolidate his claim to the English throne, then it would be useful to present the Whitehall courtiers with the one credential in which Elizabeth had famously failed: James had time to produce an heir. First he must be provided with a wife. It was in 1589 that he married Anne of Denmark. There had been only two people James had imagined that he might wed: Elizabeth, a daughter of Frederick of Denmark, or Henry of Navarre's sister, Princess Catherine de Bourbon. Apparently it took him fifteen days of solid prayer to decide. James not only prayed hard, he did his sums: he expected whoever he married to fetch him a very good dowry. Catherine's brother, however, was just as hard-up as James. The Danish option was altogether more attractive. James by now was twenty-three; the would-be Danish bride was a teenager. To James this immediately gave her the advantage over Catherine, who was thirty-one. The Scottish King's courtiers liked the idea of the French match. They thought it altogether more prudent. James was more interested in the dowry and preferred a teenager to a bride twice that age, good at her housekeeping, but with little money of her own to do it.

Now we come to the twist in James's love life: when he sent his tutor, Peter Young, to the Danish court in 1587 to arrange the marriage, James thought he was getting Princess Elizabeth. King Frederick of Denmark had two daughters, Elizabeth and Anne. Here is an interesting reminder of how in the twenty-first century we think we know everything and, when we do not, we can so easily find out through our instant system of communications. James had never seen the two princesses. He knew very little about them and nor did anyone else in his court. These were not the days of emailing photographs.

When Young arrived in Denmark with an offer from King James VI of Scotland for the hand of Princess Elizabeth he was told rather shortly that this was not at all possible. She was engaged to the Duke of Brunswick. This put Peter Young in a difficult position. To marry the younger daughter of another monarch would be considered something of a come-down. It implied that royal protocol had been denigrated and that the King of Scotland did not have first choice.

The Danes were phlegmatic, almost to the point of indifference. They agreed that Princess Elizabeth was prettier and a better catch, but to their minds there was nothing wrong with Princess Anne, who was then only twelve years old but reasonably presentable for her age.* There might just be a bargain here, thought James, especially if he could get a good dowry plus a raft of concessions, trade agreements, defence commitments, and especially if the Danes should give up their claim to the Orkneys. King Frederick died in 1588 while the negotiations continued. As far as the Danes were concerned, the bit of gold that Frederick had left his younger daughter was the only money she would bring to Scotland. The marriage looked in great doubt.

Soon, however, stories began to reach Scotland of the great efforts of Anne's mother, Sophia. She apparently was organising a silver coach, boxes of jewels, a grand and expensive trousseau. This appealed to James VI's sense of market values. He thought it best to come to some arrangement before these baubles attracted another suitor. In this, James was foolish. Not that he was in a position to make a grand occasion of the marriage. We know that he had little regard for personal appearance and formality other than that no man should forget he was king. The Scottish people were taxed to the tune of £10,000 to pay for the wedding. Elizabeth I sent him £1000 and arranged for £2000 worth of silver plate to be made in England for the wedding. It was but a loan.

The wedding itself was a fiasco. On 20 August 1589, James and Anne of Denmark were married by proxy in Copenhagen. The bride was then put on a ship for Scotland. Just as in the previous year when the weather had put paid to well-laid plans of Spanish admirals in

* In English law, Anne was therefore of the age of consent.

the English Channel, so now foul conditions prevented the Danish admiral from delivering his royal cargo. Again we must think of the times and vague communications compared with our own. The mobile phone was unknown, so there was no chance of a call to James along the lines of 'I'm on the ship, but there's a delay.' Anne of Denmark had been diverted to Oslo to sit out the storm. James did not know this. If the foul weather prevented her sailing across the sea, so it also stopped a messenger from getting across to tell him she had been delayed. All he knew was that she had left. August turned to September, turned to October, and still no news. Imagine James's state of mind. And then on 10 October a vessel from Norway came with the news that his bride was in Oslo. On 22 October James sailed to get her. This was totally against Court protocol and also the wishes of any of his courtiers. Why should this be? What would happen if he were captured by some foreign devil demanding ransom? What if he never returned?

More urgently, while James was away who would be able to control the spiteful factions in his court? James, in his early twenties, may have believed in the Divine Right of kings to rule and his superior intellect above any at his court, but this one act of sailing to collect his bride was, to that point, probably the biggest single moment of defiance in his life. It took courage and it took guile. He made it to his bride's side and on 23 November at the bishop's palace in Oslo, King James VI left not a royal palace of Scotland but his lodgings in the city for his wedding. Interestingly, the wedding was performed in French. James gave his bridegroom's speech in Latin. It seems by all accounts that James was very much in love with his blonde Danish lady.

There seemed no hurry to return to Scotland and the weather did not encourage the voyage. Imagine then the consternation in Scotland. In January the couple arrived not in Scotland, but at Elsinore and Kronbourg Castle, the bride's Danish home. There they stayed until the last few days of April 1590. It was not until 1 May that James and Anne arrived back at Leith and not until 19 May that they made their formal entry into Edinburgh. This was not much of a Scottish honeymoon for Anne. The back-stairs courtiers either plotted against her or drew her into their plots. Nor did she get on with the Kirk. She was, after all, a Lutheran, so did not think highly of Presbyterians. She was not much used to clergy publicly damning royalty. There was greater religious consternation to come. Some time during the 1590s, Anne converted to Roman Catholicism. There were no great public consequences other than fury among the clergy, and after a little time that did not matter.

This arranged marriage was, apparently, a tender union during those early years. Yet after the first flush of union, the two discovered their differences. They did not fight. They were simply on different planes. James rather admired male company and was, whatever else is said about him, an intellectual of his day. Buchanan may have succeeded in his aim of making James the most learned man in the kingdom. Anne of Denmark showed some elegance, but very little scholarship.

There is an extra moment that we should think about before James enters England. In 1599 he had written to Pope Clement VIII. The letter was a formality and concerned nothing more than a request that one William Chisholm be appointed a cardinal. The significance of the letter is in the way it was addressed to the Pope: *Beatissime Pater*. Also, he used the phrase *Obedientissimus Filius*. So what do we make of that? An obedient son? Was James contemplating conversion? Of course, Clement VIII would have celebrated his conversion because James would become King of England. To have a Catholic King of England would be a Roman triumph. As the King of England would be independent of the influences of the French and Spanish, that would be a bonus for the Pope. We do know that Clement responded to that letter in April 1600 suggesting conversion. We know also that James did not reply, but his wife did. Then Clement wrote again saying how pleased he was that Anne had converted and hoped so much that their son, Henry, would be brought up as a Catholic.* Much later, James claimed that he simply scribbled his signature to the letter without much noticing its content and styling. This ruse (still used in the twenty-first century by even the most highly placed political leaders) convinced no one.

There were other letters, more secret, to less benign characters. For example, James wrote to the Earl of Tyrone, Hugh O'Neill, in the most friendly tones. Tyrone was an enemy of Elizabeth I in Ireland. James protested that his letters were innocent and publicly issued proclamations forbidding any Scot to help Tyrone. He did so in the full knowledge that the proclamations might easily be ignored. He also kept up correspondence with the Earl of Northumberland anticipating his, James's, monarchy of England. He wanted to reassure Northumberland, one of the more important of the Catholic peers, that he would not persecute Catholics once he came to his kingdom. This was not a bad tactic. Although many said logically he would be king on Elizabeth's death, he could not be sure, and the Catholic minority was not to be ignored. By the time James became king it could be that as much as a third of the nation was Catholic – albeit many of them secretly so.

The hard-line Catholics, for example the Jesuits, were sceptical of James's avowal of tolerance towards them. Some saw him simply as wanting to reassure potential enemies that he would be a good king and therefore they should support him. There is some reason for this scepticism, particularly as he was making opposite noises to the Protestants. There was, too, a more public conundrum that James had to consider – not being able to anticipate famous moments to come. James had to decide what to do about the Earl of Essex.

The war between Essex and Cecil for the control of the English Court was a difficulty for James, as Essex claimed his friendship. Just

---

* Prince Henry died of typhoid fever in 1612. It was their second son, Prince Charles, born in 1600, who became James's heir. A daughter, Princess Margaret, born in 1598, died in infancy. Their eldest daughter, Princess Elizabeth, born in 1596, became Queen of Bohemia.

supposing Essex succeeded and there was an attempt to overthrow Elizabeth, what then should he do? At that stage James could not know that Essex was a bad ally and that he would go to the block for his treachery. Perhaps the axeman saved James from his intellectual's habit of indecision. Elizabeth, thanks to Cecil, was hardly unaware of the Essex–James connection. She wanted at least public reassurance that King James had not been involved with and had not encouraged Essex's rebellion. If Essex were a difficulty for James, then so he was too for Robert Cecil. Cecil could hardly arrange a neat succession if the man he championed were marked with Essex's treachery. With Essex gone Cecil could now get down to the business of guaranteeing a smooth succession to the English throne.

Robert Cecil was one of two sons of William Cecil. Robert's grandfather, Richard, had established the family estates at Burghley in Northamptonshire and had been a favourite of Henry VIII. By the time Richard died in 1552, the family was already considerably powerful at court and moderately wealthy. It was William who was to become the first Lord Burghley. Elizabeth in 1558 had appointed him her chief secretary and so for forty years, as we have seen, he designed and executed the policies that shaped her reign. One son, Thomas, inherited the barony, became the first Earl of Exeter (a title created for him by James), and spent his life not as a courtier as his father had done, but as a soldier. He fought in the 1573 Scottish war and against the Armada in 1588 and suppressed the attempted coup of Essex in 1601. William's eldest son was Robert. It was he who took over from his father in Elizabeth's court the duties of secretary and took on the constitutional task of masterminding the transition to James. A mark of Cecil's statesmanship was his overwhelming desire for stability in the kingdom, and that meant stability at the centre of the realm, that is the throne. It is wrong to say that Cecil and James became conspirators in any sinister sense, but their relationship was a constitutional conspiracy for reasons which amounted to transition and uncomplicated continuation of English monarchy.

By now Elizabeth was sixty-eight and in less than two years would be dead. Robert Cecil, as her secretary of state, had worn very easily the mantle that had been his father's and that had been draped about his shoulders by the ageing Queen. It was he who would become the first Earl of Salisbury and the first Viscount Cranborne. Imagine the delicacy of the constitutional and personal position of Cecil. The Queen's life was hardly to be prolonged, yet her wit was not dulled. For much of her reign she was tormented by the lack of a natural heir. Towards the end of that reign she understood the consequences of not providing her people with a prince. There were other candidates to the throne of England or at least those ambitious for it (see page 73 above). The true succession had to come with James VI of Scotland with his direct claim to the throne through the fact that he was the great-grandson of the wife of James IV of Scotland, Margaret Tudor (1489–1541), the eldest daughter of the English King, Henry VII. Therefore, the constitutional issue was hardly debatable. Much rested on the sensitivities of an ageing Elizabeth and the insensitivities of an eager and sometimes utterly undiplomatic James. Cecil, the supreme courtier who had missed no lessons in his father's diplomatic schoolroom, now made friends with King James, who only months earlier had been close to, if not in league with, the executed Essex.

James, sensing that the starting bell had tolled for the last lap to the throne, went out of his way to promise Cecil his undying friendship, his every ounce of sincerity, and promises of boundless honours once Cecil had achieved their joint aim of him becoming James I of England. Cecil plotted, but on his own terms and never in a manner to bring him into danger. He knew well that a successful transition from Edinburgh to London would make James inclined to scatter sweets in his direction. Cecil was too wise to do anything that might be seen, especially by his enemies, as a plot against Her Majesty and against his own interests. Thus Cecil declared there had to be absolute secrecy so that neither anxiety should be caused in the Queen's heart nor accusation of treacherous intent be directed at either James or Cecil (by which he really meant at himself alone). 'The subject itself is so perilous to touch amongst us as it setteth a mark upon his head forever that hatcheth such a bird,' he wrote. At the same time Cecil was careful to remind James that any honours would be gratefully received and, although he did not say so, Cecil knew that his prize would be to continue as secretary of state and to have absolute power, for he understood that James would inevitably bring with him the rough and money-hungry hordes of his Edinburgh Court. Cecil could and did anticipate the constitutional as well as financial pillage being hatched in and about Holyrood House. In this, he would be proved alarmingly correct.

He had also the difficult task of continuously reassuring King James that he was looking after the latter's interests. Often, the devious ways of the English court were a mystery to the Scottish King and therefore he might easily have wondered if Cecil had other ambitions for the throne. For example, there were those who said that Cecil was inclined to Spain to rule England. Was there not after all a case for the throne going to Isabella Clara Eugenia, the daughter of Philip of Spain? The Spanish claim, although patently contrived, was through their descent from John of Gaunt. There was nothing new in this. Ever since 1594, the more than mischievous zealot and Jesuit Robert Parsons had made out a moral, religious and even hereditary claim on the Infanta's behalf. It was all very well for Cecil to dismiss the matter, but he did not have the sense of insecurity of James VI. Given James's turbulent life story thus far, there is little need to explain the uncertainties of the Scottish King. While James was speaking of anxieties and at the same time writing to his 'dearest and trusty Cecil', to his worthy, wise and so provident friend, Cecil had to tone down the King's humour and instil a greater sense of courtly propriety. The reputation of William Cecil is that of the greatest statesman in English history. His son Robert, during those long months leading to March 1603, should not be forgotten. It was Robert who impressed upon James that he should not push Elizabeth towards open agreement and proclamation about the accession. He should simply gain Elizabeth's affection and thereby her reassurances. He should avoid lobbying either Catholics or Protestants because he might find himself promising that which he could not deliver, and he might too easily find his approaches catching the ear of Elizabeth who had long heard every murmur among high placemen as the catechism of the plotter. In short, Cecil's first task was to convince James that he should leave the whole matter in his hands.

James took good note of Cecil and even used his own undoubted literary skills (although he never did master English subtlety) to good effect. His letters to Elizabeth in all manner of things were quite brotherly, and became more so when he received her sisterly replies. James the poet breathed affection and what he called contentment from her letters. His 'dearest sister and cousine' apparently inspired James to believe that she was his oracle. Elizabeth, properly amused, noted that there was never 'any prince nor meaner wight* to whose grateful terms I did not correspond'. Such affection, such declarations of loyalties, such confidential diplomacy suggested that James now believed that any plotting on his part for the throne of England was quite out of her mind, and anyway, with Cecil's guidance, it was quite unnecessary.

Cecil had repeated that his relationship with the King had to be secret. Imagine the consequences of the Queen of England discovering that her most trusted servant was effectively arranging her funeral. Also, Elizabeth had never actually said that James would succeed her. Cecil was sure of his constitutional duty, but he was equally sure of the Queen's response should she learn of the way in which he was exercising that responsibility. It was impossible, however, that the dialogue between Cecil and James could remain their secret

---

* Wight is probably of Germanic origin, certainly Old English. In the sixteenth century it sometimes meant a spirit. Often it would be used to signify a person for example, a cheerful wight. In this case, 'meaner wight' is not a miserly person, but as in 'no mean man'.

alone. Meetings, correspondence and arrangements would mean a small number of trusted friends should be aware that something was afoot, even if they did not know the details. Thus in Scotland James trusted his schoolroom chum the Earl of Mar, his cousin Sir Thomas Erskine and his envoy David Foulis. In England three were in on the secret. It is not absolutely clear who these people were, other than that Lord Henry Howard, the brother of the Duke of Norfolk, probably knew. The Earl of Nottingham and Lord Howard de Walden possibly knew, too. The importance of this coterie was that any one of its parts might be indiscreet. Henry Howard was the least trustworthy. Elizabeth had never much cared for him. She liked neither his nature nor the family connection with Mary Queen of Scots – which had resulted in the topping of a Howard for treason. Today we would probably call him a greasy schemer. Curiously, Cecil trusted him and most certainly used him. Given the attitude of the Queen towards the Howards, and this one in particular, Lord Henry Howard was just as nervous as Cecil of being discovered as part of the unofficial committee organising James's assumption of the English throne. One person who knew something was going on, and whom Cecil did not trust, was James's wife, Queen Anne. Mindful that James should never be put in a position of doubting Cecil, the latter told Lord Henry Howard that he must warn James about his wife. This was not an easy task. Although by now James was hardly devoted to Anne there was no way that he would accept rudeness from an English Catholic lord. Equally, he was no fool and had already made up his mind to be wary of his over-inquisitive wife.

There was one particular group of people who would be against James, and about whom Cecil instructed Howard to warn the Scottish King. This single act was no aside in the constitutional dialogue. It would have enormous consequences for the leader of that group and eventually his would be one of the most famous executions in seventeenth-century history. Cecil's great rival at court was Sir Walter Ralegh. Cecil well knew that if Ralegh got wind of what he was doing then the Queen would know and that he, Cecil, would fall. It was even possible that his head would fall, too. So Lord Henry Howard took up his quill. Where he had been nothing less than obsequious in wording his warning to James about Queen Anne, he was now as spiteful and condemnatory as only a practised courtier can be. His letter explained to James that a trio of such untrustworthy conspirators – Sir Walter Ralegh, Lord Cobham and the Earl of Northumberland – could not be found anywhere else in the Scottish monarch's future kingdom. He implied that Ralegh, Cobham and Northumberland would rather see James assassinated than crowned. Little wonder then that when James arrived in England he greeted Ralegh with the words 'O my soul, mon, I have heard rawly of thee.' So indeed he had. It was no surprise that he agreed quickly that Ralegh should lose almost all his privileges and property as soon as could be decently arranged.

An amusing side to this tight-knit plotting was that many courtiers and nobles believed the open secret that James would be the next king and therefore, seeing the way the land would lie, started approaching James in Scotland and Cecil in London with confidential promises that they could bring about a peaceful transition, little realising the secret arrangements in hand. The general reaction of James was that he would never ask favours of others in such a matter and that the Divine Right of kings would prevail, if that was indeed the Divine wish. Cecil used the approaches to pretend anger against the King of the Scots. He never left anything to chance.

By March 1603 it was clear that Queen Elizabeth was close to death. Cecil, at the beginning of that month, had two important tasks to make doubly sure of the rightful and peaceful changeover. At the opening of the seventeenth century there was no established structure of seamless authority with a huge bureaucracy to continue the running of the nation during the discreet arrival of the removal van at the garden entrance of No. 10 Downing Street. It would, moreover, take many days, perhaps weeks, before the new monarch could arrive in London from Edinburgh. Cecil therefore first had to have an absolute guarantee from James that he understood that

Queen Elizabeth's council – that is, the government of the day – would remain in place until such time that James was physically on the throne and settled enough to give reasonable orders. Accordingly, Cecil wrote to James for this assurance and it was given.

Elizabeth's secretary of state had a second task. The death of a monarch is the signal for mischief-makers, both frivolous and deadly serious, to take their chance. If there is to be an uprising or palace revolution, either is best put into motion during the hiatus between the last gasp of the monarch and the first breath of the successor. Therefore, the first true indication throughout the kingdom that Elizabeth I was nearing death was when Cecil gave orders that all dissidents should be arrested, that the capital should have its guards doubled and noticeably so, and that the strategically important cities of England should have their soldiery put on high alert. For three weeks in March 1603 England stood to attention and on its guard. Some stood nervously; after all, the woman they had honoured was their patron. On her death, they would be friendless where it mattered most – their offices, status and even their estates could be forfeited. One who worried for his future was her kinsman Sir Robert Carey, the son of Lord Hunsdon.*

At forty-two, Carey was the Lord Warden of the Middle Marches, the border with Scotland. He would weep at Elizabeth's passing. Prudently, he would contrive to be the messenger of her death and be the first to bend in homage to James VI of Scotland – unless Cecil could stop him, which most certainly he would attempt so to do. In March 1603 Carey, believing the border country to be peaceful and quiet, felt it safe to leave the security of the wild country in the hands of his deputies. He was fearful that he would lose his position when Elizabeth died. Just as many would rush to James's side to renew or gain patronage, so at this point others rode to Richmond Palace in case

---

* Later Earl of Monmouth. His account of Elizabeth's death and his ride to inform James was written as late as 1627 and kept private until Lord Cork allowed it to be published in 1759. A copy is to be found in the British Library.

some last and lasting favour might be gained from the dying monarch. Carey also travelled to the Court. This part of his memoir tells of the final days of Elizabeth, or rather the last days as he remembered them and understood from others what had happened.

I found the Queen ill disposed, and she kept her inner lodging. Yet she, hearing of my arrival, sent for me. I found her in one of her withdrawing chambers, sitting low upon her cushions. She called me to her.

I kissed her hand, and told her, It was my chiefest happiness to see her in safety and health, which wished might long continue.

She took me by the hand, and wrung it hard; and said 'No, Robin, I am not well!' and then discoursed with me of her indisposition, and that her heart had been sad and heavy for ten or twelve days: and, in her discourse, she fetched not so few as forty or fifty great sighs.

I was grieved at first to see her in this plight: for, in all my lifetime before, I never knew her fetch a sigh, but when the Queen of Scots was beheaded . . .

I used the best words I could to persuade her from this melancholy humour; but I found, by her, it was too deep rooted in her heart; and hardly to be removed.

This was on 19 March, a Saturday. That evening Carey noted that Elizabeth ordered that her chapel should be made ready for the Sunday. Yet he tells us that she did not go into the 'Closset' but was rested on cushions at the door to hear the service.

From that day forwards she grew worse and worse. She remained on her cushions four days and nights . . . all about her could not persuade her, either to take any sustenance or go to bed.

I hearing that neither her Physicians, nor none about her, could persuade her to take any course for her safety, feared her death would soon ensue.

I could not but think in what wretched estate I should be left: most of my livelihood depending on her life. And thereupon bethought myself with what grace and favour I was ever received by the king of Scots, whensoever I was sent to him. I did assure myself it was neither unjust nor unhonest for me to do for myself; if GOD at the time should call her to his mercy.

Hereupon I wrote to the king of the Scots knowing him to be the right heir to the Crown of England; and certified him in what state Her Majesty was. I desired him not to stir from Edinburgh: and if, of that sickness she should die, I would be the first man that should bring the news of it . . . On Wednesday, the 23rd March she grew speechless.

That afternoon by signs she called for her [Privy] Council: and by putting her hand to her head, when the king of Scots was named to succeed her, they all knew he was the man she desired should reign after her.

At about six at night, she made signs for the Archbishop [Whitgift] and her Chaplains to come to her. At which time, I went in with them; and sat upon my knees full of tears to see that heavy sight. Her Majesty lay upon her back; with one hand in the bed, and the other without.

The end was hours away. Those left with their monarch prayed for this life and for the next. Whitgift told her that her time had come and examined her in faith. She answered in blinkings. Also there was Carey's sister, Eleanor, married to Lord Scrope.* Lady Scrope was a key actor in the drama that was to immediately follow Elizabeth's death. After prayers had been exhausted, Elizabeth was left with her ladies-in-waiting. Carey went to his lodging and gave orders to one in the Coffer's Chamber to call him if Elizabeth's end looked close. He paid the porter an angel to let him back in at any time.

* In some documents at the time called Philadelphia, Lady Scroope.

In the early moments of Thursday 24 March Elizabeth turned her face to the wall and died. There was blessed relief, but also work to be done. Carey was called some time between two and three in the morning. The Privy Council had given orders that no one should be allowed into (or out of) Richmond Palace without a Council warrant. Fortunately for the story, one of the Council, Sir Edward Wotton, met Carey and took him inside the palace.

The word had got about that Carey intended to ride north, and the Council, under Cecil's instructions, told him not to move without permission. He was trapped inside. Cecil did not want him spreading the news, especially to James. However, Carey's brother, George, Lord Hunsdon, was in the palace and he bluffed his way through, with Carey at his side. There were factions within the Council, and, more importantly and in spite of Cecil's authority, there were certain individuals and families with much to lose, or gain, by following their own instincts for survival and position. Carey escaped from Richmond, found a horse from the royal stable, and turned for London.

> I got to horse, and rode to the Knight Marshals lodging by Charing Cross and there stayed until the Lord [that is, the Privy Council] came to Whitehall Garden ... they were very glad when they heard I was not gone and desired the Marshal to send for me and I should with all speed be despatched for Scotland.

But this was a plot. They wanted Carey apprehended – probably placed under house arrest – and one of Cecil's own men sent to Scotland. It was the marshal, knowing the plot, who warned Carey and told him to be off before he was caught.

> I took horse between nine and ten oclock and that night rode to Doncaster [162 miles from London and 235 miles from Edinburgh].

The Friday night [25 March] I came to my own house at

Widdrington [Withrington, 99 miles from Edinburgh] and . . .
took order with my Deputies [of the Middle Marches] to see the
Borders kept in quiet . . . and that the next morning the king of
Scotland should be proclaimed king of England at Widdrington,
Morpeth and Alnwick.

Very early on Saturday [26 March] I took horse for Edinburgh
and came to Norham about twelve noon, so that I might well have
been with the king at supper time; but I got a great fall by the way
and my horse with one of his heels gave me a great blow on the
head, that made me shed much blood. It made me so weak that
I was forced to ride a soft pace after: so that the king was newly
gone to bed by the time I knocked at the gate.*

I kneeled by him and saluted him by his title 'England,
Scotland, France and Ireland'.

He gave me his hand to kiss; and bade me welcome.

After he had long discoursed of the manner of the Queen's
sickness, and of her death, he asked, what letters I had from
the [Privy] Council. I told him None and acquainted him how
narrowly I had escaped from them. And yet I brought him a
blue ring from a Lady that I hoped would give him assurance
of the truth I reported. He took it, and looked upon it and said
'It is enough. I know by this you are a true messenger'.

This is the famous story of the secret ring. It is sometimes said that
the ring was taken from Elizabeth's dead finger and given to Carey.
Documents in the Carey Papers† suggest that James had kept a long
correspondence with 'Lady Scroope' (or Scrope), Carey's sister. In
this source, it is said that the ring was not on Elizabeth's finger but
that James had sent Lady Scrope a sapphire ring with instructions
to return it to him as a sign that Elizabeth was dead. It is said that

* Carey's arrival is variously recorded as having been midnight Saturday or the
early hours of Sunday 27 March.
† British Library shelfmark 12269.

she threw the sapphire to her brother from a window at Richmond Palace and so began his journey. Was Carey's effort to maintain his titles and offices worthwhile? At first, yes it was. James was naturally grateful. He looked after Carey and gave him into the care of Lord Home (an ancestor of the twentieth-century Foreign Secretary and Conservative Prime Minister) and announced that he would carefully consider any reward Carey thought reasonable for his effort. Carey knew exactly what he wanted, and so James gave Carey the title of Gentleman of the Bedchamber with this promise: 'I know you have lost a near Kinswoman and a loving Mistress: but take here my hand I will be as good a Master to you and will requite you this service with honour and reward.'

But as March closed, mourning for his kinswoman was no longer Carey's most pressing concern. How he could ever have imagined that Cecil would let him off lightly, or that the King would fight his corner against Cecil, is hard to fathom. Cecil told the King that Carey should be dismissed, and James, abandoning his fine phrases, agreed. Carey was distraught.

Most of the Great Ones in Court envied my happiness, when they heard I was sworn of the king's Bedchamber; and in Scotland I had no acquaintance I only relied in GOD and the king. The one never left me: the other, shortly after his coming to London deceived my expectation, and adhered to those that sought my ruin.

No one, not even a kinsman of Elizabeth, put anything over a Cecil.

Charles II would apologise for taking so long to die. Elizabeth had no such compunctions. She truly hung on for grim death. It held no attractions for this monarch. In death, she was abandoned as she knew she would be, yet not even to the devils that had haunted her bed, but to the callousness of those about her who now saw nothing much more than a hag's corpse. Some, like Lady Anne Clifford's mother, remained loyal and watched over her body as it lay, all but discarded, for two days at Richmond Palace where it had breathed its last.

Lady Anne Clifford (1590–1676) was born at Skipton in Craven in a Norman castle, the home of her parents, George Clifford, third Earl of Cumberland, and his wife Margaret Russell, the youngest daughter of the second Earl of Bedford. Lady Anne's father was, in spite of his rank (or so today we would think), a pirate. Generously, we would call him an adventurer in the service of Queen Elizabeth. Clifford was hardly ever at home. He did follow the life of a corsair but had no great need to protect the family plate. He simply loved doing his job and in this he was not unique. Gentleman piracy was by no means uncommon and the taking of prizes an honourable following. (Prize money in the Royal Navy was not abolished until the twentieth century.) The family was, as might be expected, well connected. In 1577 Elizabeth had been at the wedding of George and Margaret Clifford. They were one of the great and powerful northern families, probably at the time dominated by George's mother, the formidable Anne Dacre who ruled the Clifford estates at Appleby, Barden, Brough, Brougham, Pendragon and Skipton. By any sixteenth-century standard, the Cliffords were big landowners and the earldom important.

Anne Clifford was married twice, and by her second marriage she became the Countess of Pembroke and lived at that family seat at Wilton, not far from Salisbury. Her previous and more celebrated marriage was to Richard Sackville (1590–1624), whose father died two days after their marriage in 1609, and so Richard then became the third Earl of Dorset.* It was through this marriage that she had five children. The three boys died. The two girls survived and through their marriages the Cliffords became linked to the Tuftons, who were

---

* The first Earl of Dorset was Thomas Sackville (1536–1608), who was also Lord Buckhurst. As early as June 1566 Sackville had been given by Elizabeth I the lease of the mansion of Knole near Sevenoaks in Kent. However, a condition of that lease was that it should remain for the time being in the hands of the Earl of Leicester. It was not until 1603 that Sackville got his hands on Knole and immediately employed two hundred workmen to restore it, which they did by 1605.

Earls of Thanet, and the Comptons, the Earls of Northampton. Henry Compton, as Bishop of London, was one of the seven directly instrumental in the overthrow of James II and became the only non-archbishop to crown an English monarch when he officiated at the coronation of William and Mary in 1688. In the longer term, Anne Clifford's descendants included the Sackville-Wests. Her marriage to Dorset did not last, strained towards the end apparently through the personalities and conflicts within the Earl's family as well as the illnesses of the whole family. The Earl died at the age of thirty-four and his brother, who succeeded him, hated Anne. She was kicked out to a Sussex dower house with the children. But she was a resilient woman; she certainly had to be.

At the time of Dorset's death she and the two girls were suffering terribly from smallpox (written in 1603 as 'small pokkes' – small pustule or pimple).* Six years later she married Philip Herbert, who was by all accounts a vile and cowardly chap as well as being, of course, the Earl of Pembroke. Pembroke insisted that Isabella, the elder of Anne's two daughters, marry his son. Isabella did not want to and the matter was eventually settled when she married an altogether more agreeable fellow, Jamie Compton, Earl of Northampton.

In Anne we have a lady of some considerable standing, with a glittering pedigree, and full of fight. She was therefore the ideal person to consult when trying to put together those exciting days of March and April 1603. She kept a diary, although the original was lost. However, what might be assumed to be a fair copy of it was written in the 1700s; it is now at the Dorset family home, Knole. The part that interests us is not day-to-day diary notes of a young girl, but the reminiscences. To some it may be stretching a point to consider the copy of Anne Clifford's diary as a first-hand account of events in 1603. She was, moreover, not yet fourteen when Elizabeth died. Nevertheless, her account tallies with other documents and it might always be argued that no single diary or memoir is anything more than the wishful reflection of the author.

* Simon Kellwaye wrote the first English treatise on small pokkes in 1593.

Overall, it is reasonable to trust Anne Clifford's notes and memory. Her family and the close friends of that family were directly involved at court. She notes, for example, that word was brought to her and her mother that the Queen had died at about two or three in the morning. She says that at about ten o'clock King James was proclaimed in Cheapside by all 'the Council with great joy and triumph' and that she was at the proclamation. Her mother was one of the ladies who waited and went with Elizabeth's corpse from Richmond to Whitehall where it was placed in the Drawing Chamber,

> where it was watched all night by several lords and ladies, my Mother sitting up with it two or three nights, but my Lady would not give me leave to watch, by reason I was held too young . . . when the corpse of Queen Elizabeth had continued at Whitehall as the Council had thought fit, it was carried with great solemnity to Westminster [Friday, 8 April 1603] the lords and ladies going on foot to attend it, my mother and my Aunt of Warwick being mourners, but I was not allowed to be one, because I was not high enough, which did much trouble me then, but yet I stood in the church at Westminster to see the solemnities performed.

The death, as might easily be imagined, was the moment of all letters and conversations. John Chamberlain was a scholar and a friend of almost anyone who mattered during this period.*

---

* Chamberlain never held high office and was perhaps best remembered, if at all, for being a member of the first commission in King James's reign for the repair of St Paul's Cathedral. At one point, he was a member of a delegation to the diplomatically important mission to Venice, but little more is known of him other than that which is revealed in his long correspondence with important people of his day, including the celebrated diplomatist Sir Dudley Carleton (c. 1573–1632). Carleton became Viscount Dorchester and had been in 1602 secretary to Sir Thomas Parry during his embassy to Paris, remaining in this post until November 1603. The two men never much got on and Carleton was back in England in time to witness the end and debacle of the Ralegh trial at Winchester.

John Chamberlain Esq to [Sir] Dudley Carleton Esq, London, 30 March 1603.

I have not written since I received yours of the 8th of this present after your style* for we were held in suspense, and know not how nor what to write, the postages being stopt, and all conveyance so dangerous and suspicious. I make no question but you have heard of our great loss [the death of Queen Elizabeth] before this comes to you and doubt but you shall hear her majesties sickness and manner of death diversely related. For even here the Papists do tell strange stories, so utterly void of truth as of all civil honesty and humanity. I had good means to understand how the world went, and find her disease to be nothing but a settled and unremoveable melancholy, insomuch that she could not be won or persuaded neither by the counsels, divines, physicians, nor the women about her, once to taste or touch any physic, though ten or twelve physicians that were continually about her did assure her with all manner of asseverations of perfect and easy recovery, if she would follow her advice . . . there was some whispering [by Cecil?] that her brain was somewhat distempered but there was no such matter; only she held an obstinate silence for the most part, and because she had all persuasion that is she once lay down she would never rise, could not be gotten to bed in a whole week till three days before her death . . . she made no will, nor gave any thing away, so that they who come after her shall find a well-furnished house, a rich wardrobe of more than two thousand gowns, with all things else answerable.

* This meant the date. The two 'styles' were the Gregorian calendar (New Style) used on the Continent and the Julian calendar (Old Style) used in England until 1752. Carleton, writing from Paris, would have been using the New Style dating.

Elizabeth died 'some two houres after midnight' as Anne Clifford thought. The Council of State assembled and decided that it was important that the people should be told immediately of the death and, at the same time, the announcement should be made that James would be the next monarch. There could be no chance for speculation. On 24 March James was proclaimed monarch by the 'Lords Spirituall and Temporall' who made up the Privy Council. The seventeenth-century wording of that first proclamation reflected the sense of uncomplicated achievement of Robert Cecil:

> James the sixt king of Scotland, is now by the death of our late Soveraigne, Queene of England of famous memorie, become also our Onely, Lawfull, Lineall and Rightfull Liege Lord, James the first, king of England, France* and Ireland, defender of the faith.†

The final lines of the proclamation announced, as ever, the complete loyalty of every courtier, noble, justice, sheriff and bailiff, constable and whoever came to mind and that those of the highest and the lowest of authority would ever be at hand to assist:

> ayding and assisting from time to time in all things that are or shalbe necessary for the preventing, resisting, and suppressing of any disorderly assemblies, or other unlawfull Acte or

---

* British monarchs would call themselves king or queen of France until the eighteenth century.

† *Fidei Defensor*: the title seems incongruous inasmuch that it was given by Pope Leo X in 1521 to Henry VIII before Rome felt inclined to revise its judgement of the English King. It was papal recognition of Henry's book *Assertio septem sarcramentorum*, an unequivocal attack on Martin Luther. Parliament recognised the title in 1544. It is retained to the present day and is marked on British coins as F.D.

Attempt, either in worde or deede, against the publique peace of the Realme, or any way prejudiciall to the Right, honour, State or Person, of our only Undoubted and deere Lord and Soveraigne that now is James the first king of all the said Kingdomes, as they will avoyd the perill of his Majesties heavie indignation, and their owne utter ruine and confusion.

The welcome for the new monarch had to be tempered by the real or contrived sorrow for the passing of the old one. The obedience and love of the people for Elizabeth had waned during her final years. Some had been anxious that her passing should not be delayed. Elizabeth had not thought to apologise for the unconscionable time she was taking to find an exit from her sovereign duties. When she went, the mourning dresses were worn, so too the indifference on the sleeves of even her close courtiers – witness the apparent disregard with which Elizabeth's cadaver was treated during those first couple of days after her death at Richmond. The delicate mask between sadness and joy was exquisitely demonstrated in Thomas Millington's opening sentences describing the procession of James VI south to London where he might claim the crown as James I. Having prefaced the description with the insistence that what followed was 'exactly set downe, as nothing can be added to it but superfluous words; which we have strived to avoyd', Millington immediately spreads himself across the superfluity of sixteenth- and seventeenth-century English – but in a good cause. Here is the prayer for Elizabeth.

The eternall majestie [God], in whose hand are both the meane and mightie of the earth, pleased to deliver from weaknesse of body and griefe of minde, Elizabeth is [sic] hand-maide, our late Royall Mistresse and gracious Soveraigne, easing her age from the burthen of earthly kingdomes & placing her (as we stedfastly hope) in his heavenly Empire, being the resting place after death, for all them that beleeve faithfully in their live [*sic*].*

The amen being loud, then it is all right to get on with the splendour of James's triumph.

* *A Narration of the Progresse and entertainment of the Kings most excellent Majestie from the time of his departure from Edenbrough; till his receiving at London: with all or the most specially Occurances.* Printed by Thomas Creede for Thomas Millington, 1603.

5

BONFIRES

AMES HAD HIS KINGDOM. With the signatures beneath the proclamation of his right to the throne and the damnation of any who fancied their chances of insurrection, he had too a sound and wise Privy Council, headed by the Lord Mayor of London, Robert Lee, followed by the Archbishop of Canterbury and, of course, Robert Cecil.* Within four days of the death of Elizabeth, James, careful only to sign himself James R (that is James Rex, not

* Robert Lee (Mayor of London); John Whitgift (Archbishop of Canterbury); Thomas Egerton (Chancellor); Thomas Buckhurst (Lord Buckhurst, first Earl of Dorset); Earl of Oxford; Lord Nottingham; Lord Northumberland; Lord Derby; Earl of Worcester; Earl of Cumberland; Earl of Pembroke; Earl Clanricard (ruled southern Connaught); the Bishops of Sussex, Lincoln, Norwich, London, Hereford and Shrewsbury; Thomas de la Warre; Thomas Morley, Lord Cobham (associate of Ralegh); Lord Scroope (Scrope); Lord Lomley (Lumley); Edward Cromwell; Robert Rich; Lord Hunsdon; Lord Chandoys; William Compton; Sir John Norreys; Lord Howard of Waldon; Sir William Knollys; Sir Edward Wotton; Sir John Stanhope; Robert Cecil; Sir John Fortescue; Sir John Popham (the judge who would preside over the trials of Ralegh and Guy Fawkes).

James, King of England etc.), was writing to the body he felt to be the most powerful in his new kingdom, the Lord Mayor, Aldermen, Commoners of the City of London – the money and its most convertible of currencies, influence. The City was the kingdom's capital. There was no Greater London in 1603.

Trustie and welbeloved, Wee greete you heartily well. Being informed of your great forwardnesse in that just and Honourable action of proclaiming us your Soveraigne Lord and king, immediately after the decease of our late dearest sister the Queene, wherein you have given a singular good proofe of your ancient fidelitie (a reputation hereditarie to that our Citie of London, beeing the Chamber of our Imperiall Crowne), and ever free from all shadowes of tumultuous and unlawfull courses. We could not omit with all the speed we might possible, to give you hereby a taste of our thankfull minde for the same: And withall, assurance that you cannot crave anything of us fit for the maintenance of you all in generall, and everyone of youo [sic] in particular, but it shalbe most willingly performe by us, whose speciall care shall ever be to to provide for the continuance and increase of your present happines: Desiring you in the meane time to goe constantly forward in doing all and whatever things you shall find necessary or expedient for the good government of our said Citie in execution of Justice, as you have bene in use to doe in our said dearest Sisters time, till our pleasure be further known to you.

Thus no doubting but you will do as ye may be fully assured of our gracious favour towards you in the highest degree, we bid you heartily farewell,

Halirudhouse [Holyrood House], the 28th of March. 1603

James R

For those who might find this little more than a trusty piece of early seventeenth-century protocol, it might be remembered that even four hundred years on, in the twenty-first century, the most important policy speeches made by the two most senior officers of government, the Prime Minister and the Chancellor of the Exchequer, are made not to Parliament, but to the City of London during the annual Mansion House speeches.

James's journey south from Scotland needed close attention to protocol as well as protection from hangers-on and would-be petitioners. On 10 April a proclamation was issued that from the moment the King left Berwick for London, then at each crossing of the county line, the sheriff of that county should meet the King, attend him, and hand him on to the next sheriff at the next county. This was more than ceremony. The King expected to be received like a king and treated like a hungry one. Each sheriff was told to make sure that there would be sumptuous lodgings at the end of each day's travel for the King and, of course, for 'such Noble personages as shall attend him, but also for the whole Traine'. There were promises made that all board and lodging would be paid for from the King's coffers and that if any of the quickly enlarging royal household be found over-boisterous, then any damage would be paid for. There was no evidence that anyone knew where the money would come from.

James of course would not concern himself with the source of the money. There is an odd parallel with James VI and some East European states at the end of the twentieth century. Once free of their former frontiers, many East Europeans saw Western Europe as a honey-pot. For years they had been impressed by the post-war economic miracle and the richness of their West German cousins and of the French, Italians and British. There had to be plenty of money in the West and surely one only had to ask for it. The Scottish Court in 1603 was penniless and draughty. The English throne, surely, sat in the middle of a honey-pot. No, it did not; nevertheless, James could not believe this. He thought he knew the people; he had sensed the wealth and touched much of it. Travellers' tales alone encouraged him and his courtiers to believe that the Palace of Whitehall housed the Promised Land.

In 1597 Paul Hentzner, a German lawyer and tutor born near Brandenburg, began a grand tour of Switzerland, France, Italy and England. He returned from England in 1600. His description of parts of the country, from an anonymous translation in Nuremberg in 1612, tells us something of the countryside and mostly of higher society.

> We arrived at Rye, a small English seaport. Here as soon as we came on shore, we gave in our names [Hentzner travelled as tutor to a Silesian nobleman] to the notary of the place . . . we were conducted to an inn where we were very well entertained as one generally is in this country.

The two then travelled to London by horseback, making not much more than twelve to fifteen miles before changing the horses. Hentzner describes the London at the close of the sixteenth century as 'the seat of the British Empire'. But it is his description of Elizabeth's Court during the final three or four years of her reign that is of particular interest, as we can see the enormous pomp of the levee. Hentzner and his nobleman arrive at the palace in Greenwich.

> We were admitted . . . into a presence chamber, hung with rich tapestry and the floor, after the English fashion, strewed with hay [rushes?] through which the Queen commonly passes on her way to chapel. At the door stood a gentleman dressed in velvet, with gold chain, whose office was to introduce to the Queen any person of distinction that came to wait on her; it was Sunday, when there is normally the greatest attendance of nobility. In the same hall were the Archbishop of Canterbury, the Bishop of London, a great number of Councillors of State, officers of the Crown, and gentlemen, who waited the Queen's

coming out; which she did from her own apartment when it was the time to go to prayers, attended in the following manner:

First went gentlemen barons, earls, Knights of the Garter, all richly dressed and bareheaded; next came the Chancellor, bearing the seals in a red silk purse, between two, one of whom carried the Royal Sceptre, the other the Sword of State, in a red scabbard, studded with golden fleurs de lis, the point upwards; next came the Queen, in the sixty-fifth year of her age as we were told, very majestic; her face oblong, fair, but wrinkled; her eyes small, yet black and pleasant; her nose a little hooked; her lips narrow, and her teeth black (a defect the English seem subject to from their too great use of sugar); she had in her ears two pearls, with very rich drops; she wore false hair, and that red; upon her head she had a small crown, reputed to be made of some of the gold of the celebrated Lunebourg table; her bosom was uncovered, as all the English ladies have it till they marry; and she had on a necklace of exceeding fine jewels; her hands were small, her fingers long, and her stature neither tall nor low; her air was stately, her manner of speaking mild and obliging. That day she was dressed in white silk, bordered with pearls of the size of beans, and over it a mantle of black silk, shot with silver threads; her train was very long, the end of it borne by a marchioness; instead of chain she had an oblong collar of gold and jewels. As she went along in all this state and magnificence, she spoke very graciously, first to one, then to another, whether foreign ministers or those who attended for different reasons, in English, French, and Italian; for besides being well skilled in Greek, Latin, and the languages I have mentioned, she is mistress of Spanish, Scotch, and Dutch. Whoever speaks to her, it is kneeling; now and then she raises some with her hand . . . whenever she turned her face, as she was going along, everyone fell down on their knees. The ladies of the court followed next to her, very handsome and well shaped and for the most part dressed in white. She was guarded on each side by the gentlemen pensioners, fifty in number, with gilt battle axes.

Hentzner's description of the English and England might well be used to make comparisons to this very day, especially his view of the character of the peoples of these islands. We might remember that apart from the measure of Britain's political, military and particularly naval position in the world, Hentzner would have considered himself to have been standing on the biggest island in the world.

> The soil is fruitful and abounds with cattle, which inclines the inhabitants rather to feeding than ploughing, so that near a third part of the land is left uncultivated for grazing ... the general drink is beer, which is prepared from barley and is excellently well tasted, but strong, and what sort fuddles ... it has mines of gold, silver, and tin (of which all manner of table utensils are made, in brightness equal to silver, and used all over Europe), of lead, and of iron, but not much of the latter.
>
> The English are serious, like the Germans; lovers of show, liking to be followed wherever they go by whole troops of servants who wear their masters' arms in silver, fastened to their left arms, a ridicule they deservedly lie under. They excel in dancing and music, for they are active and lively, though of a thicker make than the French; they cut their hair close on the middle of the head, letting it grow on either side; they are good sailors, and better pirates, cunning, treacherous and thievish; above three hundred are said to be hanged annually in London; beheading with them is less infamous than hanging ... hawking is the general sport of the gentry; they are more polite in eating than the French devouring less bread, but more meat, which they roast in perfection; they put a great deal of sugar in their drink; their beds are covered with tapestry, even those of farmers; they are often molested with the scurvy

[which the English still claimed had been brought over by the Normans] . . . their houses are commonly of two storeys, except in London where they are of three and four; they are built of wood [as the Great Fire would remind us], those of the richer sort with bricks; their roofs are low, and, where the owner has money, covered with lead.

They are powerful in the field, successful against their enemies, impatient of anything like slavery; vastly fond of great noises that fill the ear, such as the firing of cannon, drums, and the ringing of bells, so that it is common for a number of them, that have got a glass in their heads, to go up to some belfry, and ring bells for hours together for the sake of the exercise. If they see a foreigner very well made, and particularly handsome, they will say 'it is a pity he is not an Englishman'.*

An aside to this scene of the Court at Greenwich draped in white silks and embroideries and not a few courtiers was the importance of the Queen's ability to speak so many languages. At the start of the 1600s, few foreigners spoke much English. There is, for an example, a note in German archives which reports that the Duke of Stettin, in 1602, had to use Latin to make himself understood. It might be remembered that when George I became the first Hanoverian king of England in 1714, he spoke no English.

Language was the least of James VI's concerns as he mentally paced his rooms at Holyrood House. As we have seen, he had worried himself this way and that for many a month on what might happen at Elizabeth's death. There was part of him that could not believe that his accession to the English throne would be an easy affair. He immediately wrote to Cecil thanking him for his efforts and reminding him that he would not be forgotten now

* *Travels in England during the Reign of Queen Elizabeth* by Paul Hentzner, from the anonymous English translation published in Nuremberg in 1612.

that James had come into his kingdom. He was uncertain even on that night of 26 March 1603 when the bloodstained, weary, elated and anxious Carey had banged at the palace door.

As that momentous night became the Sunday morning of 27 March, James 'despatched the abbot of Halirud-house [Holyrood]' to take command of Berwick, the town that guarded the border section of the road to England. James remained unsure of his authority. He was uncertain of the reaction of the people and those who, like some nobles, opposed him. Might some see him as a usurper and grab the moment to depose him? This was no single paranoia. Had not Cecil, even before Elizabeth breathed her last, ordered the militia and army to the streets and strongholds to protect the realm against mischief and insurrection? James was quite right to be nervous of his position. His breath need not have been long held. The people of Berwick welcomed his envoy and he was 'honourably entertained'.

The following day, 28 March, the governor of Berwick, with the mayor and dignitaries looking on, surrendered his staff of office to the abbot. The mayor handed over the town keys. These two symbols of authority in his grasp, the right reverend cleric then administered the oath of allegiance to them all. The people of the town were rallied and told that their allegiance was to the new monarch. When the news came back that the people of Berwick had not opposed the abbot's command, James breathed a little more like the greater monarch he was now expected to be. He had had his first victory.

By this time, knights and sundry gentlemen were arriving in Edinburgh by the hour. They had come not, as so often in the past, to contest authority, but to pledge their allegiance and stake their hopes of preferment. One of the first to arrive from England was John Paiton, the son of the lieutenant of the Tower of London, Sir John Paiton. The Tower represented constabular authority in the capital. Since William the Conqueror, it had cast its own authority across the minds of even the most powerful, although its sinister reputation owed something to a sense of pragmatism that would persist among the English elite until the eighteenth century. The significance of Paiton's arrival was not lost on James. Perhaps, then, James felt a little more assured when, on Thursday, 31 March 1603, he was proclaimed King of England, Scotland, Ireland and France in Edinburgh. That night bonfires were lit in Scotland and burned brightly beyond dawn the next day. Clearly, James could not rush headlong to his new throne, in spite of the long preparations and warning. There was still much to arrange.

For example, who would look after the King on his long journey south? Servants and courtiers were easily found, perhaps too easily. But this was the new monarch of all England, Scotland, Ireland, Wales and, so they said still, France. How far would his train travel in one day? How long would he wish to tarry? Which gentlemen and peers could be relied upon to give over their family piles to the Scottish visitor? There was too the small matter of decorum, not always James's strong point, nor that of his court. It would be unseemly to arrive before the dead Queen was formally laid to rest. That would be three weeks or more. Nor would James wish to wait too long in Scotland. His court was not a grand affair. He was each day gathering hangers-on. It was time to move, but with certain sedate progress.

The following Sunday, 3 April, James went to morning service in St Giles in Edinburgh. This was more than just divine service. It was here that James stood before his people to bid them sad farewell. The people of course were joyous for him and for themselves. A monarch of Scotland was now to be monarch of England and even king over all the people. There was enormous pride expressed, though a more sombre mood, a more realistic one, hovered at the edges of pride and joy. It was all very well feeling pleased that their king was now the supreme governor of the islands and even king of France, albeit only in title. The reality was more thought-provoking: Edinburgh was losing its royal Court. It was losing the pomp and, such as it was, elegance of having a king sit in his court in his homeland.

With James as King of Scotland, at his castle in Scotland, the nation had a leader with whom any would-be enemy, usurper or diplomatic opportunist would first have to reckon. Yet if James were going south to England and, worse still, to London was it not true that Scotland was not at all gaining authority and kudos, but was losing a monarch and therefore power?

James, of course, because of his nature, was inclined to construe any sense of gloom about his departure as a feeling of sadness for him personally. Rather magnanimously James assured his people that he would always love them even though far away and he would make a point of visiting Scotland once every three years. Even in an early seventeenth-century society used to what we would call great time differences, James's promises were not particularly reassuring. Millington observed: 'the peoples hearts against his departure were even dead and griefe seised every private mans rayns [emotions],* saving only those that were made happy by attending his Royall person into England'.† Of course, Millington was right. The truth was that most members of James's Court were simply longing to get away to London with promises of everything Edinburgh did not have: good living, authority and more importantly a bottomless exchequer to pay for it all – or so they thought.

The Scottish contingent included those ambitious for preferment and those who felt there were wider interests to be safeguarded. Had not, for example, France a direct interest in the influence of the future monarch over relations with continental Europe, the sides that might be taken with popes and diplomatic usurpers of the *status quo* on that continent? So it should be no surprise that the French ambassador was to be found in the excursion from Edinburgh to London. So too

---

* The 'reins' (or 'rayns') were literally the kidneys or loins, from the French *rein* as in *ceindre ses reins*, to gird up one's loins. Following biblical usage – cf. Psalms vii. 9, 'the righteous God trieth the hearts and reins' (AV) – the word was also used as a metaphor for the centre of the emotions.

† *A Narration of the Progresse* . . . (see page 114).

was his wife, a less than durable lady, who was carried all the way to the English capital by eight pioneers, 'one foure to relieve the other foure by turns, carrying her in a chair with slings'.

The adventure opened with the departure on 5 April, with James already surrounded by his closest advisers determined that their collective and individual authority would survive the journey and the opportunities for powerful office. Some of them, like the Earls of Mar, Casil and Home, he trusted implicitly. Some of the others he trusted Mar, Casil and Home to keep under control. The one person whom we might have expected to be with the King was not present. His wife, England's new queen consort, but not queen, did not travel south.

Queen Anne was pregnant, and for the moment it was thought better that she should not make the journey, although she rebelled at the idea of being left out of the grand procession. James decided she must remain, at least for the moment, and with all courtliness and not a little tenderness the two bade each other farewell. Anne did not simply retire to her boudoir. She was a quarrelsome consort and now did not hide her misgivings, in particular about the Mar family. Not surprisingly, she had always felt that the Mars had too close a relationship with her husband. It was a natural reaction in someone arriving in an alien country which was, in the late sixteenth century, a somewhat crude environment with a reputation for plotting and murder. The Mar family had always been in James's life. They did not budge up to make space for her in his affections.

One source of the animosity between them was that Anne had long disputed the terms of the custody of the young Prince Henry. In 1595 James had sent Henry to Stirling Castle to be in the custody of the Earl of Mar. James thought this an excellent idea for Henry's education as well as influences. After all, a similar arrangement had done him no harm as a child when he too had been in the care of the Mar family and the present Earl had become his playmate. Anne was furious. She insisted that Henry should be with her at Holyrood. Her nature (and presumably her maternal instinct) set her on course for a collision with the Earl and his family and she plotted with Mar's enemies against him. This made James even more sure that he had made the correct decision. By 1603 Henry's affection for the Mars and James's contentment with the arrangement had not wavered, even though it was agreed that once Anne was well enough to travel south and join her husband, Henry too would leave his guardians and go to London. Anne's nature was not to relax at this prospect and accept the inevitable. She wanted possession. The guardianship was not to be discarded. Anne exercised her considerable temper. She worked herself into such a state that she suffered a terrible miscarriage.

What of James in all this? He felt himself well out of this business. He had left for greater moments. That first night, 5 April, James and his retinue rested at Lord Home's house, Dunglass (still the seat of the Homes and the final resting place of the twentieth-century Conservative prime minister, Sir Alec Douglas Home). There was food and wine to be taken and decisions to be considered. For example, here was the first inkling that Robert Cecil's authority was paramount and it would take a superb political intriguer to overcome the crouch-backed secretary of state. Sir Robert Carey was about to discover that even at a distance of London to the Borders, Cecil's influence and writ ran firmly. Remember, Carey had been the first to get to the new monarch, and while James was in a good mood at the news Carey carried he had agreed (at Carey's suggestion, of course) to appoint him a Gentleman of the Bedchamber (no mean office in those days). Cecil now acted. Carey's good fortune was elegantly nudged aside by a stream of official and unofficial courtiers and petitioners. He lost his office almost as calmly as he had gained it. Robert Cecil, who had masterminded the handover, still had work to do and he was not inclined to allow his authority to be usurped. He sent his own secretary, Sir Thomas Lake, to brief the King on the position in London and on the protocols of the accession and also to gather the King's thoughts. After all, Cecil was no longer dealing with a grateful would-be king, but his monarch. Therefore, Lake's ride north and a series of despatch riders with him were of the utmost importance that beginning of April 1603.

It was on 5 April, almost two weeks after Elizabeth's death and with the journey south just started, that Cecil finally managed to get the King's approval that the existing office-holders, including the royal councillors, the Privy Council, should stay in office for the interregnum. There were far too many people jockeying for position and power, whereas Cecil was able to explain to James that while the King was thinking about the events that would come and lead to his coronation, Cecil had to run the country quietly and smoothly on His Majesty's behalf. Cecil's view was that it was better gradually to seek out the King's opinion rather than risk volatile change and also the effects of James's habit of handing out honours and positions to almost anyone who gladly caught his eye that day.

Cecil was not alone in trying to ascertain the King's position. The Archbishop of Canterbury, John Whitgift, did not idly await the new royal presence. His interests in James went far beyond the coronation arrangements. Whitgift sent his dean to pay respects to James because he wanted to know James's thoughts on the Church of England. James could be relied upon to have many thoughts on this subject. There was hardly an interest group which did not find its way north during the first few days after Elizabeth's death. The period between 24 March and the middle of April might be counted as a series of feast days for opportunists.

On 6 April the royal party set out from Dunglass to Berwick. The town had been the scene of decades of fighting between English and Scots. James halted half a mile from the town and prepared for a grand entrance (perhaps wondering if the earlier promises of allegiance had survived). He had no need to worry. Berwick, by contemporary account, was now the scene of a fearsome salute of cannon which made the very earth tremble and the houses shudder. When the volleys ceased (and there must have been many a loader and gunner in Berwick that April who remembered without forgiveness the ruthlessness of the wars and the auld enemy) James entered the town and was received safely in grand style and, indeed, at length.

Far from being a simple journey made in haste, this was a glorious procession. Lowland and Border chieftains were his guard of honour into Berwick where the multitude waved their tartans and cried 'God Save King James'. There was great feasting and demonstrations of Border prowess as armed men paraded and cannon were fired again and again. The sun shone brightly on the joy of Scotland and its monarch. When it rained, the downpour represented the tears of his faithful people at his departure. That at least was James's version of the natural phenomenon. After the rain came the sun once more and so the journey was set fair for England.

Parkinson, the recorder of Berwick, surrendered the town's Royal and English Charter. James, of course, told the burghers not to fret. The Royal Charter would continue. To show all that this was to be a new union (although not for another century constitutionally), James issued his first proclamation on the one subject by which all men and women not concerned with legal trappings could indeed understand that sense of union – parity of money. English and Scottish coinage should have the same values.

This idea that, coin for coin, two nations were as one, was echoed when the West German Chancellor Helmut Kohl declared the parity of the East and West German marks after the fall of the Berlin Wall. James I and Chancellor Kohl may have 'ruled' four hundred years apart, but political instincts change very little. The Scots loved to be linked to the 'rich' English as much as the poorer East Germans did to the bankers of Bonn and Düsseldorf.

After dinner on 8 April James mounted and rode out of Berwick to cross the border for England, pausing only to knight one Ralph Gray. Why? A description of Gray's standing in the Borders is enough to tell us that James, with all his own history, was intent on leaving as many allies as a good dubbing could provide. Gray was 'a gentleman of great command and possession neare the borders'.* This would be the first of more than three hundred knighthoods James would dole out by the time he reached London just a month later.† He was on a well-trodden track for the English capital. As now, the arterial roads of England flowed along diplomatic and trade routes. The heart or nub of the network was London. Even in 1603 the roads were centuries old. The main roads from London went south to Dover through Gravesend, Rochester and Canterbury to the Channel port from where most crossed to and from France. The great west road from London led to Bristol, the seaport for southern Ireland, or to Chester, one of the routes to Dublin. The road from London to Scotland was the London–Berwick highway.

As he crossed from Berwick into England, James was met by Nicholas Forester, the high sheriff of Northumberland, who escorted him, appropriately enough considering those recent events, to the Carey seat at Withrington. The Careys, for all Cecil's handling of Robin's courtly ambition, were an old and powerful northern dynasty. Those who understood these late sixteenth- and early seventeenth-century matters compared the Careys to the tribe of Dan, presumably because in the Bible Dan was the son of Jacob whose land was, like the Careys', in the northernmost part of the Promised Land.

On Saturday 9 April

his Majestie prepared towards New-castle. But before his departure from Withrington he knighted M. Henry Withrington, M. William Fencke and M. Edward Gorge. After wich taking his leave with Royall curtesie, he set forwards towards New-castle being 16 miles from Withrington.††

---

* Millington, *A Narration of the Progresse* . . .
† James understood the value of patronage and the honours system. It was he who originated the baronetcy (hereditary knighthoods) in 1611 as a means of raising money for his wars in Northern Ireland and the Ulster Plantations.
†† Millington, op. cit.

The redoubtable Bishop of Durham, Tobie (Toby) Matthew, seems to have taken every opportunity to preach the Word. We find him popping up in pulpits from Berwick to Durham preaching and politicking like 'an ordained furie'. Presumably James, whose sense of moral responsibility was surmounted by his self-righteousness like some crusader's helm, listened and vociferously marked the good Matthew out of ten. On 10 April another service, another sermon. While the house of God was expected to meet with the new monarch's approval (especially on the matter of the Divine Right of kings) so the houses of the people also made him welcome.

It might be remembered that a monarch was expected to pay his way and that of his followers. Considering the size of the Stuart troupe and that typically it might well arrive on Saturday and not leave until Wednesday, and how the people would have made such special effort, this was considerable outlay on hospitality. James and his Scottish friends were well pleased with all that was given them and wanted more wherever they went. Little wonder James added the Newcastle mayor, Robert Dudley – who had told the aldermen and people to open more practical facilities than just their hearts to their king – to his list of knights.

The day after the announcement about the value of Scottish money, James was having to approve a draft declaration on foreign affairs. Cecil could not allow any subject to be forgotten during this transition. On 10 April, another announcement came that those who thought they would easily get round the protocols of court and make their private submissions to the King were to be discouraged. A metaphorical No Hawkers, No Circulars, No Supplicants notice was put on the door of James's royal mobile home. This was enforced on 12 April by a full proclamation against undue resort to the King. On the same day James broke off from his hunting to approve the plans for Elizabeth's funeral.

The following day there is another example of the way that constitutional life had to continue, however new the monarch.

James was asked to put his signature to the order that Zouch should be the new Lord Lieutenant in Wales. This was no sinecure. Four hundred years ago the Lord Lieutenancy had more than distinction as a royal office. The Lord Lieutenant truly ran the county, or in this case the country, on behalf of the monarch. It was a demanding responsibility as well as an honour. It was an opportunity to make a lot of money and a lot of enemies. The ideal position was that the Lord Lieutenant made the money for the monarchy and kept the enemies for himself. As ever in constitutional life, the successful office-holder ruled peacefully and wealthily. The concern of Cecil for the maintenance of law and order was not to be taken lightly. A report appeared on 17 April suggesting that although the nation was supposed to be in mourning, this had little effect on many people's behaviour. What we would now call protests were common, and a breakdown in law and order was always on the cards.

By 13 April James was in Gateshead, or Gateside as it was then, from there to Chester-le-Street (then Chester a streete), and thence to Durham and more homily from and to the bishop of that see. Matthew, having preached well, now adjourned to petition his receptive monarch on a more immediate matter than the discourse on a good text. The Bishop's politicking would have sad consequences for Sir Walter Ralegh.

Ralegh was out of favour. Cecil regarded him as a rival and that was hardly a good thing to be, considering Cecil's high standing with James. Ralegh's London home was Durham House, owned by the Durham diocese, but rented and hugely restored – probably saved – by Ralegh over his twenty years or so of living there. Whether or not he knew the significance of what he was doing, James agreed to the Bishop of Durham's request to have the house back from Ralegh (see page 267). The business of Ralegh's house, or Durham's, depending on one's senses of justice and politics, was swiftly if unfairly resolved. On 14 April James moved on to stay with Mistress Genison at her house, Walworth. The next day he left for York.

This was no ordinary comfort stop for King James. York was the second most important city in his kingdom. The journey until now had been a travelling festival, but it lacked stateliness. James had left Scotland with what he imagined in English terms to be a modest wardrobe. Fine for Berwick. Fine for Newcastle. Now here, as the columns approached the capital of the northern province, James could leave nothing to chance. It was important to make the right impression on York. James understood only too well his history lessons. After all, the people of York were not always the most sympathetic towards outsiders, even royal outsiders (sometimes *particularly* royal outsiders). James, probably egged on by his retinue, issued a command to Cecil tinged with a very twenty-first-century cry of woe: 'I have absolutely nothing to wear.' He demanded that Cecil send a state coach and finery for his grand entry. Cecil and his ministers (maybe councillors might be a better seventeenth-century expression) had naturally believed that the King should be decked with all the royal trappings they could muster for his entry into the capital. The plan had been to send coach and all north, but not to reach James until he arrived at the great Cecil seat of Burghley in Northamptonshire.

As James approached York something of the new monarch's insecurity revealed itself. The jewels, the coaches, the fanfarers, the silks and the outriders should be sent immediately. To James, the northern gentry was no rough caste. Much to Cecil's annoyance (he had more than enough to make ready) he too was considered part of James's regalia. He was commanded to attend the King at York.

Cecil was concerning himself with the continued running of the nation, including the not always easy news from Ireland. State affairs could not be abandoned, even for a monarch, especially as Cecil had a much better notion of the state of the English treasury than did James.

Whereas Cecil wanted calm, quiet counsel with his monarch, James wanted to be fêted. In fact, there is little sense that James was at this stage at all interested in the nation's condition, only in the glory of his coming. True, there were matters of sensitivity and protocol to be arranged. For example, apart from keeping away from London until after the funeral of Elizabeth, it would not be possible to have a coronation until his queen, Anne, had come to London. More immediately, James followed his pressing concern: he wanted to know how much money Cecil had brought with him. Promissory notes did not fetch much favour in 1603. James's retinue from Scotland had all the swagger of a new set of prefects, now in the upper sixth of James's realm. They expected to be treated with some style. And style cost money.

James, even before he reached York, had designed the new coinage of what he (the first monarch to do so) would forever call Great Britain. On one side would be his regal head; on the other the entwined arms of Scotland and his new kingdom. While on the matter of money and appearance, James told Cecil that he must supply the finest gowns, cloaks and jewels, above all jewels, for the Queen when she travelled south, and that he should also provide for her ladies-in-waiting. There was no way that Anne wanted the sneering glances of the English Court at the sight of her less than dazzling attendants.

Cecil had already supposed that it was going to be more costly to run their Scottish king than it had been to support their English queen. There was trouble enough in the state with Scottish hands in the nation's bullion. Lord Treasurer Tom Sackville, soon to be Earl of Dorset, was always going to be at the centre of jealousies and suspicions about fund-raising, spending and not a few financial irregularities arising from the methods of accountability and the general acceptance that people in even modest office would expect commissions or, in modern terminology, back-handers. Secretaries of the Navy, for example, expected to regularly collect percentages on contracts. When, as Lord Treasurer, Sackville was also handling royal affairs it is little wonder that he was known as 'Lord Fill-Sack'. His house, Knole, is an example of what monument might be built with dubious funds.*

In the short term Sackville's efforts were directed to finding provisions for James. It was not unreasonable that the 1603 equivalent to the twenty-first-century 'Civil List' should be increased for James. There was an informal means of doing this, and it was not until 1697 that the first Civil List Act was made for the monarch. We might remember that the monarch used to go to Parliament to raise money so that he could go to war. In other words *he* paid for his troops and ships. In 1689 (with the reordering of the Constitution after the installation of William and Mary as joint monarchs), Parliament declared that a regular amount should be given to the monarch, half of which was for the defence of the realm and the other half for the royal household. The 1697 Civil List Act allowed the King £700,000 'for the support of the civil list'. Out of this money came far more than payment for the royal household. The Civil List paid for the judges, the government courtiers and offices, and even the small number of ambassadors who then, quite often, simply made journeys from London to another government and returned. It was not until the nineteenth century that the Civil List was used as we know it today. William IV was probably the first beneficiary in that manner.

In 1603 that was all two hundred years away. The monarch's cost of living, even allowing for some inflation, was not so difficult to meet. Elizabeth was often known for her meanness, perhaps a euphemism for being broke. Sackville had discussions with Cecil and they agreed that considering the new monarch had what Elizabeth did not have, a family, then the 1603 cost of living allowance should be increased. Minimum expenses would be £80,000 a year. James, new to the business of English monarchy and keen to get his hands on the baubles that went with it, did not think much of this offer,

* Cecil became Lord Treasurer on the Earl of Dorset's death in 1608.

but had to accept it. There were Scottish nobles who thought this unfair, just as everyone in Edinburgh seemed to assume everyone in London terribly rich. Had not Elizabeth sent in fine plate for the wedding breakfast? In the twentieth century Percy French wrote of London that 'they don't plant potatoes nor barley nor wheat and there's gangs of them digging for gold in the street'.* Just as French's immigrant was disappointed, James and Anne soon learned parsimony was a euphemism.

For six days in April Cecil knelt at James's feet. For six days the thoughts of the new King, and of course his demands, were furiously scribbled down. Cecil, for all his previous doubts, was much impressed: 'I have made so sufficient a discovery of his royal perfections, as I contemplate greater felicity to this Isle than ever it enjoyed.' Having dealt with Cecil, the King really wanted to press on, but in spite of all the finery supplied to the royal party and the pockets of gold, James's travelling Court had grown so large that for the moment, as they found on 15 April, there were not sufficient stout horses for the rest of the journey. They had to wait for a fresh supply.

At York the King was met outside the walls by the sheriffs and gentlemen who offered their white staves of office and thanked him profusely when James handed them back, signifying that they would remain in their posts. This suited everyone. The sheriffs because they had fine jobs, James because everyone knew that when he was in London he would need friends in the north. The pageantry and traditions were played out to everyone's amusement and relief.

> The Lord Mayor delivered the Sword and Keyes to his Majestie together with a Cup of Gold, filled full of Gold, which present his Majestie gratefully accepted delivering the keys againe to the Lorde Mayor; but about the bearing of the Sword there was some small contention, the Lord President taking it for his place,

* Percy French, 'The Mountains of Mourne' (c. 1958).

the Lorde Mayor of the Citie esteeming it his. But to decide the doubt, the Kings Majestie merily demanded, If the sword being his, they would not be pleased, that hee should have the disposing thereof. Whereunto when they humbly answered, it was all in his pleasure, his Highnesse delivered the Sword to one, that knew wel how to use a sword, having beene tried both at Sea and on Shoare, the thrice honoured Earle of Cumberland, who bare it before his Majestie; ryding in great State to the Minister. In which way there was a Conduit that all the day long ran with white and claret wine, every man to drinke as much as he lifted.

Enough clear heads were kept to ensure that the York visit went well. On Sunday 17 April, having ordered the great coach of state to be sent north, James went to the Minster service on foot because he decided that, such was his welcome, it was clear that the people of York wanted to see as much of him as possible.

Not everyone drank at the conduit of claret that day. For example, a seminary priest managed to reach the King with a protest at the manner in which Catholics were treated. This was not a lone voice. James knew this and decided that rather than have the man bundled away, as the courtiers would have done, he would hear out the fellow. Having done that, he was handed over to the Bishop's staff who immediately 'committed' him.

By Tuesday 19 April, York was well attended to and the royal party drifted on its southerly way, first to Doncaster where the King, by now delighted in his own authority, restored a most valuable manor and his house to the proprietor of the Bear Inn where he put up. From Doncaster, it was on to Worksop to stay with the Earl of Shrewsbury, and then to Belvoir Castle and the Earl of Rutland. This was no ordinary trudge through Middle England.

The King was a great sportsman. He had a zest particularly for hunting. Not a hind could catch his sight without, whatever the distance, His Majesty galloping in full pursuit to make a kill. Stags were chased. Hares were coursed. This was an early spring party of hunting, feasting and continuous delight in what lay ahead. As we shall see, not only four-legged buck were felled.

On 21 April to Newark on Trent. Here, according to a short note in Millington's account, the celebrations were subdued.

> In this towne and in the Court was taken a Cutpurse doing the deed: and being a base pilfering theefe, yet was all Gentleman-like, in the out side: this fellow had a good store of Coyne found about him; and upon his examination confessed that hee had from Barwick to that place, plaied the cut-purse in the Court: his fellow was ill mist, for no doubt hee had a walking mate: they drew togither like Coach-horses, and it is a pitie they did not hang togither: for his Majestie hearing of this nimming [thieving] gallant, directed a Warrant, preferably to the Record of New-warke, to have him hanged, which was accordingly executed. This being smal comfort to all the rest of his pilfering facultie, that the first subject that suffered death in England, in the raigne of king James was a Cut-purse, which fault if they amend not, heaven sodainly send the rest.

Law and order concerned far more than the fate of a cutpurse. There was ever the tension of rebellion in the air, and on 21 April the King instructed the receiver of Yorkshire to raise funds that would finance a militia to put down skirmishes of rebels on the Border. On 22 April James wrote from Newark to his commissioners at Carlisle. These were the men who had asked for help in providing militia and horsemen. They were hardly satisfied. The King urged them to deal with the matter in all haste:

> we advise you to persevere against lewd assemblies, and send advertisements of your proceedings; when further instructions are needed they shall be sent. As to your complaint that the horsemen of the Berwick garrison and those of the laird of

Johnston cannot act because of the spoil of the country, their pay is to be raised from 8d. to 1s. 6d.*

On Saturday 23 April James arrived at Burghley, the home built by the famous Cecil, William, who was later Lord Burghley. Here, as the King approached Stamford there was a curious meeting. According to Millington, James met with giants, or rather exceptionally tall men. They were fenmen, or so it seems. But Millington's description tells us something of common knowledge of far-off places – in fact as far away as Cape Horn.

[N]ot far from Stanford, there appeared to the number of an hundred high men that seemed like the Patagones, huge long fellowes, of twelve and fourteene foote high, that are reported to live on the Mayne [coast] of Brazil neere to the streights of Megallant [Magellan]. The king at the first sight wondered what they were, for that they over-looked horse and man. But when all came to all, they proved a company of poore honest sutors, all going upon high stilts [as was common in the fens] preferring a petition against the Lady Hatton.

Easter Sunday that year was 24 April. The Bishop of Lincoln's sermon on moderation did not prevent James suffering on the very next day for his sport of hunting. He fell, remounted in great pain, and by the following day was diagnosed probably with a shoulder dislocation and forced to take his place in a coach back to Burghley. He was, as ever, royally entertained, but responded with difficulty. Given the state of seventeenth-century roads and coach springings, the King might have been more comfortable on horseback. On the Wednesday, still in considerable discomfort, he left Burghley to be entertained by Master Oliver Cromwell at Huntingdon. This was the uncle of the one day to be famous Cromwell, who in 1603 was

* Millington, *A Narration of a Progresse* . . .

just four years old. The university at Cambridge turned out in style. It was much a scarlet day with fine Latin orations and pleadings for lucrative royal charters to be renewed. They were.

The following day, 28 April, there was modest festival in Cambridge and James showed restraint in his pleasure-taking for in London a sombre occasion was taking place – the funeral of the late Queen Elizabeth. It would be indecent to expect to pass beneath any triumphal arch until the nation had paid its respects at the final rite of passage of their late Queen.

Elizabeth had died at Richmond. The Queen is dead. Long live the courtiers. Many, but not all, had returned to London in preparation to fight for their authority under the new monarch. However, she was not entirely abandoned. Elizabeth's corpse was embalmed and bound in waxed cotton. The lead coffin was brought after two days, the body placed in it, and then left for a further five days. Elizabeth's remains were then taken to the river at Richmond, placed upon a torch-lit barge, and carried to Westminster where they lay in private state at the Palace of Whitehall. Westminster Hall was hung with mourning cloths and banners and the casket removed there. It was the King's duty – not the Church's, nor Cecil's – to give the orders for her funeral. He of course wanted to get it over very quickly so that he could enter his capital. Arrangements for royal funerals take time. Even kings-in-waiting must learn patience. Thus it was not until 28 April that the coffin was borne in a hearse drawn by four horses draped in black mourning velvet to Westminster Abbey.

We might think it bizarre, but lying on the coffin was a life-size model of the Queen. It was fully robed and crowned; in one wax hand the orb, in the other the sceptre of state. Six earls held her regal canopy above the wax doll. Behind the hearse, again in a tradition observed even today, the Master of Horse led the Queen's riderless but saddled horse. Elizabeth's chief mourner, the Marchioness of Northampton, was followed by a column of noblewomen each, like the Marchioness, black-cloaked and hooded. Behind them followed almost thirteen hundred, similarly dressed in black. Here was her realm, representative of the highest peerage and office to more than two hundred of the very poor. The City of London followed with their Lord Mayor and, bringing up the rear, the halberdiers of the Gentlemen Pensioners headed by the doomed captain of their guard, Ralegh.

Thousands in the street watched and wept as the image of their late sovereign passed. The coffin was carried into the abbey, and Archbishop Whitgift read the service. That same afternoon the coffin was taken to the vault in the Henry VII Chapel and placed with the casket of Mary, the Queen's sister. Then came the final act of the symbolism of authority: the most senior of Elizabeth's courtiers, her gentlemen, stepped to the vault and each snapped his white stick of office and tossed the broken rod onto the coffin. Their duty discharged, her authority ended.

The following day, the rite of regal passage observed and a generous breakfast down him, James left Cromwell's house with good feelings towards the fellow, no doubt warmed by Cromwell's gifts of gold cups. The road then took James and his growing band to Royston via Godmanchester (the locals called it Gumster). He dined well at Royston, and the clerks and secretaries attended his wishes to make certain the benefits he heaped on or restored to many individuals. Once more there was opportunity to be magnanimous and therefore to gather the thanks of grateful subjects – but also to store up their obligations until such times he might need them. Thus John Littleton's dependants at Royston found the King in good mood and ready to tell his law officer to put matters right in their favour.

April 29. Royston. The king to the Attorney General. We wish to restore to the widow and children of John Littleton all the lands, goods, and chattels forfeit for his treason, and grants are to be drawn up accordingly.

This at first sight seems generous. The Attorney General did as the monarch said. There were, however, complications which James in his enthusiasm had not fully understood. The estates could not simply be given back without some detailed and legal (and therefore complex and costly) juggling. Less than two weeks later, by now in his capital, James completed the formalities of establishing the Littleton estates.

> May 10. The king to Attorney General Coke. We have restored to the widow and children of John Littleton, lately attainted of high treason, all lands, goods, &c. by his attainder escheated to the late Queen; Littleton, in his lifetime, assured part of his lands to Sir Charles Davers [Danvers] and others attainted, until he and other sureties were discharged of some debts for which they stood bound for Littleton, which lands escheated to the late Queen by the attainder of Danvers and not of Littleton yet as they were conveyed but for a security to Sir Charles Danvers and others, for discharge of debts which Littletons wife has now a mind to pay, we require you to contain all those lands in the grant to the wife and children of the said John Littleton.

There was an equally important letter to be written from Hertfordshire. Note the date of James's letter to the Archbishop of Canterbury – 29 April 1603. The previous day, Elizabeth had been interred. That business done, James could more openly set his image on the nation. The most obvious first way was the style of his coat of arms. The old order had to be changed.

> April 29. Royston. The king to the Archbishop of Canterbury. You are to require all the bishops to give orders that the nominee of John Gibb, one of our Bedchamber, be permitted to alter, at the expense of the several parishes of the country, the coats of arms of the late Queen there put up, according to the quarterings of our own coat of arms.

And on 30 April, to Standon near Bishop's Stortford. Here he was met by the Bishop of London and 'a seemely company of Gentlemen in tawny Coates and chaines of Gold'. Now, James was nearing London. The protocols of mourning had been observed – elsewhere anyway. The people started to gather in greater numbers than ever.

On 3 May James moved on to Theobalds, Robert Cecil's house. The great officers of state gathered with their monarch: the Lord Treasurer, the Lord Keeper, the Lord Admiral, and the now King's Council. It was time to mix and match his privy councillors. Scottish nobles were added to Council, including the Earl of Mar, the Duke of Lennox, the Treasurer of Scotland, Sir George Home, and Lord Kinloss, now to be Master of the Rolls. Of the English, he picked (or had recommended to him by Cecil) Lord Thomas Howard (whom he trusted as one who had warned him of devilment by some – notably Ralegh) as Lord Chamberlain. He managed to find time to create another twenty-eight knights. Many of these knighthoods did not bring power, but the recipients already had some at least and, of course, they did bring, for the moment, unquestionable loyalty.

Hordes in their thousands had gathered around Theobalds to catch sight of the new monarch. The people had rightly mourned and so now they celebrated their good fortune at having a quiet transition. Yet again we have to remember how people would have lived during this period. While lives were simpler than those in later centuries, certainly our own, there was a need to recognise rank for what it could provide. The symbolism of leadership is very important, particularly in a society ruled so unequivocally. If Elizabeth was indeed the last monarch to command the absolute obedience of her people, then this thought suggests that the people quite liked the idea of being obedient. The people's obedience was not to a constitutional convention and thus it relied heavily on the personality not of the monarchy, which was accepted, but the monarch, which sometimes was not. As that personality faded so the people waited anxiously for a new era. By March 1603 they had waited long enough. By the end of April the torches of welcome were lit both in James's honour and in the expectations of the people.

The sheriff and livery of Middlesex greeted James as he approached the capital, just as the sheriffs of each county had met him at the Borders to hand him with dignity to the next sheriff in accordance with Cecil's instructions. Finally, James was met as he came to London by Robert Lee, the Lord Mayor, who still had five months of his office to run, and five hundred velvet-cloaked and gold-chained attendants. Even now this was not the moment to enter the city. This new pageant rode across the fields to Charterhouse and the home of Lord Thomas Howard. Here James rested for three days, but found the energy to eat sumptuously and dub 103 more people as knights. From Charterhouse the procession on the fourth day approached the Thames at Aldergate and there James embarked on the royal barge accompanied by a flotilla of cadet vessels. It appears that the line had intended to make Whitehall, but the journey did not go quite as planned. Because the coxswain shot the bridge, that is missed the landing, James went on to the Tower – always a disturbing thought for monarchs. He gazed on the great cannon and then landed at King's Stairs where Sir Thomas Conisby, Gentleman Usher of the Privy Chamber, presented James with the sword of the City. James stayed the night in the Tower, relaxed in the knowledge that he was master of all he at last surveyed and everything that he had not.

6

CORONATION

MEANWHILE, ANNE, JAMES'S QUEEN, WAS SUFFICIENTLY RECOVERED FROM HER MISCARRIAGE TO TRAVEL SOUTH FROM SCOTLAND. We have seen the scramble of courtiers, hangers-on and petitioners to greet, escort and ingratiate when James left Berwick. Now, with the departure of Anne and her ladies-in-waiting, bedecked and bejewelled courtesy of the English Treasury at James's instruction, there was a new rush of all sorts to gain the favour of the King's consort. The Earl of Cumberland's daughter, Lady Anne Clifford, and her uncompromising mother the Countess rode north at such speed and with such determination not to slacken pace that three horses died from exhaustion carrying them to the travelling court of Queen Anne. There was one aspect which caused considerable expressions of contempt for the Scottish courtiers. It seems that the Scots did not have the same standards of hygiene as the English and visitors to the court complained of catching fleas sitting in the waiting chamber of Sir Thomas Erskine.

Anne Clifford does not tell us the date of her first meeting with the Queen but it was probably somewhere about 20 June. We do know from the Clifford memoir that the week which followed included staying with the Queen at the Spencers' home, Althorp. It was then, probably the weekend of 25–26 June, that a performance of Ben Jonson's *Masque of the Fairies* was given. The meeting with the Queen took place at Dingley's, the home of Mr Griffin. Apart from Queen Anne, the most respected person in the royal entourage was Lady Bedford, who had travelled with the Queen from Scotland. She would eventually fall from favour, not because of her manner – which was rarely less than superior – but because the mood of the Queen's Court changed once ensconced in London, Hampton Court and Windsor.

> Thither came my Lady of Bedford who was so great a woman with the Queen as everybody much respected her, she having attended the Queen out of Scotland. The next day we went to Mr Griffin of Dingley's which was the first time ever I saw the Queen and Prince Henry when she kissed us all and used us kindly; thither came also my Lady of Suffolk, my young Lady Derby and Lady Walsingham, which three ladies were favourites of Sir Robert Cecil.* That night we went along with the Queen's train, there being an infinite number of coaches and, as I take it, my aunt and my Mother and I lay at Sir Richard Knightley's where Lady Elizabeth Knightley made exceeding much of us . . . the 27th [June] being Monday, the Queen went to Hatton where the king met her, where there were an infinite number of lords and ladies and other people that the county could scarce lodge them.† From there the Court removed and were banqueted with great royalty by my father at Grafton where the King and Queen were entertained with

* Cecil was leaving nothing to chance in the management of his introduction of the new royal family to the ways and politics of the English Court.

† The Court would have been put up in houses in the country whose owners more or less matched the positions of those in the Queen's train.

speeches and delicate presents at which time my Lord and the Alexanders did run a course at the field where he hurt Henry Alexander very dangerously.

By the time Queen Anne had fobbed off, sometimes with contempt, the self-interested well-wishers, they had reached Windsor. It was here, that June, that James was reunited with his Queen, their seven-year-old daughter Princess Elizabeth ('my little Bessie') and Prince Henry. There was no mention of the three-year-old Prince Charles, the future Charles I.

Of all the honours bestowed by James during those first few weeks of his monarchy, none gave him greater pleasure than that personal gift to the young Prince at their banquet at Windsor Castle – the Garter. Henry was James's heir. His pride. It was to Henry that James had written *Basilikon Doron* ('Kingly Gift') (1599), his thoughtful epistle on kingship. It is said that he had a dream in which he might die before his time and so set about writing to his four-year-old son in the style of a sage with great classical understanding. A pompous work? Possibly. To be generous, this is more than the advice of a father to a son. It is the advice of a father in an exceptional position to a son who has yet to grasp the notion of the responsibility that will, or so it was then imagined, be his to execute. In this was the future conduct of monarchy. The work is three books in one: the king's duty to God; the king's duty as a monarch; the behaviour of a king as an individual. It is a comprehensive guide to what is expected of a monarch in all manner of days and difficulties and duties. It was given to Henry in 1599 in a private edition. Now, in 1603, James commanded that it should be reprinted for the public to read and hear about. It became a bestseller. This was hardly surprising. People who concerned themselves with these matters most certainly wanted to know the character of the new monarch and here in the *Basilikon Doron* was the key to his personality and motives. It is a document to be read because it tells so much about the monarch who would rule for more than two decades. His successor, Charles, surely discarded its principles.

It begins with verse, the first four lines of which set the tone of monarchy:

> God gives not Kings the stile of Gods in vain,
> For on his throne his Scepter doe they sway
> And as their subjects ought them to obey,
> So Kings should feare and serve their God againe.

Its pages tell us so much of James's expectations as well as how he saw himself, perhaps as a man of great perception and wisdom beyond the mortals about him. James never fancied there was a streak of ordinariness in him.

'Basilikon Doron' or His Majesties instructions to his dearest Sonne, Henry the Prince
according to the copie printed at Edenburgh 1603
(Printed by Felix Kyngston for John Morton)

To Henry my dearest Sonne and naturall successor
Whome-to can so rightlie appertaine this booke of instructions to a Prince in all the points of his calling, as well generall, as a Christian towards God; as a king towards his people whom-to, I say, can it so justly appertaine, as unto you my dearest Sonne? Since I the Author thereof as your naturall Father, must be carefull for your godly and vertuous education, as my eldest Sonne, and the first fruits of Gods blessing towards me in my posteritie: and as a king must timouslie provide for your training up in all the points of a Kings office; since yee are my naturall and lawfull successor therein; that being rightlie informed hereby, of the weight of your burthen, ye may in time begin to consider that being borne to be a king, ye are rather borne to 'onus' then 'honos' [burden rather than honour]:

not excelling all your people so faire in ranke and honour, as in daily care and hazardous paines-taking, for the dutifull administration of that great Office, that God hath laid upon your shoulders. Laying so a just symmetrie and proportion, betwixt the height of your honourable place, and the heavie weight of your great charge: and consequentlie in case of ailing, which God forbid, of the sadnesse of your fall, according to the proportion of that height, I have therefore for the greater ease to your memorie, and that ye may at the first cast up any part that ye have to do with, devided this treatise in three parts. The first teacheth you your dutie towards God as a Christian: the next, your dutie in your office as a king: and the third informeth you how to behave yourself in indifferent things, which of themselves are neither right nor wrong, but according as they are rightlie or wrong used: and yet will serve according to your behaveur therein to augment or inspaire your fame and authoritie at the hands of your people. Receive and welcome this booke, then, as a faithfull Preceptour and counsellor unto you: which because my affaires will not permit me ever to be present with you I ordaine to be a resident faithfull admonisher of you. And because the houre of death is uncertaine to me, as unto all flesh, I leave it as my Testament and latter-will unto you. Charging you in the presence of God, and by the Fatherlie authoritie I have over you, that yee keepe it ever with you, as carefullie as Alexander did the Iliads of Homer. Ye will finde it a juste and impartial counsellor; neither flattering you in annie vice, nor importuning you at unmeete times. It will not come uncalled, neither speake unspeered at [unbidden]: and yet conferming with it when yee are at quiet, yee shall say with Scipio that yee are *numquam minus solus, quam cum solus.** To conclude then, I charge you, as ever ye thinke to deserve

---

* Never less alone than when alone. Based on a saying of the Roman general Scipio quoted in Cicero, *De Officiis* iii, 1.

my fatherlie blessing, to follow and put in practise, as faire as lieth in you, the precepts hereafter following. And if yee followe the contrarie course, I take the great God to record, that this booke shall one day be a witnesse betwixt me and you; and shall procure to be ratified in heaven, the curse that in that case here I have unto you. For I protest before that great God, I had rather not bee a Father, and childlesse, then be a Father of wicked children. But hoping, yea even promising unto myselfe, that God, who in his great blessing sent you unto me; shall in the same blessing, as he hath given me a Sonne; to make him a good and godlie Sonne; not repenting him of his mercie shewed unto me: I end, with my earnest prayer to God to worke effectuallie into you the fruits of that blessing, which here from my hart I bestow upon you.

Your loving Father

JR

So here we have the hopes as well as the example imagined by James for his heir. They were, however, not much alike. King James was not a pacifist, but he saw no sense in war. It destabilised his kingdom and throne, there was never enough money for it and he never imagined the odds of winning a battle, never mind a war, to be suitably favourable. Henry became a student of warfare, dressed for battle, and tried to understand the minds of campaigners. He did this without gusto and bravado, but grave respect and thoughtfulness of what might come about in conflict. A very young student of conflict maybe, but Henry was not a huntsman in the way of his father. James enjoyed the chase, the hunt for a hart or hare. Henry was, at the very least, indifferent to hunting inasmuch that he could not be concerned to pursue a beast to the end. The biggest difference between father and son was intellectual ambition. James believed himself, with some reason, to be a scholar. Henry, while a respecter of books and learning, never followed his father's appetite for learning and knowledge. Henry was popular whereas James became unpopular, partly because he tired of the throngs and their curiosity about their monarch. Whereas Elizabeth had been adored and had let herself be metaphorically touched, James became acerbic when approached. The people turned their affections, if that is what they were, upon the Prince. Francis Bacon thought Henry would have grown into a fine man. A fine king? None would know and none then could imagine the tragedy that would confront the Stuarts when, on 6 November 1612, Prince Henry, at the age of sixteen, died from the effects of typhoid fever. His younger brother would become Charles I. This was all nine years hence and for the moment thoughts of the crowning of the present monarch were enough for court and people.

At this stage there had to be a respectful distance between the funeral of one monarch and the coronation of the next. There was also, in those few weeks of April and May 1603, much to get out of the way in order that the King could continue to do what he enjoyed doing most: acting like a king, which to his mind was spending money, hunting and dishing out his sermons and homilies to anyone who would listen – and to many more who would not. So April was a month of scurrying courtiers and the carefully timed arrival of the King in his capital.

Even before the triumphal procession reached the Palace of Whitehall, the intensity of James's formal business increased. The interregnum could not be a holiday, even for kings. Cecil, in his important way, still had a country to run. James's pen and seal were needed almost daily. Some of the decrees and orders were very close to James's heart, particularly the proclamation issued on 27 April 1603, the day before Elizabeth's funeral. As we have seen, he had been weaned on a diet of plots and ruthless ambitions. Often at the centre of those episodes had been the Ruthvens (see page 87 above). No wonder then that the court intelligence system, unsurprisingly well placed and sensitively tuned, had the full and gracious support of the monarch when it drafted the proclamation against those who would plot against the King's majesty.

Given at Burghley the 27 day of Aprill
Whereas the Kings Majestie is enformed, that William Ruthen and Patrick Ruthen (two brethren of the late Earle of Gowrie, a dangerous traytour to his Person) have crept into this Kingdome with malicious hearts against him, disguising themselves in secret places, where hee is enformed, that they doe not onely utter cankered speeches against hime, but are practising and contriving dangerous plots, and desperate attempts against his Royall person; for effecting whereof, either by themselves or by such as they can perswade and suborne thereunto, they leave no means unessayed: Be it therefore knowen to all men by these Presents, That for the speedie apprehension of the malicious and dangerous persons William Ruthen and Patrick Ruthen aforesaid, The Kings most ecellent Majestie doeth straitly command and charge all and singular Sheriffes, Justices of the Peace, Mayors, Bayliffes, Constables and all and every other his Highnesse Officers within this his Realme of England, That they, and every of them make diligent search and enquirie for the said malicious persons.

The funeral having taken place on 28 April, James maintained his modesty and did not enter London until 7 May – forty-four days after the death of Elizabeth. Now came the celebrations, with parades and great proclamations and addresses and verses of welcome from almost anyone with access to a quill and a platform. Typical was the address of Richard Martin. Mark the wit and clear precedent of City speeches which are expected to contain at least one, if not joke, then witty introduction. Like all good Mansion House speeches in the twenty-first century, the jokes done, the speaker gets on with the real business of displaying self-satisfaction as well as warning of the truths of office and authority. Thus Richard Martin here sets the standard to which orators through the centuries to follow might aspire. It was certainly published so that others might contemplate Master Martin's fine words.

A Speach Delivered to the Kings Most Excellent Majestie in the name of the Sheriffes of London and Middlesex by Maister Richard Martin of the Middle Temple At London Imprinted for Thomas Thorpe, and are to be found at William Aspley, 1603*

The common feares & difficulties which perplex most confident Orators, speaking before Princes, would more confound my distrustful spirit speaking to your high M[a]jestie (most mighty king & our dreade souvraigne Lord) did I not know that the message which I bring is to a good king always gratefull. Curiosity of wit and affected straines of Oratory I leave to those, who more delight to tickle the Princes eare, then satisfie his deeper judgement . . . I offer your benigne grace that loyall and harty welcome, which from that Honourable and ancient Cittie (the heart of this kingdome) is brought by them, whole deepe and inwarde griefe, conceaved for the losse of our Peerelesse and renound Queene Elizabeth is turned into excessive joy, for the approach of your excellent Majesty by whom the long and blessed peace of five and forty yeres is made perpetuall.

It is in this speech that the sheriffs of 'the heart of this kingdome' remind James – if he indeed needed reminding – of the breadth of his realm: Scotland, England and Wales, Ireland and, mythically but doggedly, France. Here then are the parallels with a supreme governor's tasks four hundred years on.

And see how bounteous heaven hath assined foure kingdomes,

* British Library shelfmark 1103.f.29.

as proper subjects for your Majesties four Kingly vertues. Scotland hath tried your prudence, in reducing those things to order in the Church and Common-wealth, which the tumultuous times of your Majesties infancie had there put out of square. Ireland shall require your justice, which the miseries (I dare not say the policies) of civil wars have there defaced. France shall prove your fortitude, when necessary reason of state shall bend your Majesties Counselles to that enterprise. But let England the schoole, wherein your Majestie will practise your temperance and moderations for here flattery will essay to undermine, or force your Majesties strong constancie and integrity.

Martin thought it right to tell James of what he felt were the real poisons in the kingdom, including the priests who preached against the social and political mores of the land. From the pulpits flowed treasonable sermons, or so the sheriffs implied, and certainly the Protestant Church in 1603 felt it a duty to warn continuously against papist intrusion and the plotting of even the most high born and well placed in James's kingdom. No one, especially James, could doubt this reasoning. His whole life had been marked with the conflict between the wider Catholic and Protestant conspiracies. Whatever the debate and the passion of proponents, none should believe that clergy of 1603 lived in a golden age of theological discovery. Priests were often as scurrilous and opportunistic as the next villain.

The money changers and sellers of Doves (I mean those which trafique the livings of simple and religious pastors) shall your Majestie whip out of the Temple and commonwealth: For no more shall Church livings be pared to the quicke, forcing ambicious Church-men (pertakers of this Sacriledge) to enter at the window by simonie and corruption, which they must afterwards repair with userie and make up with pluralities.

There is too a reference here to piracy. For decades, Elizabeth's privateers had cheerfully pillaged merchantmen on any high sea that proved good passage from the riches of the New World. The end of English piracy, considering its main victims, could also lead to a more peaceful relationship with Spain. The City's aldermen were much aware of this and had little to lose except percentages from some of this British maritime pastime. Piracy was, after all, a business – almost an honoured profession. Certainly it was a trade for the very top drawer of English society. Peace with Spain could advance attractive mercantilism and most of all just might protect their own cargo vessels – after all, piracy was not an exclusively English trade. Martin's reference to corsairs may be construed as a plea to defend against foreign pirates, but the reference was not lost on James who really did need peace with Spain. As we shall see, he would that very year proclaim that piracy, whatever the Elizabethan precedent, was not exercised with this majesty's pleasure. The City would applaud James for dealing with what Master Martin called 'sea wolves'.

Martin reflected the strength of the City. He was in a position to tell James what he and the aldermen thought in the straightest of language. It is not insignificant that one of the first letters James sent, even before he left Scotland, to England was to the City fathers in London. Yet not all the greeting was gloomy. Not all the Church corrupted. Not all the advice for personal gain.

The neglected (almost worne out) nobility shall now (as bright Diadems and burning Carbunkles) adorne your Kingly Diadem. The too much contemned Clergy shall hang as a precious earing at your Princly eare, your Majestie still lystning to their holy Councels. The wearied Commons shall be worne as a rich ring on your royall finger, which your Majesty with a watchful eye will still gratiously looke upon. For we have now a king that will heare with his own eares, see with his own eyes, and be ever jealous of any great trust, which (being afterwardes become necessary) may be abused to an unlymitted power.

Having said that, implied Martin, the terrible truth was that there were those who would take all advantage possible of the monarch. The City fathers, of course, would never do such a thing. Of course not. Others, said Martin, might well lack the moral and sturdy altruism of the mayor and sheriffs. 'They mean to sell the king to his subjects at their owne price and abuse th'authority of his majesty to their private gayne and greatnes, who perswaded him, that to shut himselfe up from the access of his people, is the meanes to augment his state.'

When James arrived in London he was expected to go through the constitutional custom of the new monarch. The king- or queen-in-waiting was supposed to establish the Court at the Tower of London. The Tower is normally associated with imprisonment and execution, but it was also known as the Castle Royal and was considered the 'chiefe House of safety in the Kingdome, until the more weighty affaires of the state' are settled.* In times when the succession might be disputed the monarch would have lodged in the 'House of safety' until the eve of the coronation, and the procession from the Tower to the monarch's palace in Whitehall was considered the centrepiece for the public's view. This was more than gaudy pageantry. Cecil understood its meaning: this was the moment when the King rode bareheaded and usually simply dressed in front of the people. It was hardly the entrance of a saviour on an ass, but the similarity was not that far removed. It was the monarch declaring himself and asking for the allegiance of the people before the formality of the crowning. The symbolism was so important that although James did not make that journey on the eve of the coronation, he was encouraged to ride in procession the following March.

On 12 May 1603 James went to the Tower. The next day he observed the new coins of his reign being minted and seemed intent on enjoying himself rather than going through any solemn ceremony.

---

* Edmund Howes (fl. 1607–31) in expanded version of John Stow's (c. 1525–1605) *Annales* or *Chronicle*.

On 15 May James, accompanied by Queen Anne and Prince Henry, began his procession from the Tower towards Westminster.

> The companies of the Citie martialled according to their degrees, were placed, the first beginning at the upper end of Marke lane, and the last reaching to the Conduict in Fleet-street, or therabout: their seates being double railed, upon the upper part whereof they leaned: the streamers, Ensignes and banners of each particular company, decently fixed. And directly against them, quite through the body of the Citie, so high as Temple barre a single raile, in faire distance from the other, was likewise erected to put off the multitude: the king richly mounted on a white Gennet, under a rich Canopis, sustained by eight Gentlemen of the Privie Chamber, for the Barons of the Cinque Ports, entred his Royall City of London, and passed the same towards Westminster, through seven gates, of the which, the first was erected at the East end of Fan-church, over the which gate, was represented the true likenesse of the notable houses, Towers, and Staeples within the City of London.*

Howes refers to the seven gates of the City of London. Modern travellers in that place will see gates still referred to, for example, Moorgate and Aldgate. The first gate on James's route in 1603 was the one at Fan-church Street (now Fenchurch Street) which had on its top the models of the most notable buildings of the City. The second gate, at Grace Street (Grace Church Street) was built by Italians and owed more for its design to images of Venice than cold and plague-ridden London. The third gate was by what we now know as Cornhill and the Corn Exchange. This had all sorts of references to the Lowlands and represented the seventeen Dutch provinces. The fourth gate was the people's gate built by the citizens at West Cheapside near Soper Lane. The fifth gate was at St Paul's

* Ibid.

and was known as the Music Arbour. The sixth gate was a triumphal arch at the bottom of what was then Fleetstreete and was celebrated for its spinning globe. The most important gate of all was at Temple Bar where James, like his successors today, crossed out of the City of London. It was at this seventh arch, a replica of the Temple of Janus, that the Lord Mayor and aldermen handed their monarch safely over to greater London.

The great pageantry that was the transition from the Tower to Whitehall was easily taken by James as his triumphal entry. The symbolic journey of March 1604 was delayed pageantry from the previous year. It might be thought, with good reason, that this was because of the presence of plague in London. It is also true that Cecil has left no evidence in his family's papers that James was ever told that the journey was to seek the authority of the people. If he had been it is unlikely that his utter belief in his Divine Right to rule would have allowed him to ride before his people as if seeking their vote. His son, Charles I, never made that same journey. Belatedly and unwittingly James I was the last monarch to do so. It is clear that James had no intention of loitering in the Tower until the coronation. He entered the Tower on 11 May and appears to have been at Greenwich two days later. We know that he stayed at Greenwich because some, although not all, of the proclamations which seemingly poured from the Crown Printer, were issued when the court rested below the park by the Thames. Petitioners and scroungers gathered to touch the hem of James's patronage. Cecil stamped on most fingers. Yet the state had to tick over as if nothing had happened at its pinnacle. Some petitions brought easy response; others were wisely given because favour and patronage allowed the recipient to dispense his own favours as well as acknowledge whence his power had come, no matter how innocent the gift might appear.

19 May. The King to the Lord Treasurer.
Wm. Lewes, of Bristol, has had for several years the collection

of the impost of sweet wines in the port of Bristol, &c., and behaved honestly therein; and having besought continuance in the same under you, to whom we have committed the general collection of the impost, as under Alderman Wood, late Collector General, we have signified our pleasure to Sir Wm. Ryder, whom we have made Collector General of our customs inwards; but it has not taken effect, from your pretending that the right of appointing officers for our collection appertains to you and our butler of England. Wherefore we require you, on his putting in good security for such moneys as come to his hands, to continue him in the said place.

Not all proclamations and decrees were so jolly. Some reflected times past and the anxieties expressed by Cecil, who had, remember, put militia on standby in case of civil disobedience and worse as a reaction to the new sovereign. Ironically, James had left Scotland with all the cheers and assurances he thought right and imagined that the Borders were quiet. Maybe his passing from Scotland might be mourned but he rather assumed there was no better territory to reflect the new beginning of his rule over a unified state.

Robert Carey had been satisfied that, for the moment at least, the Borders which he was patrolling were quiet enough for him to leave them in the charge of his deputies before riding to Richmond Palace to see the dying Elizabeth. Just as Carey had indicated and James had nervously wondered before entering Berwick, the land between Northumbria and Scotland was never quiet for long. It was hardly a surprise then that James had only been in London a couple of days and was not even crowned when news of skirmishing and antagonism in the Borders, which he had left just five weeks earlier – supposedly at peace – reached the capital. Cecil urged a royal proclamation to order the protagonists to desist. Local rivalries, bitterness and not a little opportunity to grab land and more would take more than a proclamation to cool tempers and ambitions. However, this form of decree made clear that those who did not observe the published wishes of the monarch would indeed be beyond the law. The proclamation was signed at Greenwich on 17 May 1603 and sent to the royal printer, Robert Barker, for publication and posting throughout the realm.

The foule and intolerent outrages lately committed upon the borders of our Realmes of England and Scotland by persons accustomed in former times to live by rapine and spoyle, praying dayly upon our good and loving Subjects without feare of God or man, hath given us just cause to use all meanes convenient both for the reliefe of our Subjects damnified, and for prevention of the like mischiefe hereafter. Wherefore as of late we gave commission to proceede against those persones that were guiltie of those foule facts: So now againe, because as yet such redresse hath not followed as both our honour and our good Subjects losse do require, We have thought good to renew our Commission to certaine persones of qualitie and of good understanding in the affaires of those our Borders. And, withall to publish by open proclamation to all men, but specially to such as are guiltie, or were partakers of the foule incursions made upon our first coming to our Crowne of this Realme of England, or any others before or since, That whereas some of them have of late submitted themselves, and some others seemed to be willing to submit themselves, to our mercy, because they and all others shall now, that as we are a Prince that before all Worldly respects Whatsoever affecteth the preservations of Justice among our people and the punishment of such as breake the Rules thereof, So that We are not indisposed to shew mercy where there is cause to extend it, and where the same is sought at our hands in such dutifull manner as is meete: We do therefore charge all persones whatsoever, who know themselves to have bene Actours, Partners, or of consent to that incursion above mentioned, or to any other breach of our peace within the Counties and Lymits heretofore called our Borders both of the English live and of the Scottish, that they do before the twentieth day of June next coming resort to such place, Where they shall understand our Commissioners to be, and there submit themselves to such mercy and favour, as Wee shall thinke good to extend towards them.

Rather like the contents of sermons, we can tell a great deal about the way favour was badgered, claimed and acknowledged from the list of proclamations of the time. Many were favours redeemed, thought better of, or even bestowed whimsically. Always there is a sense of the courtier's hand, the whisper from the Wardrobe and Privy Purse corridor that this or that sign of a monarch's gracious favour would be wisely spent on this or that person. For example, what had happened to Bagshott Park could hardly have bothered James I. He probably had no idea of its existence. Cecil and his secretaries knew full well its importance: here was a chance to pay off debts to Guildford, who was loyal to Cecil, thus maintaining the authority of patronage. This altogether subtler instruction appeared the day before the order to stop skirmishing in the Borders.

May 16. The king to the Lord Admiral.
Her late Majesty granted to John Lidcott the custody of Bagshot Park; he sold his interest to one Furst, who conveyed it to Sir Hen. Guilford, and afterwards sold it again to another, by which double sale great disturbance has grown, and meantime our deer and woods are neglected. As we hold Sir Henry Guilford meetest to have the keeping, and as he has the best right from Lidcott, we require you to order that he be put into quiet possession.

May 16. Grant to Simeon Furner of the office of merchant and agent in the East parts for buying pitch, tar, hemp, flax, oakum, sailcloth, cables, ropes, masts, iron, firs, deals, &c. for the Navy; fee, 33L. 6s. 8d. yearly.

May 20. Note of the reversion of a grant to Hen. Guevara, one of the captains of Berwick, of the office of master of tents and pavilions; fee, 30L. a year. Endorsed on a grant by Queen Elizabeth, 20 Jan. 1560, to Hen. Seckford, of the reversion of the said office after Sir Thos. Baldwarden.

May 21. Note of a grant to Roland White, in reversion after John Harrington, of the office of constable of Carnarvon Castle, North Wales; fee, 60L. a year. Endorsed on a grant by Queen Elizabeth, 11 May 1579, to John Harrington of the like reversion, after his father, John Harrington.

May 21. The King to the Officers of Exchequer.
Being informed that Sir Francis Knollys, Geo. Blande, Edw. Duffeild, Ellice and Toby Gaylor, &c., without commission, on 16 July 1599, took out of the house of Francis Parkins, at Uston, co. Berks, of the goods and treasure of Thos. Vachell, 1,484L. in gold, 8L. in silver, plate value 200L., and two gold chains worth 100L. and 100 marks, on pretence that Vachell was convicted of recusancy, and that the late Queen seised all his goods and chattels, and two parts of his lands and tenements; – question now being made whether the said gold, silver, and plate yet remaining in our Exchequer as *in deposito* appertains to us or to Vachell, and to whom the rest of the said treasure not yet brought into our Court belongs; – We, now allowing such taking without commission, and pitying the case of the said Vachell, whereof he has made petition to us, grant to Sir Thos. Vachell, his cousin and next heir, all the said gold, money, jewels, and plate, &c., as our free gift.

May 22. Instructions to the Commissioners appointed to sit upon suits, to be careful what suits they listen to, lest the king should have to give offence by denying what they grant, and not to grant any reversions of places of consequence, as those are the rewards to be looked forward to by faithful servants. In requests for peerage or for the garter, to examine into the rank, &c. of the claimants, and not to add to the present number of 24 privy councillors.

May 25. Grant to Oliver Cromwell [James's host during his journey south], gentleman of the Privy Chamber, of the keep-ership of the game in the forests of Weybridge and Sapley, and in Gaynes and Ramsey Parks, and elsewhere in cos. Huntingdon and Cambridge, as also within five miles of Babraham co. Cambridge; with authority to search and find out all persons unlawfully keeping or using guns, nets, &c. for taking or destroying game, and to seise and take away the same, and to prevent any hunting or hawking, without consent of the owners of the land.

May 25. Greenwich. The King to [Sir Thos. Knyvet], warden of the Mint.
We are determined to proceed with the moneys wrought by warrant of the late Queen; viz., angels, half angels, and quarter angels, of fine gold; crowns and half-crowns, shillings and sixpences, of silver. Also pieces of two pence, pence, and half-pence. Minute directions for the engraving and legends of the said coins.

You are to order Charles Anthony, graver of our Mint, to cause to be graven irons needful for the striking of our said moneys, and we authorise you to take up skilful gravers for the said works, within our Tower of London.

May 28. Greenwich. The King to the Mayor of Gloucester.
Being informed that Wm. Oldisworth, late recorder of Gloucester, has departed this life, and that Jasper Selwyn, of Lincoln's Inn, an ancient utter barrister, dwelling within the liberties of the

said city, is a very fit man for the place, we command you to elect him thereto.

May 15. The King to the Lord Treasurer.
The customs on silks, the farm of which was granted by the late Queen to Sir Robert, now Lord, Cecil,* are no longer payable in strict law, being granted by her only for life; but not doubting their renewal next Parliament, you are to order their payment as usual in the meantime.

Once the dutiful decrees and proclamations were tied up, James could proceed to the most important day (after the death of Elizabeth) of 1603. The way was clear for the coronation. Because of the plague, the ceremony was modified. There were fewer nobles and gentry in the procession. The plague frightened the court and with good reason. London was well used to the feared consequences of the pestilence, which returned only too regularly to the capital. More than 37,000 were to perish that summer and autumn. The week before the coronation was subdued and even the date was in question. A coronation normally would take place on a Sunday or holiday, not so that more people could attend, but because this gave emphasis to the religious aspect of the occasion, remembering that a holiday in the early seventeenth century was still observed as a holy day, even if accompanied by fairs and sports. (These preferred dates continued until the coronation of William and Mary.) The day chosen, being St James's Day, was even a Red Letter Day in the Book of Common Prayer. But proclamations had already been issued cancelling many festivals, including the celebrated St James's Fair.

The ceremony itself was truncated. The tradition of electing the monarch in Westminster Hall was abandoned. The custom, an ancient one, of raising the monarch into his stone seat at

* One of James's first duties was to create Robert Cecil a baron, ostensibly for his service not to James but to the late Queen.

Westminster was discarded. The formalities began on 22 July when the King and Queen arrived at Westminster and then the next day, a Saturday, the King held an investiture in his garden. The Knights of the Bath, on 24 July, rode in procession from St James's to meet their new monarch and receive their knighthoods. Other, not so illustrious, persons had an investiture of quite different meaning. As the knights jingled for their honours, the King ordered a warrant issued that a Coronation Pardon should be made for all offences committed before 20 March. The great (if not entirely good) also received a remission for their sins.

> July 20. The King to the Lord Treasurer.
> Whereas Robert Earl of Sussex owes us divers sums grown due to the late Queen our sister, and her and our progenitors, by him and his ancestors . . . as appears by a note by him to us, which we send herewith . . . which debts we are pleased to remit; We require you to examine any documents touching such debts, and cause our learned counsel to draw a discharge of the same; and send it to us for signature.

Coronations produce more than street parties, even in time of plague and uncertainty. The coronation was on the feast of St James, 25 July 1603, but the smell of dying loitered over London. The recently arrived Venetian envoy, Giovanni Carlo Scaramelli, tells us that in the King's name a proclamation was issued from Windsor Castle on 11 July which ordered those not invited to keep their distance from this royal affair.

> Various orders were issued so as to prevent the presence at the ceremony of any of the dwellers in London, whereby people are dying by the thousand every week. Tickets of admission have been issued to those attached to the Court, and to a certain extent the very private character of the ceremony has been modified . . . Land access was forbidden by a strong body of

guards placed at the gates of London, while on the water it was the penalty of death to bring people in boats from the city.*

The proclamation, drafted by Cecil, was uncompromising in its language.

our castle of Windsor the xi day of July, 1603. In the first yeere of our reigne of England, France and Ireland, and of Scotland, the sixe and thirtieth.

The care we have to prevent all occasions of dispersing the infection amongst our people, doeth sufficiently appeare by our former proclamations, and that for that cause Wee are contented to forebeare at our Coronation all such Ceremonies of honour and pompe used by our Progenitors, as many draw over great confluence of people to our Citie. For which cause also being informed that usually about the day of the coronation intended, and for some dayes after, a faire hath bene used to bee kept in the fieldes neere our house of S. James, and Citie of Westminster, commonly called S. James Faire, which if it should holde at the time accustomed, being the very instant of our Coronation, could not but resort of people to that place, much more unfit to bee neere our Court and Traine, then such as by former Proclamations are restrained. Wherefore wee have thought it necessary to put off the keeping of that Faire for some few dayes: And to the ende that all men may take notice thereof, doe publish the same to all mens knowledge, Requiring those who are Lords of the Faire, or otherwise interested therein, That according to this our pleasure, they doe forbeare to holde the sayde Faire, and to resort thither, for the space of eight or ten days after the first day of the usuall holding thereof: Licensing them after that time to keep the same, as they have used to doe.

* PRO, Calendar of State Papers, Venetian, 1603–1607.

Furthermore, to avoyd over great resort to our Cities of London and Westminster at that time, for the cause of our Coronation, we have thought good to limit the Traines of Noblemen and Gentlemen, having necessarie Service of Attendance there, to a number certaine, Viz. Earles to fifteene, Bishops and Barons to ten, Knights to five, and Gentlemen to foure: which numbers We require each of them to observe, and not to exceed, as they tender our favour.

That business done, James was anxious to get on with the coronation where he could take oaths of office and, equally important, receive oaths of allegiance. Until he was crowned and anointed, his natural sense of insecurity prevailed.

It was necessary also to guard against any demonstration against James. The sense of uncertainty and sensible precaution was evident in instructions to the lords lieutenant to provide guards of honour and, more importantly, protection. Here is the King's order to the Lord Lieutenant of Surrey.

July 18. Hampton Court . . . As we hold it necessary at the day of our coronation that some number of men, armed, be placed in guard about our city of Westminster, for preventing sedition or tumult, we require you to levy and arm 100 of our trained bands of Surrey, in places next the city of London, under some sufficient gentleman, and send them to such place and at such time as you shall be directed by our Council.

The coronation may not have had all the customary pageantry, yet it most certainly was not a dull occasion. Archdukes, viscounts, princes of France, Lorraine and Brunswick were in procession. Twelve heralds, splendid in their tabards depicting the arms of James's kingdoms, were followed by the mayors and scarlet-coated aldermen. Judges in scarlet and the Lord Chief Justice with his gold collar were followed by the sixty Knights of the Bath in their blue and violet satin and white plumes and scabbards of white leather; the ermine-caped barons, twenty earls in crimson velvet, each with a small plain gold coronet, their slender sceptres of office in their right hands. Behind the earls came the Lord High Treasurer bearing a cushioned crown and sceptre, followed by the Earl of Southampton with the royal sword of state. Then as a reminder of the true right of this king came the cup-bearer with the golden chalice holding sweet communion wine, and another holding a paten. Behind the bearers processed four pages carrying the four staves which supported the silken canopy beneath which the King solemnly walked, dressed in a crimson velvet mozetta (cape) lined with ermine.

Following the King's canopy were the courtiers of his consort. An earl carried her crown on a cushion. He was followed by twelve countesses in crimson and white who preceded the Queen. Just as the King was simply dressed, so Anne wore no embroidery and her hair was unpiled and about her shoulders; her headdress was a simple gold crown. She was followed by ten of her ladies-in-waiting, also in crimson. Then came perhaps one hundred and fifty halberdiers, the King's guard in their new Stuart liveries. In their procession also were twenty of the King's military pensioners in their knee-length crimson coats with lances in their right hands.

As those in the procession split to left and to right to take up their positions in the three rows of the choir stalls, the King, for a moment alone, took a seat below the throne. The countesses and ladies-in-waiting to the side, the Queen curtsied to her monarch and sat also in a chair below the throne. The royal king of arms called the ceremony to order, three times sounding with loud voice, 'Listen! Listen! Listen!' A long pause and then the Archbishop of Canterbury intoned to the four sides of the abbey that if anyone would deny that James, King of Scotland, was not the lawful King of England, France and Ireland, he should say so at once, or then he would be held a traitor, and that he, the Archbishop, was about to confer on James the ensigns of the kingdom, trusting firmly that he would defend and govern his people well. The King and Queen were then led to the altar for prayers and then back to their seats again for the sermon.

Preached by Thomas Bilson, Bishop of Winchester, the sermon was more than a homily. The Bishop laid out what was expected of a monarch. The chance of birth, the privilege of monarchy, the accompanying wealth and authority did not come alone. The monarchy still had a direct duty towards the people. This moment in the abbey of Edward the Confessor defined the arrangement of a promise by the monarch that he would protect his people and in return would expect their allegiance: the father's duty to his children. That sermon on the feast of St James in 1603 was in real terms the final expression of kingship in the history of the English monarchy.

Equally, Bilson struck a high chord in the constitutional symphony composed by James himself.

If James might ask common folk whether they had studied his treatise on the Divine Right of kings, he had no need to fret over Bilson's scholarship, nor his sensitivity when expressing it. James had written that the monarch was like a father and that his pleasurable fatherhood was ordained by God. The Bishop preached well. God was indeed the authority of monarchy – certainly this monarchy.

God ordained the power of men over other men, & with manifest woordes authorised Rulers to take and keep their places. Private and inferior powers, as the husband over his wife, the father over his children, the maister over his Servantes, were to be allowed and ratified by God, from whome is all power, before they could be lawfull . . . I thinke it fitte for this present time, and place, to observe, not onely, how the Princes function in generall is established by God, more specially, how the braunches thereof, namely, their power, their honour, and their service are ordained and confirmed of God. To express them more distinctly. Their Authoritie is derived from GOD, resembling his image; Their dignitie is allowed of GOD, to

partake with his homage: Their Duetie is enjoyned them by
GOD, to preserve his heretage. The first they have received
from GOD; the second they must receive from men; the third
they must yeelde to both . . .

The likenesse that Princes have with the kingdome of GOD
and of Christ, consisteth in the Society of the names, and signes,
which they have in common with Christ; in the Sufficencie of
the spirite, wherewith God indueth them; in the Sanctitie of
their persons, which may not be violated in the Soveraigntie
of their power, which must not be resisted.*

One can well imagine James nodding wisely and delightedly at
these last two points. The sanctity of the monarchy was close to
his heart. That its power should not be resisted was an even closer
sentiment.

Princes can not be Gods by nature, being framed of the same
mettall, and in the same moulde, that others are; It followeth
directly, they are the gods by Office; Ruling, Judging, and
Punishing in Gods steede, & so deserving Gods name heere
on earth. As it was said of Moses, Behold, I have made thee
Pharaohs God [Exod.7] that is his people, his person, his land,
his life, and all hee hath, shal be in thy power, and depend on
thy word . . .

The greatnesse of the power which Princes have received
from God, resembling his image, leadeth us to the greatness of
the Honur they must receive from men, in partaking with gods
homage. The one is Gods ordinance as as the other, for God

* A Sermon preached at Westminster before the king and Queenes Majesties, at
their Coronation on Saint James his day, being the 28 [sic]. Of July. 1603 by the
Reverend Father in God the Lord Bishop of Winchester. Printed at London by V.S.
for Clement Knight and are to be sold at his shop at the signe of the Holy Lambe
(this was in St Paul's Churchyard) 1603. British Library shelfmark 695.a.b.

hath not put Princes in his place, and given then his power, to be despised or disobeyed, but to be honoured and served as his Lieutenants and Viceregents here on earth.

Then followed the very thoughts that might have emerged from the mouth of the King himself.

What kinde of honour is due to Princes, is shortly delivered in that commandment, Honor thy Father. They are Fathers in Gods Law, that hath or should have fatherly care over us, whether it be to ayde us in the things of this life, as masters and teachers; or to guide us the true way to heaven, as pastors and ministers; or to keepe us in peace and godlinesse, as Magistrates and Princes: God giving Princes that name, because they should be as vigilant for the good of those that are under their charge, as parents are for their chidren; and receive the same honor and service for their paines, which are due to parents from their natural children, if not greater . . .

Reverence due to Princes must come from the whole man, and have the whole man, that is, it must have the love of our hearts, the prayer of our lips, and the submission of our bodies. They are Gods ministers for our wealth. They must therefore be loved even from the hart. We must love their places appointed by god to partake, as wel with his honor as with his power.

So here Bilson is making it as clear as James himself would have that the monarch was Our Father on Earth and hallowed indeed is the King's name. Should such a god be beyond the reach of the common man, even the courtier, who after all could be little more than minor angels in such a courtly heaven? Bilson had thought of this:

because it is growen a great fashion in needelesse curtesie to bow and touch the anckle, and in necessarie duetie to stand starke and stiffe, let us see in a word or two whether the Custome of this Countrie, in kneeling to their Princes, be servilitie or flatterie, as some reckon it, or part of their due honor and dignitie.

The preacher was spoilt for biblical references in making out a case for each and every forelock, never mind hem, to be touched. Joseph suffered the brethren to bow down to the ground before him; Jacob urged his son to keep the sceptre of his office close to him and, at its sight, fathers and sons would bow before him; did not everyone bow before David? Then honour and custom and respect would rule the way in which the monarch was honoured.

There remained the matter of kingship, the contract between the monarch and the people. If James were to receive God-given honour, then, proclaimed the Bishop, the people must receive God-given protection and honour due to them. If the biblical King David was wise in these things, so should King James I be.

Let not your power or honour deceive you, your Kingdome hath limits, and shall have an end, only the Kingdome of Christ is over all, and forever. Serve therefore the Lord. You are great Lords above others, but there is a farre greater above you. Your soveraignty over men must be a Service under God. You are not called to do your own willes, but his that exalted you. His Law must be your levell, his worde your warrant. If you serve not him, you serve sinne . . .

[B]esides the procuring of publike and private peace to each place and person, it is no small service, that Princes do unto GOD by repressing the unbrideled lusts of mans corruption, and revenging the wicked attempts of mans presumption; I mean Adulteries, Incests, Rapes, Robberies . . . Conspiracies, Witch-crafts, Murders, Rebllions, Treasons and such like hainous and impious enormities, which would overflow each Kingdome and Countrie if the Princes Sword did not take Revenge of the Doers and Committers of such Outrages . . .

Princes themselves no lesse then other sent and authorised
by them, doe execute the Judgements, not of Man, but of the
Lord; and in that respect, as the Seate is Gods, wherein they sit,
so it must bee guided by Gods lawe, and they must imitate Gods
steppes, who sitteth and judgeth in the middest of them.

Bilson's sermon was a calculated and clever affair. None could
ignore that James was crowned by the archbishop of the southern
province of the Established Church. None could ignore the Millenary Petition from the non-conforming ministers sent already to
James. Thus, Bilson's sermon would not have been written to do
anything but please the monarch. Bilson was making certain that
James understood that it was the Established Church, now his
Church, that had power and authority and that James was now
part of the collusion between English monarch and the accepted
English religious persuasion. The curious relationship of the English
monarchs and their bishops, whereby the king or queen frequently
expressed frustration and the bishops their anachronisms, so often
made and continued to make a religious mockery of the Established Church whose supreme earthly governor was the monarch.
The very crowning, but particularly the anointing, of the English
monarch expressed a belief in the Divine Right to rule and, for
many centuries, absolutism that the Church continued to condone
for its own survival. The ritual of anointing the monarch was more
important than the crowning. This was the duty of the archbishop.
The thick oil or soft ointment was contained in a small vase covered
with white linen and stood apart from the more gaudy regalia on
the altar. It was said that this oil was one of the most precious
objects kept in the Tower. It had been blessed and consecrated many
monarchs before, including Edward VI and Queen Elizabeth. Now
came a point in the ceremony that would marry the monarch and
his people.

Edmund Howes in his *Annales*, published later (1631) in London,
gives us a good account of what followed.

They put upon him over the dress of white a vestment of crimson velvet lined with white, with tight sleeves, and over this a royal surplice (*cotta*) with the tunicle of a deacon, embroidered, I think, with the arms of his kingdoms. Then the Archbishop having taken from the altar the sword, the garter (*Giarthiera*) and the grand collar of the order, the Admiral and two others, Earls, put them on him. Over all was put a mantle without folds, like a cope, of violet brocade with a large orphrey (*lista*) of white cloth of silver. The king being thus vested went and sat in his private seat; and then the Archbisop took the Imperial crown from the altar, showed it to the king, and put it again on the altar; then the king was led to the royal chair, and the Archbishop returned to the altar, took the crown, came back to the king and put it upon his head. This being done the king came back to the altar; having taken a book like a missal he read in it, and the king having touched the book with his hand, certain earls took from the altar a sword adorned with gold but in a plain scabbard of leather, drew it, and so carried it before the king. Some say that this ceremony shows the defence of the Gospel: others say that the king took an oath; but I do not believe this, because it was said to me that he took an oath as the last of all the ceremonies.

Then the king came back to his royal chair, and the Archbishop took the sceptre and a verge from the altar and carried them to the king, and put the sceptre in his right hand and the verge in his left. The sceptre is imperial and a palm and a half long. It has the globe at the top, and over it the cross. The verge is of gold, and touches the ground; it has a globe at the top and a crown above.

Now was the King crowned. The two bishops held up the crown and all the earls and barons covered their heads with their caps and took the oath of allegiance. They each approached the throne and bowed at its foot. Each rose and then knelt on a cushion at the

King's foot. Each peer then kissed the King's right hand. There was one exception which lightened the solemn moment. The young Earl of Pembroke, still in his twenties and a favourite of the King, stood to kiss the King's crown and then kissed his cheek. From that point the mood lightened and James shook and squeezed hands with all the jollity of one newly ordained. The herald called for the people's silence and the Lord Chancellor declared in strong voice that James VI, King of Scotland, was now James I, King of England.

While James sat in his glory, Anne had sat in silence and contemplation. Now it was her turn. The Archbishop took the imperial crown and sceptre and she was presented as the loyal queen of her most loyal subjects. After this point the service moved to the first communion of James as the new monarch. This was the great confirmation of the public acceptance of the authority of the Established Church of England as the vicar of God on earth. Pointedly, Queen Anne did not leave her throne and refused to take the Protestant communion. According to some Vatican papers and evidence offered by the seventeenth-century English Catholic priest Dom Oswald Hunter-Blair, O.S.B., Queen Anne had been received into the communion of the Church of Rome some time before 1603, and at the time of her coronation was a member of that communion.* Anne was not alone in her refusal. As some mark of the differences between Catholics and Protestants, certain representatives of foreign powers felt they could not remain in the abbey during the communion service. Certainly the French ambassador and the envoy from Lorraine actually left the abbey at that point of the service and returned later as they believed the English Established Church service to be heretical.

* Vatican transcripts 1604–10, 21 January 1604. Roman transcripts, 11 August 1603, PRO. See also J. Wickham Legg, Chairman of the Council of the Henry Bradshaw Society, *Coronation Order of King James I* (F.E. Robinson & Co., London, 1902).

The grand procession from the abbey was short. While the ceremonies had proceeded, outside the plague looked on. From the abbey James and Anne processed speedily to Westminster Steps and their barge, keeping those who waved at a proper distance. That night they lodged at the palace at Whitehall. The next morning they went with all haste beyond the germs to the palace at Hampton Court.

The ceremony done, James and Anne at last had all the authority of monarchy. One of Anne's first acts was to issue her own warrants and decrees. The protocol of monarchy would now have to be challenged rather than decided by officials. Even the smallest royal warrant could mean the transfer of large amounts of monies and these would have to be watched by Lord Treasurer Buckhurst (now translated from Ireland). The day after the coronation, a simple warrant by Queen Anne for running up a few royal frocks contained an accounting column that was a reminder, if any needed reminding, of the cost of the trappings of monarchy.

July 26. Hampton Court.
Warrant by Queen Anne, appointing Audrey Lady Walsingham, one of the ladies of the Privy Chamber, guardian and keeper of the robes; yearly fee, 40 marks; with authority to buy all stuffs of gold, silver, tinsel, silk, &c. needful, and to convert the same into apparel, according to Her Majesty's direction. Also to choose tailors, embroiderers, haberdashers, &c. necessary; none to be used or have access but at her choice.

The Court was perhaps the most expensive business in England. As Elizabeth had shown, even the simple need to feed that Court each and every day could cost a small fortune. James was not more extravagant than Elizabeth had been, but each day money had to be found for maintaining forty tables of food, beer and wines. This was not a banquet; it was the amount needed to cope with a royal household.

In 1603 James took to London his own staff and hangers-on and inherited those of Elizabeth. The single act of feeding these people made alarming inroads into the royal budget, no matter how cheap the food or wheresoever it came. James had his own table in his own quarters; beyond that would be another table, sometimes with as many as forty dishes for lords and ladies. The Lord Chamberlain would entertain daily and the cost of that would come from the royal coffers. In the great chamber, the courtiers would sit down to eat, as would another table of privy councillors. The Comptroller of the Household would have his own private table (paid for by the monarch, of course) and so would the Lord Treasurer. Add to these gatherings and dinings tables for the likes of the Master of the Horse, clerks of this and that, the dean and chapter and the Master of the Crown Jewels, plus the twenty-five other tables for servants and minor officer-holders, including tables for laundrymen and -women, servants of the scalding house, pastry-makers, chandlery and larder, porters, musicians and spicery, and enormous inroads were made into the monarch's purse. James and Anne seemed unworried by this thought. Perhaps their priorities were right, as an awesome enemy was eating away at the population of their capital city.

7

PLAGUE

THE CORONATION CARAVAN HAD SETTLED TO THE BUSINESS OF MONARCHY. It had also shown a determination born of a sense to keep much of the capital at a clinical distance. The plague was spreading.

Most people were aware of the history of plagues throughout Europe. At one time, a third of the Continent's population had perished. The continental Black Death had arrived in England (probably from the Crimea) through the ports of Dorset in June 1348. The population of England in that year was probably about five million people. It is variously estimated that as many as two million people perished in that plague. By 1603 the population had only recovered to reach not much more than four million, so now many knew that this was not a new disease but the return of a hateful visitor.

Although everyone would be familiar with its consequences, few, if any, would know how to deal with it. Basic hygiene was rare. Inoculation centuries away. So what could the mighty organisation commanded by Cecil do? The answer was dreadful in its simplicity: nothing but hope to cut the risks of infection.

In 2003 an epidemic – among humans or bovines – would be accompanied with cries of 'What is the government doing about it?' In 1603 there was no government in the sense we understand the term. To start with there was no continuous political system. Parliament met only when the monarch called it. James would not convene a Parliament until 1604. There was no other effective forum, and as there were no organised political parties, there was no form of accountability. There was no prime minister (that office would not appear for more than a hundred years, with Robert Walpole as the first First Minister – a title of derision initially); there was no cabinet. The political power in the land was in the hands of Robert Cecil and those agreeably, or sometimes disagreeably, about him. Ultimate authority was the monarchy. The parish councils, aldermen and burghers would cope as best they could, and, considering the plague was less virulent outside the cities, particularly London, this demanded no great effort. The national direction – what today we would expect as the big announcement of emergency measures – could come only from the throne. This was the only way in which the people and the governing elements from the parishes to the elite of the ruling aristocracy could know what was expected of them and, equally importantly, of others. The jealousies of twenty-first-century politics are nothing compared with those in the early seventeenth century. The ultimate patron was the monarch, and the monarch was new, and therefore the jockeying for position and power was as excitable as the wretched spores sweeping the nation. Placemen and, worse still, yesmen answered a long roll-call. So the timing, the wording and the effectiveness of the King's word were eagerly awaited. The authority of the monarch was in his proclamations, carefully and politically penned before being delivered to the royal printer, Robert Barker, for distribution. Proclamations were issued regularly in the hope that gatherings could be prevented and infections reduced. These were eagerly awaited decisions. Many proclamations were the only legal means of cancelling, for example, a legal sitting.

The wax effigy of Elizabeth I. Like Charles II,
she took an unconscionable time to die

A detail from Elizabeth's funeral procession;
her ladies-in-waiting in long black robes, as from some silent order

James dressed as King of Scotland.
The cupids are adding the Scottish
emblem to his British coat of arms

Anne of Denmark, James's consort. On
the journey south to London, he
demanded that Cecil send fine gowns
and jewels so that the English court
should not look down on her style

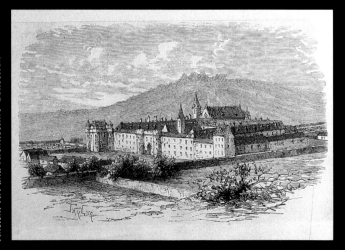

Holyrood (Halirud) House, a sometimes splendid and
often sad place for the Scottish royal family

James's Coronation on the feast of St James. Numbers were restricted because of the plague and Queen Anne, a Catholic, pointedly refused to take communion

Tom Derry, Anne's jester, by Marcus Gheeraerts. The importance of the court wit was diminishing, but Shakespearean theatre reflected Derry's role

Prince Henry, the firstborn of James and Anne. He died in 1612 and so it was his young brother Charles who succeeded their father in 1625. If Henry had survived, Cromwell may never have had a place in British history

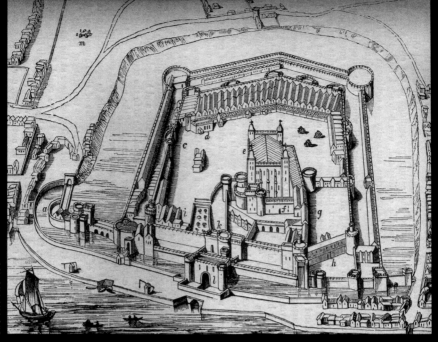

The Tower. Note the green fields of London. Started by William the Conqueror, the Tower is remembered as a place of imprisonment and execution, yet its smart apartments were used by the Royal Court

The imposing Richmond Palace on the banks of the Thames, favoured by Elizabeth. She died there in March 1603

Lancelot Andrewes (1555–1626), the erudite preaching bishop of Winchester and one of the editors of the King James (Authorised) version of the bible

Reverendiſs. & Doctiſs. Domini.
Lancel Andrewes, Episcopus
WINTONIENSIS. Obiit 1626 Ætatis ſuæ 71

A
SERMON
OF THE
PESTILENCE.
Preached at Chiſwick, 1603.
By the Right Reverend Father in GOD,
LANCELOT ANDREWES,
late L. Biſhop of Winchester.

LONDON.
Printed by Richard Badger, and are to be ſold
in Saint Dunſtans Church-yard, neere
the Church-doore. 1636.

The title page of Andrewes' famous sermon on sin and the pestilence

Londoners fleeing the plague. In 1603, more than 37,000 Londoners (out of a population of 210,000) perished between the spring and autumn

Panorama of London about 1600. The large church is St Paul's which was replaced after the Great Fire later in the century by Wren's domed cathedral

Robert Cecil (1563–1612), the secretary of state to Elizabeth and then James. Arguably the most important man in England during this period who secretly arranged James's translation from Scotland to England. He became the 1st Earl of Salisbury and Viscount Cranborne

Sir John Popham (1531–1607), Lord Chief Justice. He presided over Ralegh's trial and two years later over that of Guy Fawkes

Anne Clifford, who as a young girl observed the comings and goings surrounding the death of Elizabeth and whose memoir proved valuable in judging these events. Her adult life as Lady Dorset and Lady Pembroke was somewhat colourful and often difficult

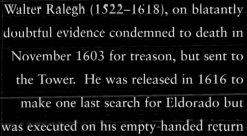

Walter Ralegh (1522–1618), on blatantly doubtful evidence condemned to death in November 1603 for treason, but sent to the Tower. He was released in 1616 to make one last search for Eldorado but was executed on his empty-handed return

James VI watching the trial of the North Berwick witches. There are those who believe James showed an unhealthy interest in such affairs and he has been controversially accused of encouraging witch-hunting

Confcientia mille testes

Tyrones   falſe   Submiſsion   afterwards   rebelling.

Elizabeth died before she heard the news of Tyrone's submission, here before Mountjoy at Mellifont in Ireland. It was her need to bring about Tyrone's downfall that indirectly led to the death of her sometime favourite, Essex

The symbol of the beginning of the British Empire –– the mercantile marine. Here, in the autumn of 1603, ships bring home the first cargoes of the East India Company

Some took to the country (Ralegh's trial was removed to Winchester), others to pamphlets and, inevitably and rightly, some to their pulpits. What had the people done to offend the Lord so conclusively that he should, in such biblical rage, send down this pestilence? Christopher Hooke would preach in St Paul's. What he said would be circulated for considered reading by all who should have instruction and consolation and who 'are heavie harted, for the woefull time of God his generall visitation, both in the Citie and in the Countrie'; the sermon was also 'fit for the comfort of Gods children at all times'.

The court met to discuss the various remedies and frankly had little to offer in judging one from the other. In 1603, as in 2003, the authority of the day had to be seen to be doing something. On 30 July 1603 James and his Privy Council met in the safety of Hampton Court (tents and marquees had been set up about the palace to keep any travellers from infected places at a safe distance – safe for the royal family, that is). The Privy Council selected certain precautions that seemed to have some authority, although there was not much distance between physician's advice and old wives' tales. The latter were not scoffed at. Herbal teas and beers, chopped onions and cloves of garlic, smoking charcoal, etc. were all listed. This, however, was not a commercial pamphlet to exploit the disaster and make profits for the author (should he survive) but the official word of the King and his advisers. That same evening the Privy Council's instructions were published, with a preamble suggesting the disease had spread.

As the most loving and gracious care of his MAJESTIE for the preservation of his people, hath already bene earnestly shewed and declared by such meanes and wayes as were thought expedient to supresse the grievous Infection of the Plague, and to prevent the increase thereof, within the Cittie of London, and parts about it; so whatsoever other good meanes may be yet remayning which may extend and prove behovefull to the

Countrey abroad (where his MAJESTIE is so to understand that the Contagion is also in many places dispersed) it is likewise his gracious pleasure that the same bee carefully provided and put in practise. And therefore having taken knowledge of certaine good orders that were upon like occasion published in times past; together with certaine rules and medicines prescribed by the best and most learned Physicians; and finding both of them, to serve well for the present time, his Majestie is pleased that the same shal be renewed and published: And withall straightly commandeth all Justices of the Peace & Others to whom it may appertaine, to see the said Orders duly executed.

Here then was the 1603 version of what we would call in the twenty-first century a national emergency and the government's response. This was a rare moment and indicative of the terrible conditions. James, the father of his nation as he liked to think, was behaving properly as the head of the national family. That the disease had spread should not diminish the consequences for London. The spores were in touching distance of the biggest concentration of the English in any one place.

At the time of the coronation, a six-page pamphlet was being sold at the entrance to the Exchange in the City of London. Its remedies were much as others had written: rooms should be aired with charcoal fires in stone pots in the middle of chambers rather than in the sooty chimneys where the chance of smoking out the plague would be lost, literally, up the chimney; in addition, 'put in your fire a little quantity of Frankinsense, Juniper, dryed Rosemary, or of Bay-leaves'. Rosemary was to be soaked and boiled in strong vinegar and the fumes allowed to 'ascend into the middle of every roome'. Angelica root was to be chewed, and sorrel steeped in vinegar was to be eaten 'in the morning fasting, with a little bread and butter, sorrell sauce is also very holsome against the same'. To slake the thirst brought on by the plague, ale was to be infused with rue, wormwood and scabious overnight and drunk every morning.

The advice came from no quack – as far as we know. It was 'Written by a learned Physition for the Health of his Countrey'. Whether he really existed is open to some doubt, especially as the publisher made so much show of telling the reader how this noble physician was revealing all for the good of the common man and woman. Whatever the origins of the pamphlet it was well written and well received.

Present Remedies
Against the plague
Shewing sundrie preservatives for the same by wholsome Fumes, drinkes, vomits and other inward Receits; as also the perfect cure (by Implaisture) of any that are therewith infected

First came the foreword by Thomas Pavyer the publisher. Once more we find the suggestion that the plague and its consequences were not confined to London. There was also a slight indication that while here was certainly good advice, there was no less opportunism.

For as much as the force and infection of the ordinary diseas called the Plague or Pestilence, hath heretofore beene too well knowne and felt in sundrie places of this Realme: and considering that it hath of late begun to increase in many chiefe Citties and populous places; I thought it goode to publish to you in time, sundry preservatives against the said disease, the better to defende those that are in health, from the infection of the diseased. And to this I was imboldened, the rather that it was written by a very learned and approoved Physition of our time, who desireth more the health of his Countrey than by discovering his name seeme vaineglorious to the world. Accept the same I pray you in good part, and thanke God for the Phisitions paines, who hath his desire if it might doe but that which he wisheth: namely expel sickness, and increase health to this Land. Which God for his mercie sake, prosper and preserve from all plagues and dangers for evermore, Amen.*

Loud amens did not dissipate the disease. The Church would, of course, seize the moment, doing what it probably did best and to its credit. But hygiene and not prayer was needed. It seemed that the wages of sin were stronger than the cleansing of hands. The physicians could use common sense and tell people to clear the ways and alleys, fumigate their rooms and parlours, and wash down with vinegar water. Yet in a society where even the monarch would consider dabbing his fingers on a damp cloth sufficient toilet for one day, what chance of sluicing the nation to rid itself of pestilence?

Medicine was hardly a new science. The understanding of anatomy was reasonable. The story of the barbers and barber-surgeons of London (there was no such organisation outside London and few were allowed licence to practise beyond a seven-mile radius of the capital) began in 1308 when Richard le Barbour was sworn in as the first known master at the Guildhall in London. In 1369 the guild had three master surgeons supervising surgical practice. In 1493 there came an informal alliance between the barbers and the Fellowship of Surgeons and in 1540 the two formally joined together to form the Barber-Surgeons Company. James, shortly after coming to the throne, granted the company its royal charter. It was, perhaps to our minds, a curious alliance that would continue until the surgeons, perhaps more scientifically confident and able to overcome the barbers' objections, broke away in 1745 to form the Company of Surgeons.

The College of Physicians was established by Thomas Linacre in 1518, received a royal charter from Henry VIII, and was a group boasting a series of codes and ethics. Its members held doctorates in medicine from either of the two universities. Here were competing forces, so we find in, for example, 1595 the physicians writing to the

* British Library shelfmark 1167.c.29.

barber-surgeons whom they described as their 'verie loving freends'. Apparently their loving friends had been practising physic and if they did not stop and so preserve 'good amytie and concord' then the physicians would take them to court. The physicians were the more respected group and attracted influential patrons, including Arabella Stuart, even though she was incarcerated in the Tower of London. As an aside, it might be noted that King James had glanced favourably at a petition to give midwives some official standing. Sir Francis Bacon, James's Solicitor General, agreed and put the King's blessing to good use in this early example of feminism. The physicians put a stop to the nonsense even though there was an obvious need to get rid of dangerous quack midwives and to give better instruction to those to be retained. Midwives were admitted before a diocesan bishop or chancellor. The physicians relented by agreeing to two or three of their number sitting on the interview board and said that it would 'depute such grave and learned men as shal alwaies be ready to resolve all their doubtes and instruct them in what they desire concerninge midwiferye'. These then were the people in 1603 who made sure that their profession was a closed shop in which the practices of dissection, anatomy and theoretical medicine were better understood than the cure for an epidemic. Even those 'learned in physicke' had little to offer that worked. The pulpit had reason on its side while the medics stood still. We should not be alarmed at this ignorance. Here was a society that did not expect the professions to have instant cures. It was too, as we see in the practice and belief in witchcraft, a society that was willing to assign superstitious and supernatural causes to the most natural phenomena – for example, epileptic fits and crops destroyed by storms. No wonder that a plague was a phenomenon that could so easily be explained by a priest who saw sin rather than brown rats and filthy conditions as the root cause.

That autumn of 1603, an Indian summer in the southeast of England, the mourning bell continued to toll out its grim commentary. So too did the increasingly vocal clerics. In Paul's Churchyard,

Christopher Hooke preached on sin and its wages, the pestilence. He was good enough to send his sermon (probably from the relative safety of his parsonage at Deptford) to the Lord Mayor-elect of London, Sir Thomas Bennet.

Read or heard, there was enough to preoccupy Bennet's thoughts for some time. Hooke's message was uncompromising. Christians were 'sonnes of God' whether or not they were smitten by plague. It was therefore wholly wrong for those who would claim that the plague or anything else for that matter was to be blamed on God and particularly on Jesus Christ, whom Hooke, with all his powers as a celebrated New Testament scholar, declared fairer than fair. No other denomination was to be believed or trusted. Here was the Church coming off the ropes to denounce those who denigrated Christianity and Christians for their beliefs at this terrible time: 'this love of our saviour is carnal, contemptible, foul, what lesse than all ful in the eyes of Turkes, Jewes, Epicures, Atheists, Papists, and al the wicked where there is no lesse than faire and al faire in the eies of al the faithfull'. Racism was never far away in apportioning the blame for any catastrophe.

The Church was not as one in explaining the plague. On one hand, there were those preachers who saw it as an opportunity to make certain that people understood that the plague was a natural punishment. On the other hand, there were the preachers who believed that if this were God's work, then rather than repent, the people would curse God. But there were practical questions to answer. Therefore, in 1603 there began to appear what in the twenty-first century we would find in newspapers under the heading Pass Notes. These were dialogues with a scholar (sometimes referred to as The Professor) and a cleric (usually called A Preacher). The Professor would pose early seventeenth-century FAQs and the Preacher would answer them. Some really did resolve tricky problems. For example, when a nation was under stress, where better for it to be than on its knees in its churches? But what if the supplicant were contaminated, taken with the plague? Should he or she really be allowed to sit in the pews with the healthy? The answer to this one might have been found in a fat bound pamphlet published by Richard Boyle that year and sold from his shop in Blackfriars, by the dank north bank of the Thames; its title, *A short Dialogue concerning the Plagues Infection.*

Professor: May it please you: we heare your selfe, and other faithfull Preachers in this Citie, reprove such as (for the comfort of their soules) come to church, either with Plague sores, or out of infected houses. As also those, that of charitie visite such as have the plague, and accompanie the diseased of that disease, unto the grave. In all which duties we thinke (with your favour) that Preachers should rather incourage then discourage us. Now because I am under your ministrie, and you have publickly willed us to resort to you for satisfaction, if we either understand not, or approve not any thing by you delivered: I am bold to come and crave your satisfaction accordingly.

Preacher: You do well, & I thank you: for there be too many that runne counter in contrarie Court. For whereas they should be swift to heare and slow to speake, they have heavie eares, and readie tongues to speake eveil of things they know not, and so scandalise (that is stumble) themselves and other, in hearing the word, which is to be heard not as the words of men, but as the word of God. But I pray you tell me, in what sense, and for what reason have you observed me and other Preachers to reprove the offendors you speake of?

Professor: Truly sir . . . I must acknowledge my infirmitie: for as soone as I heare you or other begin to checke Pieitie and Charitie (so seeming to me) I am presently so troubled, that I cannot understand, much lesse rightly remember, what hath beene delivered.

Preacher: If it be with you, who professe the obedience of faith, how is it with the rude multitude, whose imaginations are in no good sort brought into captivitie to the obedience of Christ? But we see the words of Christ fulfilled: that we do not understand his talke, because we cannot heare his word [John 8.43]. Me thinks, professers should attribute so much to their teachers.

There may have been a place for philosophers, but there were those who claimed the wisdom to alleviate if not cure. Let us take one known in 1603 simply as 'S.H. Studious in Phisicke'.

A New treatise of the pestilence
Containing the Causes, Signes, Preservatives and Cure thereof.
This like not before this time published
S.H. Studious in Phisicke
Printed by John Windent, for Mathew Law and are to be sold at his shop at the signe of the Fox in Paules Church-yarde. 1603

The pestilence is nothing else then a rotten . . . fever, which being ingendered by a rotten and corrupt ayre by a hidden and secret propitie which it hath, doth kill and destroy mortal creatures. The causes are said to be four fold, as the first & chiefest cause is supernaturall, as being immediately sent from God for the punishment of sinne and disobedience of mankind, as doth appear in Deut. 2.15 . . .

The second cause is attributed to an evil constelation which Astronomers affirme to proceede by the placing of the Sunne, Moone, Stars, being in the firmament of circles of the heavens by their conjunctions, oppositions and other aspects the one to the other.

The third cause is attributed to the corruption of the ayre, which being corrupted is apt to infection of mans body, for all living creatures drawe their breath from the ayre that is round about the [thee], which if it be stinking, venomous, and corrupt, the body of man living therein is in danger to be corrupted: whereby often times the pestilence is ingendered.

The fourth cause is the aptnesse of the body of man, through corrupt and rotten humours fitte to receive the effects of a venomous ayre, putrifying and corrupting the body whereby the pestilence is ingendered. And this aptnesse to infection by the abuse of the fit things which are called by the Phisitions no naturall, which are

1. Ayre
2. meate and drinke
3. Sleepe, and watch
4. Exercise, and rest
5. Emptinesse, and repletion
6. The perturbations and affections of the minde.

. . . The signes to know when a body is infected, are for the most part an Apostum or tumor about the eare, necke, under the arm holes, or flanke, with a fever, and sometimes there ariseth in some other parts of the body, a dark greene or evill coloured sore . . .

As I have already declared that there is a fourefold cause of this cruelle disease of the pestilence: so also there is a fourfold meanes to cure the same.

The first consisteth in evacuation and mundification of the body.

The second, in a due observation of diet.

The third, in comforting and strengthning of the principall members; which are the hart, the liver, and the braine, with asseveration of the potentiall and operative powers.

The fourth, in giving and administring of Antidots, Alexi-pharmacon, and other preservatives against venomous and contagious aygres, with the office of the Chirurgian, for Phle-botomy, bloud letting, maturation, ettraction, and healing of Carbuncles.

. . . And first of all for preservative before the body be infected may be used this following.

Take Oxysaccharum
Syrup of Sorrell

Oxymel Symplex, of either of them halfe an ounce

Waters of Endive, Scabios, Cardusbenedictus, of either one ounce

Let all these be mixt togither and taken in the morning fasting, and to coninue it every other day during the time of the Pestilence . . .

We have already set downe in briefe manner precautions and preservatives against the Pestilence. Now if it happen any man to be infected, let him presently with all the speed that possible may be, take two drams of this powder following in halfe a draught of good white wine. Take

Tormentil
Dictamni
Zedoari
The roote of Gentian
Of the roote of Carlinæ
Of the roote Verbascus, dried in the shade and powedered of either 1. Dragme

Make all these into fine powder and as soone as it may be, let the patient that is infected take 2. Dragmes in halfe a draught of good white wine, then let him go to his bed & be covered warme with cloathes that he may sweate throughly. And to the entent he may sweate the soonest you may put into the bed earthen bottles filled with hot water, and so let him sweate for the space of two or three houres keeping him from sleepe and drinke, all that while . . .

And thus by the grace of God and his blessing, whosover shall follow the foresaid precepts, and rules, shall preserve both himselfe and his familie from the Pestilence. And I beseech the Almightie to hold his holy hand over this realme of England which by sinne hath deserved farre greater punishment.

How many died in London alone? In about the third week of November 1603 Ralph Blower printed the words of one William Muggins, sent as a record of the sorrows of the town in verse form to Sir John Swinnerton, one of the worshipful aldermen of the City of London.

William Muggins
London mourning garment, or Funeral tears worne and shed for the death of her wealthy Citisens
Ralph Blower, London 1603

>Ay me poore London, which of late did florish,
>With springing March, the tidings of a king:
>And April showers, my blossomes so did nourishe,
>That I in Maie, was calde a famous thing,
>Yea Townes and Cities did my glory ring.

The preface of Master Muggins is obsequious, and it is difficult in cynical times not to wonder what profit he expected.

Right Worshipful and grave Senator: if my knowledge and my learning, were answerable to my good will and affection: this my poore labour now mourning in a sable Weede, should be as great and precious, as to the contrary it is weake, and slender. And knowing that the Vertuous minde, respecteth not so much that valuwe of the guift, as the good will of the giver, emboldenth me to prese[n]t this smal Pamphlet to your Worships view; most humbly craving pardon for my rash attempt, which if to your wonted clemmencie I doe obtain. I shall liken my selfe to a poor Debtor owing much, freely forgiven of all his large reckonings and dangerous accounts, and bound in duty to pray for your Worships long life, with increase of honor.
Your Worships at Command
William Muggins

At the end of the verse there is a 'Godly and Zealous' prayer unto God for forgiveness and saving of the 'plague and grievous Pestilence' and then most usefully the record of 'al that have bin buried of all diseases, in every funerall Parish . . . within the citie of London & liberties from 14 July to 17 November'.

There were funerals in ninety-six wards of the City and twenty wards without the walls of the City. This latter group would have included Southwark, Smithfield, Clerkenwell (then Clarkenwell) and St Martin-in-the-Fields. This gives some idea of the tight boundaries of the wards and the small acreage of the City and its few suburbs.

In this area, between the middle of July and the middle of November 1603, 37,717 bodies were buried – that was more than 17 per cent of the population of London. Imagine the consequences and fears if that level of disease arrived in any capital today. Help from quacks was at hand, although some had proper title, and for the main it was a case of the blind leading the blind.

Francis Herring, Doctor in Physicke and fellow of the college of physitians
Certain rules, directions, or advertisements for this time of pestilentiall contagion: with a caveat to those that weare about their neckes impoisoned amulets as a preservative from all the plague
Printed by William Jones, London 1603

[L]et care be taken that the streets, especially the narrow lanes and allies, be kept from the annoyance of dunghilles . . . let not the carkasses of horses, dogges, cats etc lye rotting and poisoning the aire (as they have done) in More and Findusburie fields and elsewhere round the Citie . . . let the air be purged and corrected, especially in the evenings which are somewhat cold, and in places which are low and neare the river (as

Thames streets and the allies thereabout) by making fires of oaken or ash wood, with some few bundles of Juniper cast into them.

Let men in their private houses amend the aire by laying in their windows sweete herbes as, Marioram, Time, Rosemarie, Balme, Fennell, Peniroyall, Mints &c. Likewise by burning Juniper, Time, Bay-leaves, Cloves, Cinamon . . . the poorer may burne Wormwood, Rue, Time. Let them cast often on the floores of their houses water mingled with vinegar . . . Perceiving many in this City to weare about their necks, upon the region of the heart, certaine placents, or Amulets (as preservatives against the Pestilence) confected of Arsenicke a strong porton, I have thought it needfull (other men keeping silence) to declare briefly my opinion touching the said Amulets: not (I professe) in hatred to any mans person, or enuie at their commoditie, wherein I might have shared with them, if I could have brought my judgement to have shared with theirs; But in conscience and discharge of my dutie. The rather because I feare greatly that through veine confidence in them, other more opposite, convenient and effectual antidotes, & Alexeties are neglected.

My opinion is, that these Placents of Arsenicke carried upon the region of the hart are so farr from effecting anie good in that kinde, as preservatives, that they are verie dangerous and hurtfull, if not pernitious to those that weare them.

It is evident that Arsenicke being a confessed poison, it is opposite, professed and perpetual enemy to our nature. Therefore being worne next the skin as soon as the heart waxeth hote by any vehement motion, labour or stirring (as it falleth out usually) it must needs send out venimous vapours to that noble and principall part; which will either penetrate by their owne force, or be drawne in with the aire, by the dilation of those arteries which are spread about the skin.

Potion dispensers were everywhere, and even grand citizens felt threatened enough to abandon all dignity and stuff wormwood up their nostrils as they went about the town, stepping across the carcasses of beasts, including dogs, either dead from the plague or with throats slit to prevent them carrying the infection from alleyway to cul-de-sac. Every palliasse that remained unburned was bare. Any linen had long been taken as shrouds. Only the clerics saw prosperity. After all, the price, even a pittance, must be paid for a burial and a sermon. And how they sermonised! Take one, Henoch Clapham, who saw this as an opportunity to explain that the people were visited with disease because of their sins. What sins? Mainly those of denying Catholicism. Clapham believed that of the three biblical plagues – sword, famine and pestilence – it was the last that brought with it most mercy. English sinners should pray for mercy. For Clapham therefore the solution was not in herbs and cleansings of vinegar water, but in prayer. His prayers and cures were copied out and printed then sold by the Widow Newbery at her shop in Paul's Churchyard 'at the signe of the Ball'. No one was beyond making a little loose change, even from tragedy.

Beloved, God having smitten our Citie with the Pestilence, Behold, booke upon booke, prescribing naturall meanes as for naturall maladies, but little said of spirituall meanes, for spirituall maladies, which should give life to the former . . . if a true Christian do but take meate or drinke, hee prayeth for a blessing; because otherwise the dead creature can give to him no life, nor yet continue health. The true Christian taketh no Physicke for the weakest ague or ache, but hee calleth upon the name of the Lord for adding his blessing; for that otherwise the thing applied, can remove no maladie.

Of course, the true cause of the plague was sin. Lancelot Andrewes, Bishop of Winchester, delivered a sermon at Chiswick in 1603 with a simple brimstone message. The plague was God's doing because the people were disobedient. The text of the sermon was Psalm CVI, 29–30. 'Thus they provoked Him to anger with their owne inventions, and the plague was great among them. Then stoode up Phinees, and prayed and so the Plague was ceased.'

As in all the big, if not great, sermons of the day, each sentence had a biblical reference. Nothing in the theological tract was left to chance nor heretical stain. So the Bishop chose Psalms to show that the plague was in response to a provocation; the book of Numbers to show how great a plague might be ('Here is mention of a Plague, of a great Plague. For there died of it foure and twenty thousand. And we complain of a plague at this time'); then the epistle to the Romans to reassure everyone that this was a warning from the Lord ('whatever things were written aforetime were written for our learning'). As were, he said, these texts.

A Sermon of the Pestilence, Preached at Chiswick, 1603, by the Right reverend Father in God, Lancelot Andrewes, printed by Richard Badger, and are to be sold in Saint Dunstans Church-yard neere the Church-doore.

The Plague is a disease. In every disease we consider the cause and the cure . . . That there is a cause that the plague is a thing causall, not casuall; comes not meerely by chance, but hath somewhat some cause that procureth it.

[T]he English word Plague coming from the Latin word Plaga, which is properly a stroke, necessarily inferreth a cause. For where there is a stroke, there must be one that striketh. And in that both it, and the other evil things (that come up on us) are usually in Scriptures called Gods judgement; if they be judgements, it followeth, there is a judge they come from. They come not by adventure; by chance they come not. Chance and judgement are utterly opposite. Not casually then, but judicially. Judged we are; For when we are chastened, we are judged of the Lord.

Here the preacher was on a collision course with the physicians. They were confident and familiar enough with plague. After all, as the Bishop had well observed, plagues had been around since at least Old Testament times. He could say they were judgements; physicians said they were man-made, not God-sent. 'The aire is infected, the humours corrupted, the contagion of the sick' spreading from one being to another. True there was biblical support for both physician and priest. The air was a furnace, it said in Exodus, describing the plague of blotches brought forth in Egypt. The humours of King David caused the moistures of his body to be corrupted and dried up as the drought of summer. And Leviticus spoke of the lepers who cried 'keep away'. It all sounded very familiar that summer. Andrewes had, he believed, theology on his side. He knew his Exodus.

> [W]e see an angell, a destroying angell in the plague of Ægypt . . . so that if there bee a plague, God is angry; and there be a great plague, God is very angry . . . there is a cause in God that he is angry. And there is a cause, for which he is angry. Fir [sic] he is not angry without a cause . . . Is God angry with the earth when he sends barrennesse? Or with the aire when he makes it contagious? No indeed. His anger is not against the elements, they provoke him not. Against them it is, that provoke him to anger, against Men it is, and against their sinnes, and for them commeth the wrath of God upon the children of disobedience . . . the corruption of the soule, the corruption of the wayes, more than the corruption of the aire [Mica]. The plague of the heart [Kings] more than the sore that is seene in the body. The cause of death [Romans] that is sinne, the same is the cause of this kinde of death, of the plague of mortality. And as the Balme of Gilead* and Physitian there, may yeeld us helpe, when Gods wrath is removed: so, if it be not, no balme,

* Misprinted 'Liliad' in original. Andrewes was referring to Jeremiah 8.22.

no medicine will serve. Let us with the Woman in the Gospell, spend all upon Physitians, we shall be never the better [Mark] till we come to Christ and he be the cure of our sins, who is the only Physitian of the diseases of the soule.

Well, the God of Lancelot Andrewes was exceedingly angry. The plague continued. It spread beyond London. Gentlemen fled the towns to their country seats and their ladies. The plague curtailed ceremony and mocked pomp. It took a harsh winter to curb it, yet it never lurked very far from the alleys and lanes of the capital, and for sixty and more years, it returned at every chance. It was a trying time to become monarch.

8

CONSTITUTION

JAMES INHERITED A KINGDOM AND SO BECAME GUARDIAN OF A CONSTITUTION. Nothing was written down excepting that a way the country was ruled and the authority of the rulers were to be found in the precedents of civil and Church law. The Constitution that had served the Elizabethans would adjust, as all unwritten constitutions must do. But although James, and later his son Charles I, had very definite ideas of their own powers and how they might be exercised, the Elizabethan Constitution continued to function until 1642 and the rebellion.

Historians have long attempted to trace the origins of the Civil War from either the beginning of the Elizabethan reign in 1558 or, more energetically and with better cause, to the beginning of the Stuarts in England in 1603. James was blamed for much. Certainly, it must be tempting to search 1603 and James's first Parliament of 1604 for some sign that the Constitution suffered immediately at his hands. If the hypothesis is that 1603 was the starting point of the decline in constitutional rule that would lead to the Civil War less than forty years later, then this path should be followed with considerable caution. It is a difficult, near impossible track to follow with any certainty. It is, however, useful to grasp what happened to the English Constitution in 1603 and why James I should not automatically be seen as some intellectual bully who began the process that led to Cromwell's startling entry in British history.

The collapse of the monarchy in the 1640s had far more to do with the foolhardiness and consequent arrogance of Charles I, the influence and misguided intellect of Archbishop Laud, and the silly concept of imposing the English Prayer Book on the Scots, as well as the confrontations of government and ambitions of monarch and parliamentarians. We might also remember that between 1629 and 1640 Charles refused to summon Parliament. Consequently there was no public body which allowed the big issues as well as the small ones of the day to be openly discussed between the legislators and the executive. Imagine then the sense of unease turning to outright animosity that this single period of more than a decade without Parliament would create. As ever, there was no single reason why the Elizabethan Constitution became null and void in the meeting of the Long Parliament in November 1640. By that time few supported the King, and, as with all monarchies, the distinction between support or opposition to a ruler and to the monarchy itself should be carefully made. When the Civil War came, parliamentarians could still raise a force in the name of the King. Even when the monarchy and the House of Lords were abolished it was not long before the leaders of the Commonwealth recognised the absolute need to have a monarch who was above politics in theory, and so offered the crown to Oliver Cromwell who was clearly sorely tempted to accept it, given the length of time it took him to turn it down.

Accusations were obviously going to be made against James from the moment his journey south from Scotland began. His extravagant ideas and his exercise of power plus his personal characteristics could never cast him as a boring monarch. There were great hopes for the new reign. This should not be surprising. There is not much evidence that many tears were shed for the passing of Elizabeth. Each period in history has as its bookends major events, constitutional dates or change in monarchy, even dynasty. Much later, with either hindsight or artistic ease, we draw pictures of these islands as we believe they would have appeared at the time of a monarch. The Elizabethan era is, by its definition, centred on the monarch herself – an almost unique individual in the line of more than fifty sovereigns since the great Saxon kings. Elizabeth's reign certainly contained spectacular events and characters which and who survived in historical memory more than those of more sturdy and important reigns. If there might be a single word to describe the reign of Elizabeth, it would be uncertainty. Even though England was at relative peace, few were certain of the economy, of the possibilities of great conflict overseas, of religious tolerance, and, most of all, of the succession. The British people are just the same as any other nation – they prefer to know what is coming next. When it comes they immediately want to know what is after that. During the later years of her reign, the lustre of Elizabethanism was dulled. Centuries on, the Virgin Queen's England was seen in an altogether more romantic light. But that is the way of all multi-million-dollar landscapes, most of which were worth little more than a loaf and a reasonable bottle of red wine at the time of their painting.

The eulogies from the poets and play-makers reeked of formal affection and political correctness in equal parts. Chettle's elegy 'in memorie of their sacred Mistresse, Elizabeth, Queene of Vertue while shee lived, and Theame of Sorrow being dead'* may read like an anthem to his dearly beloved and departed sovereign mistress, but it is a preamble to what the poets thought was a much more joyous occasion and one which better pleased the crowds – the arrival of the new monarch. It is little wonder that the bureaucracies of Court and justice eyed James's coming with a healthy suspicion, mindful of the need to keep him under control. The people thronged to see him. Elizabeth liked these moments of image-making. After the initial welcome, James appears to have soon treated *his* throngs with

---

* Henry Chettle, *Englandes Mourning Garment: worne here by plaine Shepheardes . . .*, VS [Valentine Sims] for Thomas Millington (London, 1603).

something approaching contempt. In 1603 this was the first time the people, in living memory for most of them, would spy a monarch who did not much like them. Not until his great-grandson George I (1660–1727) became the first Hanoverian king of England in 1714 did we have another monarch who so openly disliked his people.

Robert Cecil and his clerks did not have to wait until 1603 to understand much of the nature of the monarch. Cecil had been preparing for the succession long before March 1603. What he does not appear to have been prepared for was the way in which James quickly made it clear that he was not much interested in the bureaucracy of being king. His keenness for the chase should have warned them of that. Fortunately for England and for James he understood perfectly in that first year that Cecil was one of the most capable administrators of the seventeenth century and was a worthy successor to his father, William.

James was also fortunate that Cecil had gathered about him other able administrators. Some were curious additions. For example, Francis Bacon, the philosophic scientist, was part of government for a decade and a half; Edward Coke was perhaps the great lawyer of this period and had already held office for a decade before James became king; Lionel Cranfield rose from apprentice boy to become a government administrator and survived almost to the end of James's reign before being impeached. For the five years after James's coronation, Cecil was the most powerful person in England after the King himself. Although James had imported many of his fellow Scots into high places, Cecil knew the system and made it work on the monarch's behalf. He had cemented this position during the latter years of Elizabeth's reign. True, he had to work with often less able but nevertheless extremely influential peers, for example, the Howards, whose family tree included powerful earldoms. (In 1605 Cecil himself became an earl, with the title Earl of Salisbury.)

By the end of 1603 the King's confidence and interests had broadened. He continued to rely on Cecil. He understood his brilliance as well as his utter loyalty, but James's introduction of one of his favourites, Robert Carr, was a sharp thorn in the side of Cecil's administration. As an administrator, Carr was hardly in the same league, but he too had the King's ear. By 1612 Cecil was dead and so was the sense of an era of Cecils who had made sure that the government of England was as sound as it possibly could be during difficult and transitory circumstances. The fact that Cecil attempted to abandon the post of secretary of state-cum-principal secretary but failed is another story. It is one of gathering oppositions in the Privy Council. It is one of the battle between the Howards and Robert Carr. It is also the story of the emergence of George Villiers. The relatively calm procedures of the Cecils had been disrupted by political jealousies with no one at the top able to control them and divert them for the King's good. This was to come, and even great men, even Cecils, may hold power only for the duration of their images, most of which never survive more than a decade or so – a blink of the eye in history.

A further important aspect of government in 1603 is that the continuity which Cecil (along with the significant fact that there was no serious rival to James's throne) had made possible extended throughout government and included the grass roots of political England.

In 1603 the government of England and Wales had five branches. The first was the most powerful. This consisted of James as the 'chairman', the Privy Council and the two secretaries of state. The Privy Council had a staff of administrators and especially clerks, as did the secretaries of state. The positions of the clerks were important because here was the basis of the loyalty of the civil service system that was to continue for four hundred years. The clerks were regarded in a far more important manner than we might expect. For example, although, as we have seen, printing was what we might crudely call a boom industry, almost all government documents with the exceptions of parliamentary Acts and proclamations were handwritten. These documents were so important and had to be so distinctive that each department had a handwriting style peculiar to itself. The Customs Office might write in an upright manner, with certain embellishments to letters. The Navy Department might be more cursive. The inks might be different. Each clerk had to learn how to automatically write in the style of his department. Thus the secretary of state or privy councillor would pick up a document and, without looking at the title, know from which department it came.

Handwriting was a mark of learning and of station. Look at (especially early) Tudor and Stuart letters and there is much to learn about society. The script of the Anglo-Saxons and Normans was laborious and practised by few. The standards of handwriting had deteriorated since the twelfth century. The larger impetus for the revival of script came through the Italian Renaissance and evolved into an Italian cursive fist, still known as italics. This would seem to have revolutionised handwriting in England and by the start of the seventeenth century calligraphers were minor celebrities. They were so much admired as artists that they could give exhibitions of their craft. James I called John Davies from Hereford to London to teach Prince Henry. In 1595 Peter Bales had beaten Daniel Johnson in a handwriting competition for a (literal) Gold Pen award. Of course, not everyone scribed clean and elegant lines. The clerks of Admiralty and Exchequer, with their precise and distinctive styles, and clerics and pamphleteers may have been in demand and admired, but rather like present-day elegance, a gentleman could never be bothered to be so fastidious.

There is, in the British Museum, a letter from Shakespeare's patron and supporter of the Essex rebellion against Elizabeth I, Henry Wriothesley,* to the famous judge Sir Julius Caesar.† The

---

* Wriothesley (1573–1624) was the third Earl of Southampton. Shakespeare dedicated to him *The Rape of Lucrece* and it was Wriothesley who put on a performance of *Richard II* hoping to rouse London against Elizabeth. He was sentenced to death by Elizabeth's court, but was released by James I. He died while campaigning with the Dutch against Spain.

† Caesar (1558–1636) was the son of Bloody Mary's physician, Cesare Adelmare. In 1606 James I appointed him Chancellor of the Exchequer and in 1614 he became Master of the Rolls.

style may represent Wriothesley's character – free thinking, a fighter and a chancer. Nevertheless, it does seem typical of the English upper classes of the time. The script had an easy flowing Italian style without any nod to clerical formality. Truly, this was from, as the expression of the day would have it, a gentleman too grand to write fair.

To return to the shape of governance, the money departments were quite naturally the most important branches of government. In earlier years the monarch's household had two financial offices, the Wardrobe and the Chamber. These had been the controllers of the treasuries and the departments of supply, particularly in wartime. By 1603 the household looked after the Court and so had no great financial influence. It did of course have political importance. This came about partly because of the office-holders themselves, who were, inevitably, influential people.

A third branch of government was the Exchequer, which was a court of law. In fact all the economic and money departments were law courts. James discovered that 75 per cent of his revenues would be channelled through the Exchequer. Independent of the Exchequer were the courts of wards. These looked after, for example, all his feudal incomes. More money came in through the royal estates of the Duke of Lancaster. This dukedom had been kept for the Crown since 1399 and even pre-dated that moment by thirty-six years when we find it mentioned in the household of John of Gaunt. By 1603 the court that handled money from the estates was the Duchy of Lancaster.* There was no treasury building or bank and not much gold was shifted into the royal coffers. The economy ran quite well on the credit system, knowing that, for example, if a feudal income was worth £1000, then this could be balanced against a debt.

The political nature of the law courts was, as James discovered,

* The Duchy was responsible for the Chancery Court of Lancaster until 1971, and still administers estates and is responsible for the appointment of all magistrates in Lancashire, Merseyside and Manchester.

not to be ignored. The three great courts of common law, the King's Bench, the Exchequer and Common Pleas, were rivals to the two other main courts, Chancery and the Star Chamber.

Within these tiers of government were concepts which stemmed from Saxon times, but are often promoted in the twenty-first century as modern thinking. For example, in 1603 Wales had its own regional council, as did the north of England. There were, too, the fringe departments: the Navy, which had reached its peak in 1603 and in which one day Samuel Pepys would become controller;* the Ordnance Office, which produced the weapons of war; and of course the Mint, literally the money-maker. Most of these departments were inefficient and usually corrupt. Poorly paid officials found their salaries by other means. Back-handers or, more politely, commissions were commonplace and expected. In this, the English system of government and administration was not at all alone.

And what of that other form of government, the Church? Here was a body as corrupt as could be imagined, as powerful as any, and as split as any constitutional debate. When James was faced with a thousand 'signatures' of ministers seeking stark reform of the Established Church, he understood this was not a petition to be ignored.†
Even the Church in opposition was not a body to be ignored. Within the Established Church sat the courts of high commission. As powerful as many secular legal institutions, they were the courts of the provinces of York and Canterbury, each with a leadership that went beyond the personalities of two archbishops. Membership of these courts included the archbishops, the diocesan bishops, privy councillors, church lawyers and administrative officials.

These influences of high court, high government and high Church

* Pepys (1633–1703) was appointed secretary to the Admiralty and made a tidy sum from the appointment. He was sacked in 1679 for supposedly being involved in the Popish Plot, although reinstated five years later when he was very much in favour. He also became President of the Royal Society in 1684.
† The Millenary Petition of 1603. See page 235.

spread to the villages and small towns. It is from the bottom up that we understand the way the government worked because human nature was no different in 1603 than in 2003. Government, like many aspects of public life, works on patronage.

In 2003 the Prime Minister has the most power of patronage. In 1603 the King had the most power, but the common link between 1603 and 2003 is that at the bottom of that patronage pyramid are the local government officers. Today a local official can and does seek the patronage of one above and everyone accepts this. It is called 'getting on' and networking. Personal qualifications do not make patronage obsolete in the twenty-first century. In 1603 in the villages, towns and counties this form of 'friendship' existed firmly on the basis of 'it's not who you know, it is who knows you'. So in 1603 local government was very much in the hands of those thought to be loyal to the Crown and who could extend that loyalty to the lowest official and constable.

In 1603 the most important men in local government were probably the lords lieutenant of the counties. Some 50 per cent of those lords lieutenant were members of the Privy Council. Their first function was to command the militias. Thus the lords lieutenant of all the counties could, in theory, hold the security of the monarchy in their hands. In practice the day-to-day duties were carried out by the deputy lieutenants. If we assume that half the lords lieutenant were privy councillors, then it follows that half of them were influential peers whose main interests and work were with the royal Court and the administration, and they would rarely be in the counties over which they had lordship. Therefore, the deputy lieutenant could be the most powerful person of the shire. He was proposed by the Lord Lieutenant, but because of the very real possibility of him wielding power in the wrong direction his appointment had to be approved by James, who in turn would have Robert Cecil to advise him. Moreover, the deputy lieutenants were peers or very senior gentry. Consequently, their influence was widespread beyond the county borders. It was the gentry of the county that took charge of justice and its administration – a system that would survive into the twenty-first century. The peace commissioners had emerged as the central link in early seventeenth-century local government; for example, the chief justice of the peace of a county, often referred to as the *custos rotulorum* (keeper of the rolls). In spite of the importance of these appointments, none was salaried. Today, lords lieutenant are purely ceremonial and although they may have an influence on a recommendation for an OBE, they have no power duties, yet by the very nature of the positions that led to their appointments, they are usually men and women with influence and patronage. In the early seventeenth century we can see that the amateur status of such an official could often lead to patronage on a lucrative scale. Part of the job of the county official was to make sure that the Crown revenues, the taxes, were brought in. Each county was separated into divisions and a tax officer would be appointed to gather in his division. Thus tax gathering and financial administration were magic markers for the division of regional rule. The most practical area of local government was the hundred.

The Saxons had created a unit of land measurement called a hundred in the tenth century. The size of the hundred varied throughout the country. The term came from one hundred hides, a hide in Saxon times being thought the area of land necessary to support a peasant family and its stock. So the smallest Saxon administrative unit from which taxes could be raised would be a hide. As hides differed in size from one region to another, so did hundreds. The size would be an indicator of land fertility. An East Anglian hide might be 120 acres. A West Country hide could be 50 acres. If we take the average hide as, say, 80 acres, then a hundred would be 8000 acres. Thus a hundred would be a considerable area of administration and tax-raising in modern terms. Every four weeks local matters of tax and law were discussed as well as tried at the hundred courts. A hundred had a number of justices of the peace and a high constable. The smallest unit in a hundred was a parish. Each parish had a petty constable. Even, or maybe especially, at this level, patronage ruled.

These arrangements might lead us to think that the people of James I were cynical about their governance; perhaps they were indeed very ignorant and hardly cared. Yet evidence suggests that James had arrived to rule a nation which took very seriously the way in which it was governed – corrupt or not. Perhaps as many as 40 per cent of the population took an active part in local government and justice. From these people were appointed the petty constables, the jurors and the churchwardens – considerably important posts.

In the towns or boroughs the system was somewhat different. These were run by the mayor and aldermen or by a senior bailiff. Some were subject to a court of common council on which would sit the freemen of the borough. This was the theory. In 1603 the reality, in spite of what many liked – and still like – to think, was that feudalism was not entirely dead and buried. The major landowners ruled within their own interests and their placemen did so on their behalf. What is very clear at this time is how few of the officials were paid officers; hardly a wonder then that lucrative patronage was extended from the court to the parish.

The Crown rarely paid anyone, so many officials made their living from bribes as well as commission on services. We have to be careful when we praise men like Robert Cecil with a sense of public purpose acting for the good of the nation. The Cecils made a fortune out of this apparent altruism. They certainly did not make their money from their salaries. Robert Cecil, for example, the most senior commoner in the land, was paid just £100 a year. Fortunes had to come through other means; and so they did. There was not, although it would be tempting to believe there might have been, any sense that these officials were doing their work entirely for the good of the nation and the people. At the highest level the attractions were power and gold. At the lowest level of the administrative order of England and Wales the attractions were the same. Even though it is probably right to believe that the Cecils were a breed apart, senses of public duty and expressions of public service are best kept for the late eighteenth century in conversations about the motives of Whiggery.

Whatever the case and cause, it was clear by the end of 1603 that James had no inclination to reform the way his nation was governed – not in moral terms at least. Also we should remember that the Scots went south in the belief that they were entering a Promised Land. Considering the state of Scotland's finances it was easy to see why they thought that to be the case. Little wonder James did nothing to curb his instincts for spending. This reduced the size of the royal treasury. In turn this meant James needed even more the friendship of governments, from the hundreds to the highest in Parliament, and was a weaker king for it.

We should not single out James for constitutional or financial maladministration. Few monarchs were as powerful as their surviving images. They all needed their courtiers to work for them even when they knew full well the corruption and positioning of power that was never much more than a corridor's distance from the throne. Once more we should be reluctant to view the workings of the court and government with twenty-first-century eyes. In 2003 we are used to the contempt in which politicians are often held. We understand the cynical consequences of what we have come to call sleaze in political life. We may be disturbed, but we accept the good Pangloss's notion that all is for the best in the best of all possible worlds.* There is, therefore, little reason to be aghast at the thought of back-handers and outrageous patronage at the courts of Elizabeth and James or indeed that of any other monarch during the centuries before and those which followed. Anyone who has tipped a builder's mate to finish by the weekend would have easily fitted into the society of 1603.

For this worldly wise system which acknowledges the power of some and the facility of others not to destabilise society, the bureaucracy has to be supremely efficient and needs to manipulate the system for the nation's greater good as well as its own individual gain. Tudors and Stuarts understood the simple hypothesis that there

* Voltaire, *Candide*.

is little wrong with corruption as long as it does not corrupt the stability of the state; for this to work, there had to be a totally commanding figure in charge of the state apparatus. Today, we call it strong government and for the most part choose to ignore twenty-first-century forms of corruption as long as it sees to the needs of the people. Elizabeth had been fortunate in having William Cecil as her commanding figure. James acknowledged the skills of Robert Cecil, for whom he quickly created a peerage.* It was the skill to maintain continuity of power that James so lacked and needed. He failed to grasp and therefore manipulate the ways of government. Yet, every aspect of that government was the prerogative of the King. Whatever the power of regional and county authorities, the royal Court was the centre, not simply of bidding, but of political thought and action.

James brought to England in 1603 an ambivalence to political theory. As king in Scotland, the concept of politics was far more to do with survival than administration. Perhaps the two went together. In England the Court as centre of politics – both personal and administrative – was altogether more complex, even sophisticated. For example, England in 1603 needed to maintain a pragmatic foreign policy as well as one which protected interests others refused to recognise. An example of this would have been relations with states vis-à-vis Catholicism. When James joined and became a leading member of the Protestant Union with the south German princes, this was part of a sensitive foreign policy rather than an instinct or predilection that might have been humoured in Edinburgh. The politics of Church relations in England, ways of raising monies for the Navy and the Crown were heavily politicised and this policy-making could only take place in the royal Court. When James called Parliament in 1604 he did not do so simply to listen, he did so to be heard. Therefore, politics and power had to have the guidance of the sensible and shrewd

---

* In 1604 Cecil became Viscount Cranbourne.

Cecil, particularly as others were now manoeuvring to take his position.

The main difference between the Scottish and English courts was that now influence had to be underwritten. James was faced with the reality that in England patronage could not be exercised with caprice. Cecil taught him that the royal patronage that created offices of state and regional authority had to be selective. James did not always agree: his writ was true authority. Once patronage was distributed, Cecil therefore was forced to make sure that the royal interest was best served by continuously supporting those in the offices and authorities James had nominally created. James could not easily be made to realise that an appointment by itself would not provide the stability necessary to keep the monarchy untroubled and therefore the nation at one with itself. Regional officers had to be encouraged and supported in the building of their power bases and the maintenance of them. The skill of successive Cecils was to protect the monarch by making sure that the powers the monarchy had distributed did not usurp the Crown itself.

There was a second function of the Court as the political centre of England, Wales, Ireland and to some extent Scotland. James had been brought up and had matured in a closed society in which intrigue was a matter of course, bloodthirst a matter of instinct, and, too often, chaos the consequence. Cecil was to show him, even during those first few months on the throne in 1603, that while he had not entirely left behind the ways of intrigue and manipulation, he was now monarch of an altogether more sophisticated, albeit equally unforgiving system. This did not mean that the Court was a place of calm and imperturbable reasoning. Even the seemingly most insignificant matter could and did arouse deep feeling. Later, when a Cecil no longer ruled the bureaucracy, the animosities and ambitions of the likes of George Villiers created schisms on immense subjects such as the distribution of power and even the pros and cons of declaring war on Spain, but this was for later.

Our focus on the need for the Court to be the centre of political power is that in 1603, especially with the change of monarchy and therefore the new generation of courtiers and petitioners, debate had to be kept in one place. The court was that place because it was the only one where debate could be controlled, personalities influenced and consequences anticipated. This was perhaps the most important lesson for Sir Robert Cecil discreetly to teach and for James implicitly to understand during the months between the death of Elizabeth in March and James's coronation towards the end of July. The streams of decrees and proclamations provide clear evidence of the importance of this lesson.

9

THE CHURCH

AS WE HAVE SEEN, THE ARCHBISHOP OF CANTERBURY WAS ONE OF THE FIRST TO SEND AN ENVOY TO SCOTLAND IMMEDIATELY JAMES WAS PROCLAIMED. The Established Church was nervous. We often think of that nervousness as stemming from the real and perceived threat of Roman Catholicism, but there was another encroachment upon the authority of the Church of England. The spread of Calvinism was certainly known throughout Scotland and England and the origins of opposition to Rome might be found there. But there was a more immediate aggravation confronting the bishops and the ancient universities which through their theological and academic positions had a deep interest in maintaining the *status quo*. What of the churchmen who wanted to rid the liturgy of everything other than that which reflected fundamental belief and to discard what it saw as the incompetent elements of the priesthood?

For the past five hundred years or so English society has concerned itself with the conflict between the Church of Rome and what became the Church of England. As we have noted elsewhere, it is too easy to describe the formation of what became the Anglican communion as entirely the whim of a sixteenth-century king frustrated by Rome's objections to his ambition to discard one wife for another. The anti-Catholic, or perhaps more particularly anti-Rome, movement was not confined to England. Protestantism had spread across Europe. The schisms within the Roman Church itself were as strong as those in the religious denominations set against it. Disorder in religious practice reflects a tendency for doctrine to be corrupted by unsystematic liturgy. This, after all, was a great contribution of John Calvin (1509–64), whose teachings had so influenced – and sometimes annoyed – the young James. Calvin was French. That Calvinism should have its origins in the land of England's old enemy is an irony not to be ignored.

The Reformation had started, of course, under Martin Luther (1483–1546). This German Augustinian monk had been ordained a Roman Catholic priest and had lectured at the University of Wittenberg. Yet it was a pilgrimage to Rome in the early sixteenth century that sparked off Luther's ideas about a reformed Church. He was appalled at the fund-raising practices of the Dominicans, especially the sale of indulgences.* It was on 31 October 1517 that he famously nailed his Ninety-five Theses on indulgences to the church door at Wittenberg, condemning any pope's right to forgive sins. Thus started the grand conflict and excitement between the Church of Rome and what Luther saw as the Church of God. No one escaped his withering cast, including Henry VIII, whom he condemned on the subject of the seven sacraments. Luther was not, as some might insist, an intellectual. He was a firebrand.

Calvin had started in the late 1520s to preach what became the reformed doctrine known by his name. By the 1530s Paris had become the focus of religious revolution and with it the persecution of the new thinking. No longer able to ignore his peril, Calvin had left France for Basel where he published in 1536 his *Christianae*

---

* The Roman Church sold remission of sins so that a sinner would have to spend less time in purgatory.

Religionis Institutio, then to Italy, then home to France, and then Geneva. The trail of new-born Calvinism was as clear as a snail's on a frostless morning. Here was the silvered hallmark of the Reformation and with it the moral and severe Protestant Confession of Faith. It was all too much for the authorities and for the movement itself, and for three years Calvin settled in Strasbourg, working on the New Testament until he could return to Geneva. Here it is important to understand what happened in Geneva so that we can see clearly that Protestantism was not simply a religious persuasion, but a theocracy that would have an authority delivered with all the self-assurance of communism nearly four hundred years later.

Calvin's doctrine went beyond the New Testament. It became the basis of law and order and the discipline of the people in their social and commercial, as well as religious, lives. Calvin was intolerant of any opposition, including more libertine Protestants. His structure of uncompromisingly systematic theology gave this persuasion a form which allowed every adherent a template for his or her life. There might even be a case to argue that it was not until the mid-nineteenth century that the Roman Church under Pius IX made such a clear statement of doctrine and order with the decree *Ineffabilis Deus* and the Vatican Council's proclamation of the infallibility of the Pope. Unlike Pius IX, who spent his last days as the virtual prisoner of King Victor Emmanuel II, Calvin spent his last days untroubled and at liberty in the theological college which eventually became the University of Geneva.

Thus a century of Calvinism and Lutherism serves to remind us that the doctrine of Protestantism was not an invention of Henry VIII.

The Reformation was in full swing in continental Europe and there was little fear in Britain that the Word of God according to the Church of Rome would be making a comeback any time soon. And while the Armada had threatened these islands as recently as 1588, that was seen as a Spanish rather than a Catholic menace.

This does not mean that England in 1603 was swept clean of

Catholics. Far from it. It is true that all the sermons welcoming James to his throne were preached by Protestant ministers, but there were far more Roman Catholics in England and Scotland than is often imagined. It was recognised that the Catholic majority of the sixteenth century had waned, but it was equally clear that the majority of the English did not immediately embrace Protestantism. Certainly by the late sixteenth and the early seventeenth centuries England was not a religious country. The English thought of themselves in terms of nationality rather than religion. It may be, of course, that had the Armada succeeded against the weather conditions in 1588 then the Catholic minority would have ruled England. It may even be that the throne would have easily slipped back to Catholic worship. There was never any deep conviction that could not easily be swayed by politics or instinct. Did not Charles II whisper his Catholic faith on his deathbed? William Cecil gave the impression of believing religious devotions a dangerous pastime and best left to a section of the aristocracy to pursue in private. There is no indication that Robert Cecil felt much different. What happened in 1605, the Gunpowder Plot, only helped the cause of Protestantism, but not in some damning way that made the very idea of being a Catholic open to persecution. In 1603 the question of Catholicism or Protestantism had more of a constitutional and political importance than a religious one. We might accept that the dispersal of the Spanish Armada effectively was the last proper hope of a Catholic revolution. Equally, growing Protestantism was the basis of the notion that within a hundred years or so, certainly by the middle of the next century, English Protestantism had less to do with its devout perceptions than its sense of nationalism and the nation's belief in its superiority. Thus Protestantism, rather like Islam, was not simply a religion; it was also a socio-economic condition of its adherents.

James at his accession was full of promises for religious tolerance and the English priests certainly made their hopes clear that this would be true, although sometimes their language was spitefully uncompromising. For example, Dr George Downame, one of

London's boisterous theologians, delivered a full-scale denunciation of popery as a vehicle of the Antichrist Movement. Here was a most scathing diatribe on behalf of those who were tacitly warning the King (whose wife, remember, was a Catholic) that there must be no let-up in the official contempt for that religion.

> A Treatise concerning Anti-Christ divided in two bookes, the former proving that the Pope is Anti-Christ
> George Downame, DD and lately reader of the Divinity Lecture in Paules. Imprinted for Cuthbert Burbie 1603*

As was the style of the day, Downame dedicated his book to the most important person he reasonably could.

> The Most High and Mightie, Most Christian and Worthy king, James, by the Grace of God king of England, Scotland, France and Ireland, defender of the Faith &c.
> The blessed dispensation of Gods most gracious providence towards this land . . . in bringing your Highnesse unto this kingdome, in the beginning of the seventeenth century after Christ, seemeth to pressage, that the happy reformation of the church, restitution of the Gospell, consumption of Antichrist, decay of Babylon happily begun in the last centenary, shall in this age or century receive a notable confirmation and increase, if not a perfect consummation. For howsoever whiles the darknesse of Popery over-spread the Christian world, not onely the inhabitants of the earth were made drunks with the goulden cup of the whore of Babylons fornications, but the Kings also and Princes of the earth having drunke of the same cup, committed spirituall whoredome with her and gave their power to support the beast: yet when as it pleased God to enlighten the world with the bright beames of his glorious

---

* British Library shelfmark 478.a.25.

Gospell, then Antichrist began to consume, and Babylon to decay: the Preachers discovering Antichrist, the people coming out of Babylon, and the Princes which before had assisted Antichrist, setting themselves against him . . . And hereof Christian Princes are to be assured, that as those which joyne with the Pope in persecuting the Faithfull, doe fight under the banner of Antichrist the beaste, against Christ the Lambe: so they in oppugning the Pope and Church of Rome, doe fight the battailes of Christ against Antichrist . . .

When we say that the Pope is Antichrist, wee meane not this or that Pope, howsoever some of them have been more Antichrists then others: as for example Silvester the Second, Gregory the Seventh, alias Hildebrand, Boniface 8, John 22 alias 24, Alexander 6 &c but the whole rowe or rabble of them, from Boniface 3 downward . . . If the Romish church be Antichristian then those that embrace that religion and joyne themselves to that church, acknowledging the Pope to be their head, receive the marke of the beast. And those that do receive the beasts marke . . . shall drinke of the wine of Gods wrath, and shall bee punished with fire and brimstone before the holy Angels, and before the Lambe. This therefore must serve as a serious admonition, and necessary caveat both to reclaime all tractable Papists, and to confirme all wavering and unstayed Protestants.

Nearly two hundred pages of argument based on scriptural text followed. The message was simple: the Pope is Antichrist and therefore the separation of the English Church from Rome remains valid. There should be no wavering, whatever the blandishments in the tracts of the Jesuit cardinal Robert Bellarmine (1542–1621), Archbishop of Capua, who had refused to succeed Clement VIII as pope and is remembered as the most authoritative defender of the Roman Catholic faith of his generation.

Here in Downame was the uncompromising language of the

Established English Church. Yet were there signs that even royalty might incline towards Rome? Just as Elizabeth I might have done, so might too the son of Mary Stuart. As for James's queen, had she not refused to take communion in the Protestant rite at the coronation that July? Should Downame *et al.* have been concerned? Certainly the state was at its most vulnerable as the old order changed. Might there really have been a revolution that year?

During August 1603 King James, who had been in correspondence and had exchanged envoys with the papal nuncio at Brussels, was being told that the Pope would not support any revolutionary tendency by the English Catholics. So, at the beginning of his reign James was confident enough to allow English Catholics greater freedoms than they had enjoyed during Elizabeth's time.

This lax, charitably enlightened mood of the monarch resulted in the English Catholics who might have attended Protestant services (to protect their skins and purses) not doing so. Cecil was not as sanguine as James. His view was that if those who had been counted as Protestants were indeed covert Catholics, then the religious balance in England could not be as comfortable as the King thought. If it were possible for them to say that they were Catholics without being prosecuted or persecuted, then what else might they aspire to? Here then was the beginning of the argument for the return to more stringent controls over religious freedoms. Remember also that religious belief was not regarded as a matter of theological discussion, but rather political concern. Which was why the supposed plots, particularly the Main and the Bye plots, were seen as motivated by political Catholic thought, especially Spain's, rather than devout priestliness. That was the sole reason for Ralegh's trial at Winchester and the judgement that he should be put to death. The whole thing was of course a nonsense but it reflected the point that it was political ambitions and not the saying of beads that threatened the King.

At the heart of the concern of the English authorities were the so-called recusants. These were simply 'registered' Roman Catholics who refused to go to the Established Church services. This is an important point to remember because the penalties against them did not apply to the Protestant nonconformists. Under Elizabeth, a recusant could be taken to court and, if a conviction followed, fined £20 a month, which at the end of the sixteenth and the beginning of the seventeenth centuries was a considerable amount. If that £20 was not found every lunar month then two-thirds of the recusant's property would be confiscated.

In 1603 the Church and the state were particularly concerned to establish the number of recusants. The diocesan return of 1603 was 'A brief sum of all the parishes, impropriations, preachers, communicants, and *Recusants* certified for the several diocese of both the provinces of Canterbury and York'.* Although the arithmetic is sometimes awry, we can see from this document that there were more than nine thousand parishes from Cornwall to the Scottish Borders and Wales. The big dioceses were Lincoln with 1255 parishes, Norwich with 1121, London with 613, Exeter with 604, York with 581, and Coventry and Lichfield with 561. These were the major centres of population, although not necessarily of worship. For example, London with a population of some 220,000 had on Easter Day 146,857 communicants. Lincoln diocese had 242,550 communicants. We might consider that by Easter London was beginning to suffer from the plague and that gatherings were discouraged.

The interesting figure in those tables is the number of recusants: approximately (there are here and there a few arithmetic discrepancies) 8590 people were declared Catholics who refused to attend an Established English Church. In very crude summary we might deduce that there were 2,250,765 Established Church communicants. Those figures suggest that about 50 per cent of the English were going to church, if we are right in assuming the population to be about four and a half million. Does this mean that half the population were not churchgoers? Not necessarily, because

* British Library, Harleian Manuscript 280, pp. 157–72; author's emphasis.

many of the missing communicants would have been children. By the same token, the figures for the numbers of recusants would not include children. Therefore, we could reasonably double that figure and assume that at least 17,000 recusants existed. However, there is a more interesting bit of detective work to be done: the figures in the diocesan return of 1603 show that of the 8590 recusants, almost 4600 were women. Now, is this because women were more religious than their husbands? No, it is not. It simply means that English Catholics were not stupid.

If we go back to the penalties to be paid for recusancy, we see that the second part entailed the confiscation of property, that is, land and goods. This property would have been in the husband's name, not the wife's. Therefore, by declaring the wife as the family recusant, the land was kept. Thus a twist on the twenty-first-century accountancy trick of putting vulnerable assets in the wife's name.

It is not difficult to imagine the unease at court when this diocesan return was read. Robert Cecil would have been quite aware of the strength of Catholic feeling among the nobility and gentry. There was no need for him, as we must, to resort to statistics. Catholic sympathies and open devoutness were apparent. Catholicism ran deep in families. Examples were the Earls of Rutland, Shrewsbury, Worcester, St Albans, Castlehaven and Sunderland. Also Catholic were Viscount Montague and Lords Wootton, Stafford, Petre, Windsor, Stourton, Arundel, Cottington and Carnarvon. When Parliament was summoned by the King in 1606, of the seventy-four peers seated twenty were openly and twelve were probably Catholic.*

The year 1603 shows James keeping his word to allow religious tolerance, with a financial benefit becoming immediately apparent. During the final decade of Elizabeth's reign recusants were fined between £6500 and £8500 a year. That first year of James's reign, the new-found freedoms meant only £1414 was paid. This might

* See Charles Butler, *Historical Memoirs*, vol. 2, p. 177 (John Murray, London, 1819–21).

have continued if it had not been for the Gunpowder Plot of 1605 – which, incidentally, was being planned as James came to the throne in 1603. The next return shows recusants were fined nearly £7000, and it was not until twenty years later that James felt confident enough to relax the pressures on the Roman Catholics.

The figures that have survived look rather good because they are precise. We should read them with a sense that they may represent ambitious accounting and that not all recusants paid the fines. After all, if a woman had no property what could be confiscated? Yet, overall they do reflect a trend of pressure against the English Catholics, a pressure maintained by the English Church for fear of losing its authority as well as reminding the monarch whose authority he was bound to protect.

As would be the case for some time, religion could not be separated from the political thought of the country. James's son would lose his inheritance because of entwined religious and political confrontation. The Stuart monarchs never had the strengths of their predecessors. Charles I might insist on absolutism, that is the absolute authority of the monarchs, but it was a sham, even in 1603. James came to the throne believing in a monarch's God-given authority to rule. His frustrations with Parliament clearly tell us that he believed that he should have absolute power. Yet he had to work within the government and thus continue the Elizabethan Constitution.

The connection between religion and politics has to be made in 1603. Clearly religion was the most contentious component of everyday English life because it inspired political uncertainties. The differences between Puritanism and the Established Church meant that there was a harsher doctrinal hold under the new King than ever before, which is surprising considering the evolution of that Established Church. For the moment any reformation had to begin with the influence of Puritanism within the Established English Church. What happened later was inevitable: the Puritans stepped outside the protection of conforming religion. But in 1603 all sides were feeling their way. Many sermons were packed not only with doctrinal but political proclamations. Those who had access to the pulpit frequently used it as a political platform.

So, for example, we find the Reverend Doctor Miles Moses of Norwich preaching on 5 April 1603. Moses recalls the virtues of the recently dead Elizabeth. These are far more than the mediaeval sentences read at the death of a gartered knight. Moses speaks to his huge community (there were more Easter Day communicants in Norwich than in London that year) at great length, demanding their attention to the late Queen's virtues. He bids them welcome the new monarch, but encourages them not to let Elizabeth's memory fade. Moses is doing more than preaching; he is challenging the community and the new Court to understand the social and political as well as the religious consequences of embracing the sentiments of Catholicism.

Our late Soveraigne Lady Queene Elizabeth was so worthy an instrument unto us of such speciall benefits, as we were not onely bound to be infinitely thankefull unto her while she lived: but also we are still bound to keep an honorable remembrance of her and her government for ever . . . Her father had made some entrance to the Gospell, and wounded deep the heary scalpe of the Antichrist . . . Her mother the Lady Anne Bulleine was a woman very religious, and vertuous, and full of good workes. According to the godlinesse of the Parents was the godlye education of the child: for she was trained up in the knowledge of tongues, and sciences, and (that which was especiall) in the doctrine of the Gospell. Answerable to her education was her profession and religion, even from her youth: keeping godly Preachers about her, and suffering for the Trueth in the daies of Queene Mary. So that in the opinion of all that saw and knew her, she had the estimation of a wise, learned, vertuous and religious Princesse. Heerof it came to passe, that upon her sister's decease, she was proclaimed successor to the crowne not onely . . . with a full consent of all estates . . . but also this consent was witnessed with such shouting, such casting up of caps, such ringing of belles, such kindling of bonfires, such discharging of ordnance, and other points of solemnity: as witnessed their hearty joy for her comming to the crowne and exemplified notably this sentence of Solomon: in the prosperity of the righteous the city rejoiceth . . . And the coming of our late Queene to the Crowne, was the releasing of the Protestants out of prison, and the recalling home of learned men from beyond the seas and the confirming of poore Christians in religion . . . I meane, The high and mightie Princess, our late most renowned and soveraigne Lady Q Elizabeth – the glory of the world as Master Beza* called her: and of whom that may be said as truly, as it was of Luther in his time – 'she was the very terror of that declining Popedome' . . . Her people were so obedient as they were ready to goe whether soever shee sent them, and ready to disburse whatsover sums her extra-ordinary charges caused her to demand. Her Proclamations were as strong as enacted lawes: and her Private letters as forceable as Publike proclamations. The world was so quiet in her time, as England for 45 yeeres never knew by Feeling, what belonged to the warres. And now her winding up was in so quiet a season, as not only her owne kingdomes were in a generall peace; but all the countries of Christiandome, in a calme unity and concord . . . have we not all (I beseech you) very great cause to mourne for so heaviy a losse betided to us all? . . . now are ye, (O ye daughters of England) to mourne for the death of Q. Elizabeth; who not onely gave you outward things in such abundance, as our plaine Ancesters, if they now rose from the dead would hardly acknowledge us to be their posteritie . . . why do I so digresse from my joyfull Text, to dolefull, Elegies of sorrow . . . why do I by weeping with David provoke the people to turne the salutation of this present day into mourning? Why

* Théodore de Bèze.

rather go I not on to shew how Gods mercie hath mitigated the depth of this sorrow, with a new occasion of joy and calleth us anew at this time also to rejoice in the prosperitie of the Righteous . . . when Moses, the servant of the Lord was dead, God raised up Joshua to carry them over Jorden and to put them in possession of the promised land of Canaan. Queene Elizabeth, that good servant of the Lord, is dead, . . . God is now raising up a Joshuah by whom we conceive great hope to enjoy the perfect beautie and complements of the Gospell. Wherein not to stand upon this, that he is a Man, and so of more power and courage to all parts of government . . . neither yet to speake of this, that he is no meere aliant unto us, but one descended of English blood, from the ancient line of the Kings and Queenes of this land, and so the liker to carry a naturall affection to this nation . . . there are three especially points which may excite us to a confident expectation of much good to be done in our church and Common-wealth by his Majesties gracious government . . . his holy and vertuous education . . . have we great hope that the sweet liquor wherewith he was seasoned in youth, will yeeld him an healthsome and savourie relish all the days of his life . . . the experience of his peaceable and mercifull government in his owne countrey. Neither hath he shewed himselfe a disturber of other Princes . . . Neither hath he beene a plotter of bloudie stratageines . . . neither have we even heard that he hath beene covetous in exacting, or cruell in oppressing his own countrey people . . . But he hath established his throne by mercie and trueth: accounting clemencie . . . the next duetie to Religion . . . and to doe good to his countrey, the speciall vertue belonging to a soveraine Prince. So that his former practice in Scotland giveth great hope of a mercifull government unto this realme of England. The last (but not the least) thing is his Religion and Profession . . . If this man were a Papist, we could expect nothing but blood, and fire and fagot: for they are their sole arguments to maintaine their religion.

But thanked be God he is a professed Protestant, a supporter of the Gospell, an enemy to Popery: and therefore what cause is there to us of feare nay what cause is there not of joy in this his Majesties new Prosperity? . . . The common peace of the land since the death of the Queene, and the generall consent in this new proclamation, may rightly be called in respect of the Papists hope and purpose. A very miracle seene in our time. For full confidently did they expect, that so soone as ever the breath was knowen to be out of the Queene's bellie, they should have been . . . fiering of houses, and spoiling of goods, and levying of armies, and bringing in of forraine power from beyond the seas: yea cutting of our throates, and burying of us in the dust . . . For our selves: let us on the one side like good citizens rejoice in the Prosperity of this religious Prince: and on the other side let us pray to God both to affect his heart with large purposes of our common good, and to prepare our hearts to intertaine the good which his coming to the Crowne seemeth to promise unto us.*

Here then is the warning of the Church that James must have the wisdom of an inspired and chosen prophet. The cry 'No Popery' would never, it seems, leave these islands.

In 1603 the new monarch saw himself as Solomon. He believed himself to be wise, erudite and full of good scholarship. He was certainly no dullard. He understood the need to reform the system of government. Yet his hopes to settle the discrepancies between religious and political movements were largely unsuccessful inasmuch as, although he saw his encouragement of religious settlement adopted, he never quite managed to set aside the polemics of those who refused the idea of reforming the Established Church. The days were numbered for the reformist Protestants. They were not stripped of their positions; they simply faded. Here the new King

* *Scotlands Welcome*, preached at Needham on Tuesday 5 April 1603.

would lead the way in defining what he expected of the Church, as well as politics.

James was perhaps the most prolific author of the English monarchy.* He easily and happily wrote at length on his concepts of theology and politics and he expected a wide audience. He expected also that audience should understand what he had written and properly act upon it. By properly, James meant be obedient. The pulpit was the forum from where this message was broadcast. The English liked sermons. They liked long sermons with a good argument. (It is interesting to note that in the twenty-first century places of religious revival in England have seen the return of the long sermon, thus overcoming the rather tepid Anglican view that a sermon should be short, sweet and over soon enough for the congregation to get home to Sunday lunch.) An early seventeenth-century congregation would not only listen to but read sermons in order to discover the mind of its new monarch. Consequently, in the second half of 1603 the sermons preached at Court and throughout the country by those clerics attached to the Court made up a big percentage of the rapidly growing output of printing presses. They were also more than guides to salvation; they were the most important political pamphlets of that year.

In understanding what was coming from the Court preachers in 1603 we have to be careful not to be overwhelmed by the genius of Lancelot Andrewes (see page 194). Andrewes, as he makes very clear in most of his sermons in 1603, preached against Calvinism. And more of Andrewes's sermons were published in 1603 than those of any other preacher. He probably preached more sermons to King James than any other bishop. We also have to remember that James had grown up respecting, if not the theology, then the power of the Scottish Church, the Kirk. So when he arrived in 1603 James was very used to a form of churchmanship that was

---

* Lori Anne Ferrell, *Government by Polemic: James I, the King's Preachers, and the Rhetorics of Conformity, 1603–1625* (Stamford University Press, 1998).

not liked by some of his bishops in England. James was willing to accept Nonconformity, but not those he referred to as Puritans. His English bishops most certainly did not care for Calvinism and its dedication to an accusatory form of preaching. Little wonder that the bishops regarded their first task, reflected in Moses's sermon at Norwich (see page 225 above), as convincing James that it was their understanding of the English Church that he should adopt. If it had been good enough for Elizabeth, then so should it be for James was the message; by and large the churchmen seemed to have overcome the Scottish King's instincts.

The sense of Catholic denigration survived into the twentieth century. It did not of course begin in 1603. Any casual student of the Tudors would understand that. But the deep concerns of the clergy that the Established Church should not be reformed and that the wickedness of Rome should be kept at arm's length preoccupied the political and religious minds watching to see the ways in which the undoubted intellect and independent mind of the monarch might tend. The upheaval of Catholicism and Established Church culminating in the Protestant arrogance of the eighteenth century was an inevitable path leading from the beginning of the English Stuart age. Even in modern times, Roman Catholics were still ostracised, even thought socially peculiar and, curiously, still were sometimes excluded on religious grounds from certain professional positions. The English view that the Established Church, and certainly the Nonconformist persuasions, represented Christianity at its most vital, and that the Roman Catholics interpreted Christianity in a simpler yet more decorous faith, was emerging at this time.

10

HAMPTON COURT AND
THE BIBLE

hOWEVER ELSE JAMES MIGHT BE REMEMBERED, PERHAPS HIS LASTING MEMORIAL STEMS FROM THE CONSEQUENCES OF THE MILLENARY PETITION AND THE INTENSE CONCERNS OF THE ESTABLISHED CHURCH. For one consequence of those events during the first few weeks of his reign was that James ordered a new translation of the Bible. That book was his legacy.

The King James Bible was, and is, a remarkable work. Biblical translations into English and other languages were hardly unknown, even though the Church had for many years been wary of allowing translations, especially liturgical translations, from the classical languages; yet the Bible continued to be printed in translation, a development that ran parallel to other changes in Western society. A printed Bible was, when we think of it, an astonishing work. The middle-class development of Europe in the Middle Ages meant that mercantile interests began to control the major cities which had been in the hands of the aristocracies. This was all taking place in the 1400s. If we should think that the late twentieth century saw a sweeping aside of prejudice, privilege and curiously enacted traditions, this is almost nothing to what was happening in the fifteenth century. The merchants were making fortunes. With money came power and the setting aside of the authority of those families who claimed hereditary right to rule. The new merchants formed the new councils and turned societies into social and economic communities of their own. As mercantilism (in England, an expression not adopted until much later) gathered authority, so the infrastructure of investment and trade became more sophisticated. For example, what had been large social festivals for traders – grand fairs – became essential gathering points for merchants throughout Europe. Here was the origin of the twentieth-century trade fair. When merchants searched for new opportunities to invest, they made, as they still do in the twenty-first century, judgements according to the social trends around them. The great social change in Europe was, of course, literacy. The clergy who had throughout much of the Middle Ages dominated literary trends, and therefore had made the positions of clerk and recorder almost exclusively theirs, was now challenged. The more people learned to read the greater the demand for that still elusive item, the book.

In the fifteenth century five main groups of inventors were trying to produce a system that would undoubtedly revolutionise the transmission of information and also would make their fortunes: Prokop Waldvogel in Avignon, Laurens Koster in Haarlem, Panfilo Casteli in Feltre and Jean Brito of Bruges competed against each other to produce a printing process. None of them would be first to do so. In his Mainz workshop, Johannes Gutenberg triumphed. Each one of the would-be inventors probably knew what the system required but Gutenberg knew how to make it work. It was Gutenberg who produced the first printed Bibles; before him, of course, they had all been handwritten. The Bible was not chosen purely for religious reasons. It was certainly a commercial venture (although Gutenberg never made a great deal of money because he was not a good businessman). It was also a technological achievement, which is what Gutenberg set out to attain. Commercially it made a great deal of sense. The scale of religious education and development in the fifteenth century meant that the Bible was the most influential document of all. In Gutenberg's 1468 version it was also a truly enormous technical triumph, all 1768 pages of it.

There then is the beginning. Caxton began printing at Westminster in 1476. The great work of printing at this stage was inevitably the Bible. It was a book common to all instincts of those who could read and those who could not, and increasingly interesting to those who could read only English.

The relationship between the Church and the people should not be overlooked. It was not always an easy one. After all, in 1381 the Peasants' Revolt against the poll tax and the Statute of Labourers resulted in the Kentish rioters getting hold of the Tower of London and executing Simon Sudbury, Archbishop of Canterbury. This short reflection on the origins of printing and the Bible cannot be complete without noting the debate between those who wanted to preserve Latin as the Church language and others, like Richard Ullerston (d. 1423), who argued the case for English to be used. Consistently, English was rejected as being an inappropriate language for the Bible. Early in the fifteenth century the Archbishop of Canterbury, Thomas Arundel, ordered that no text whatsoever should be translated into English or read in that language. A century later, in 1512, John Colet was threatened with removal as dean of St Paul's for the heretical offence of translating the Lord's Prayer into English. These were positions being voluntarily taken rather than enforced. It might be remembered that English even in the early sixteenth century was not an exclusive language in these islands. This distinction between Latin and English had a certain amount to do with national identity. The Church, well into the sixteenth century, continued to use Latin. Increasingly, the law and government were scripted in English. The clerics held out against the laity. They were supported by the two universities, Oxford and Cambridge, which used, exclusively, Latin.

The same thing happened in France. The University of Paris used Latin. This was so distinct from the rest of the city that the area in which the university was sited became and has remained known as the Latin Quarter. Not surprisingly, academe was the last grove to give up Latin as its prime language.

In 1522 Luther had published in German his version of the New Testament. It could only be a few years before there was an English Testament, even if it might have to be published outside England. A pointer to this is that William Tyndale went to live in Cologne in the 1520s. The first gospel, St Matthew's, was finished in 1526. The text was brought, surreptitiously, to England, and not unnaturally this encouraged those who wanted a full Bible in English. There were not many printers, and certainly not many who would risk reprinting Tyndale's work. The booksellers of St Paul's Churchyard (the Hay-on-Wye of its day) were warned off by the Church should they imagine they could get away with what were called 'untrue translations'. Cardinal Wolsey even had his agents abroad telling printers to keep the English language at a distance. Tyndale was considered such a revolutionary that he was eventually captured and with little ceremony sent in October 1536 to the executioner at Vilvorde, near Brussels, where, much to the Church's delight, he was strangled and his body then burned. No wonder Tyndale is honoured to this very day. He was executed just a year after the first complete Bible in English was produced by Miles Coverdale. Coverdale was no great scholar, but he knew how to draw together texts, including Tyndale's, to produce this first completed English Bible. By now of course English was unstoppable for church use. Not even a year after Tyndale's execution, Archbishop Cranmer obtained royal approval for English translations.

In 1539 the so-called Great Bible was printed. In 1560 the famous Geneva Bible (because it was printed there) appeared. It was a masterpiece of translation and language, and one of its keenest students was William Shakespeare. It remained popular for more than a century and is still read today. There was opposition, mainly on the grounds of its marginal notes, which were thought to promote Puritan interpretations of the text, but it remained the most commonly read Bible during Elizabeth's and James's reigns.

When James became king in 1603 there was considerable pressure for him to take the Geneva Bible into his library and give it royal endorsement. There were even those who said it should be called the King James Bible. What they did not understand was that James had an even bigger ambition – his own Bible. It is here that we come back to the battles, sometimes no more than skirmishes, of the factions within the Church. Calvinism had been successful in Scotland. Little wonder that the English Puritans were delighted that James had become king. They could foresee nothing else but the marginalisation of the Established Church. They had forgotten James's belief in the Divine Right to rule and that therefore he would have little time for Puritan England and much time for the bishops. They were the Lord's vicars on earth and therefore would do the Lord's bidding and keep James on the throne. Certainly James would never extend his divine argument as far as, for example, Scottish Presbyterians had. They asserted that if it was God's will that he should be king then he should acknowledge that God was the true king and, as the Scottish churchman Andrew Melville had declared, that James himself was nothing more than 'God's silly vassal'.*

So, we find that although the Geneva Bible was the most popular in England, James had other ideas for his nation. He was a good enough scholar to question the Geneva translation when it was at variance with his authority. The petitioners for change had not yet realised this. The most famous of the petitions was the Millenary Petition presented to James in 1603 on his journey south from Scotland. It gives us the fundamental description of the differences within the Church that so frightened the bishops and academics. The thousand or so churchmen did not call it the Millenary Petition but *The Humble Petition of the Ministers of the Church of England*

* Melville to James in October 1596 at Portland Palace.

*desiring Reformation of certaine Ceremonies and abuses of the Church,** and it was delivered to King James with all good wishes for a long reign and even more fervent hopes for change. To begin with, they had to assure the monarch that they were humble men with sincere objectives. They could not rely on James's arrogance, his belief that all would be humble before him other than the out-and-out plotters, for whom the nooseman and his quartering butchers had easy remedy.

> [W]e the Ministers of the Gospell in this land, neither as factious men, affecting a popular Parity in the Church, nor as Schismatikes ayming at the dissolution of the state Ecclesiasticall; but as the faithful servants of Christ, and loyall subjects to your Majestie, desiring and longing for the redresse of diverse abuses of the Church; could doe no lese in our obedience to God, service to your Majestie, love to his Church, then acquainte your Princely Majestie with our particular griefes.

It is always a good tactic for the petitioner to quote the patron of his petition, and so the anxious clerics did so, knowing full well that James set much store in his own writing on his Divine Right to be king and expected the likes of his ministers to hold it in equal regard.

> For as your Princely penne writeth, The king as a good Physition, must first know what peccant humoours his pacient naturally is most subject unto, before he can begin his cure.

There now followed more soft words before the four points of grievance were addressed. Under the Church service section were:

> That the Crosse in Baptisme, Interrogatories ministered to

* British Library shelfmark 698.g.4.

Infants, Confirmation, as superfluous be taken away. Baptisme not to be ministered by Women, and so explained. The Cap and Surplice not urged. That examination may goe before the Communion. That it be ministered with a Sermon. That diverse termes of Priests, and Absolution, and some other used with the Ring in marriage and other such like in the booke, may be corrected. The long-somenes of service abridged, Church songs and Musicke moderated to better edification. That the Lords day be not prophaned. The rest upon Holy daies not so strictly urged. That there may bee an uniformity of doctrine subscribed. No popish opinion to be any more taught or defended. No ministers charged to teach their people to bow at the name of Jesus. That the Canonicall Scriptures only be read in Church.

Concerning Church ministers they asked:

That none hereafter be admitted into the Ministery but able and sufficient men, and those to preach diligently and especially upon the Lords day. That such as bee already entred and cannot preach, may either be removed and some charitable course taken with them for their reliefe: or else to bee forced according to the valew of their livings, to mainetaine preachers. That Non-residencie be not permitted. That king Edwards statute for the lawfulness of Ministers marriage, be revived. That Ministers be not urged to subscribe, but, according to the law, to the Articles of religion and the Kings supremecy onely.

Points made under the heading of Church livings and maintenance complained of episcopal patronage and greed as well as the holding of multiple benefices:

That bishops leave their Comendams some holding Prebends, some Parsonages, some Vicarages with their Bishoprickes. That double beneficed men be not suffered to hold some two, some three benefices with cure: and some two, three or foure dignities besides. That Impropriations of Laymens fee, may be charged with a sixt, or seventh part of the worth to the maintenance of the preaching Minister.

The final point covered a range of issues concerning Church discipline:

That the Discipline and Excommunication may be administered according to Christs owne institution. Or at the least, that enormities may be redressed. As namely, That Excommunication came not forth under the name of Lay persons, Chancellours, Officials etc. That men may not be excommunicated for trifles & twelve penny matters. That none be excommunicated without consent of his pastor. That the officers be not suffered to extort unreasonable fees. That none having Jurisdiction or Registers places, put out the same to farme. That divers Popish canons (as for restraint of marriage at certeine times) be reversed. That the long-somenes of suites in Ecclesiasticall courts (which hang sometime two, three, foure, five, sixe or seaven yeares) may be restrained . . . that Licenses for marriage without Banes asked be more cautiously granted . . . Your Majesties most humble subjects, the Ministers of the Gospell, that desire not a disorderly innovation, but due and Godly Reformation.

No wonder the bishops were agitated. The Puritans had seemed to have made their case before the King, leaving the Established Church indecisive and polishing its titles and impropriate tithes – the lucrative practice of getting money from the parishes to fund the bishoprics. The scholarly bishops, for example Richard Bancroft, Bishop of London (in 1604 to become Archbishop of Canterbury), were only too aware of the upper hand held by their opponents in Christ, the Puritans. Bancroft, along with every other senior churchman, academic and courtier, knew the King's feelings about his divine appointment. Those who had not done so when it was published in Scotland were now getting copies of *Basilikon Doron*, James's 'Kingly Gift', which was being printed in London immediately after the proclamation of his accession. As we have seen, James had written it as an instruction to his son on the values and duties of a monarch divinely ordained. Now, the Puritans did not see it that way. This was their weakness if they were to keep the King on their side. The answer, as Richard Bancroft saw it, was to explain to James that the Puritans and most certainly the Roman Catholics were instinctively, because of their churchmanship, not to be relied upon and in some cases were in downright opposition to the principle of monarchy. Who would then guarantee this Divine Right which James so jealously guarded? None other but the Church of England bishops. If James wanted the monarchy, then he needed his bishops. The more that Bancroft could raise James in his own image as some mighty kingly vision, surely the more the bishops would be his host of angels in support. As Lancelot Andrewes preached to James, 'make thee trumpets of silver . . . thou shalt have them to assemble the congregation'. Here was the symbolism of Church and state. Bancroft's position became more to James's liking. The Archbishop of Canterbury, John Whitgift, had of course received James as the new monarch, but his health was failing. James would need Bancroft to succeed Whitgift and thus make the silver trumpets sound forth sweetly in his authority.

The Bishop of London may have been successful in countering the ascendancy of the Puritans in James's mind, but James was not such a fool as not to realise that little was to be gained, certainly at the beginning of his reign, by totally alienating one or other group of churchmen. The one thousand ministers had to be reckoned with. With all groups in 1603 trying to get into the best position for the King to see, hear and be impressed with their opinions, there were moments when James, it seems without much thought, condemned, praised, confiscated or enhanced the positions of many who crossed his line of sight. Usually, the politics that encouraged James's reactions were tight-knit. After all and for example, how many people would truly be hurt if he endorsed the fall of Sir Walter Ralegh? The answer is not very many. Yet the Church and state, with two silver trumpets, needed more sensitive handling. James may have agreed that the monarch needed the bishops, but he was immediately aware that a thousand churchmen who could be so bold and agitated as to sign the Millenary Petition represented not, say, just two-hundredths of the population of London, but the opinion of thousands of others in the parishes across the country. The Millenary Petition was a movement and could not be dismissed as little more than a lobby.

In his wisdom, James issued a proclamation on 24 October 1603. It was this decree that called together what would become known in constitutional and Church history as the Hampton Court Conference. He announced that he would be in the chair, churchmen and their bishops would attend, so too the academics and his Privy Council. On reflection, the idea was a nonsense. The Puritans, for example, thought that this conference was the answer to their petition. In part, indeed it was. They had some cause for optimism. After all, whichever monarch or prince had ever agreed to hear them before? Bancroft *et al.* were naturally bothered that in spite of their efforts James was siding with the Puritans. This was not simply a matter of religion; it was, to the bishops, a way of life which was anyway increasingly dominated by Puritan influences in the country and, worse still, in Parliament. James had yet to call his first Parliament, but the Puritans already saw themselves in the ascendancy within that institution. For our purposes, what happened at Hampton Court is some distance off. The conference, rather like the Parliament, was not convened until the following year. However, we should take note of its results because they were not so much set at Hampton Court, but by the moods abroad in 1603.

Not surprisingly, the Puritans were told whom they could send as representatives. For example, the academics included the famous

Laurence Chaderton who was master of the Puritan-based Emmanuel College, Cambridge. John Reynolds (or Rainolds), the president of Corpus Christi College, Oxford, was there. So, too, was John Knewstubs, a fellow of St John's College, Cambridge. The Established clergy had, if not the intellectual authority of the meeting, then the seniority in churchmanship. Whitgift led his Bishops of Carlisle, Chichester, Durham, London, Peterborough, St David's, Winchester and Worcester. The two deans of the great London churches, Westminster Abbey and St Paul's Cathedral, attended them. James gave the Puritans hope when he recognised the importance of the Millenary Petition. He was cautious in advocating change, and the churchmen, some anxious, some complacent, recognised that their single hope might be in the King's reluctance to make great changes, but at the same time make those which would improve the standing of the churches without causing instability in the formal and informal worship in these islands.

So, for once, James behaved diplomatically. He gave assurances that he had not called 'this assembly for any innovation'. He made the point that ecclesiastical government must be approved by God. At the same time, he thought that nothing can be so absolutely ordered that it cannot be added to, and even the most perfect institution could be corrupted. He noted that he had 'received many complaints, since our first entrance into this kingdom of many disorders and much disobedience to the laws'. He saw himself as a physician called to diagnose the ailment and then prescribe a curative.

It was John Reynolds who spoke most fluently in the Puritan cause. He, and they, wanted to establish four points. Church doctrine should be preserved in a pure form according to what the Puritans saw as God's Word. Ministers, or pastors, should be worthwhile and learned characters and should replace many of the duffers of the Established Church. He also wanted better administration of the Church. He was not alone in this matter and the bishops shifted uneasily. His final point was that the Book of Common Prayer should be more pious. In fact the Puritan notion was that it had very little to do with the Bible and should therefore be either rewritten or tossed out.

The bishops thought the Puritan demands, which of course they had not heard here for the first time, to be worth little consideration. And James had little patience with Reynolds's intervention. He had grown up with dissent all about him and saw his task as the new monarch of Scotland and England as maintaining stability and thus being able to rule with fewer difficulties. He knew very well that any suggestion that he approved of the proposed rewriting of the Book of Common Prayer would have the opposite effect. Religious infighting had no history of yielding stability as an outcome.

The matter of the Geneva Bible was not on the Hampton Court Conference agenda. There is little evidence to suggest that when James called the conference in October 1603 he intended to do much about that Bible. However, the conference, as it progressed, seemed to be going entirely the way of the bishops. Bancroft was particularly pleased. He had successfully opposed everything that had come from the Puritans and had done nothing to harm his authority over his brother bishops. James had protected their prayer book. So what could be done for the Puritans? There had to be some backstairs negotiations.

The Bishop of Durham, Tobie Matthew, who had preached to James's delight in his cathedral when the new monarch first set foot in England, recorded that the Puritans wanted 'one only translation of the bible'. This single work would be considered authentic and therefore the only one at the lecterns. James recognised that an authorised Bible translation might be the answer to any critic that the Hampton Court Conference had not produced innovation. The King did not like the Geneva Bible and nor did the bishops; the Puritans, though critical, thought it the best of what was available. Moreover, everyone knew that following the 1582 Roman Catholic version of the New Testament, soon the whole Bible would be completed by priests at Douai and Reims. No matter the conflicts within the Protestant Church in England (and in the text of the

Millenary Petition the ministers had pleaded against schism), there was one matter that could bring them all together: not a single person at the conference could bear the thought of any Roman Catholic influence. Against the Catholics Puritan and Established churchmen could unite. How much better to have a new translation in place. It was not the King, nor the bishops, but John Reynolds who publicly proposed a new translation of the Bible. The politicking of Hampton Court was successful. James declared that the scholars of Oxford and Cambridge should begin work on a translation that would be 'made of the whole Bible, as consonant as can be to the original Hebrew and Greek and this to be set out and printed without any marginal notes and only to be used in all churches of England in time of Divine service'.

The Puritans had not really got everything they wanted. Equally, the Established Church was not convinced that the King was wholly with them and not inclined to the Puritans. However, two people had done rather well. Bancroft had got a Bible which would be an improvement on Geneva, if for no other reason than that the King's instructions were that it should have no marginal annotations. (The annotations in the Geneva Bible margins slanted doctrine in such a way that the Established Church was always vexed with it.) Also, Bancroft took charge of the project and therefore imagined (to some extent correctly) that he could lean on the translators. Third, for Bancroft, he had improved and consolidated his position as the most important bishop, apart from Canterbury, and Whitgift did not look at all well. The other person who had come out of it rather well was King James. It is doubtful that he would realise it at the time, but that 1603 Millenary Petition and the angst of the Established Church had led to the only achievement readily accredited to him in the whole of his reign: the King James Version of the Bible, still read in the twenty-first century.

11
WITCHCRAFT

THE DEBATE OF THE CHURCH AND THE STATE AS TO WHICH WAS THE TRUE RELIGION AND WHICH WAS THE REPOSITORY OF THE DOCTRINE OF ANTICHRIST DID NOT NECESSARILY SPARK THE ENTHUSIASMS AND DEBATES THAT MIGHT HAVE BEEN IMAGINED. The people in the towns and the countryside had to be wary that they were not caught up in that controversy. Yet it is true also that there is little evidence to show the deeper feelings of the population, especially in the rural areas. In 1603 a rural area was not something that took hours by train and motorcar to reach from the cities. Even a city such as London was surrounded by fields, and it might be hard to imagine now that Chelsea was rural England.

The numbers of communicants recorded at Eastertide do not necessarily reflect the religious beliefs of the people. Right up to the beginning of the twentieth century country people often went to church according to their allegiance to a landlord. A deeper belief might often be understood as the suspicions of the countryside. The dark woods and relatively unsophisticated minds combined to make a society which owed many of its practices to a limited number of doctrines, and many long memories could not be expected to do anything other than respect the laws of superstition. With that allegiance came the fear of the unknown and the reliance upon the few who apparently had special powers. In 1603 witchcraft was centuries old. Because it was feared, because it was threatening and, most of all, because it was sometimes inexplicable, it provoked uncompromising punishment.

For the historian, witchcraft remains something of a mystery because its reputation in this period was based on anecdote and folklore. Today few believe in witchcraft because most expect a logical explanation for almost any phenomenon. In a period when superstition and curious powers did not seem so unlikely, a largely ill-educated and particularly rural population would have believed in some form of witchcraft. This would be particularly the case when there was sufficient report of an individual's ability to cast fear as well as spells.

Documentary evidence which explains prosecution and punishment of a witch does not tell us anything of the facts beyond the prejudice of the accusers. The evidence produced to relate the witch with the bewitched is necessarily circumstantial. Only the accusation that a person practised witchcraft is reliable. That a woodlander would go to an old crone and pay over a coin for a spell to be cast in the heart of his beloved or against the heart of his rival is hardly surprising. That a child should die or a crop fail and a mystic stand accused of both tragedies is, again, hardly surprising in early seventeenth-century society. Such were the restrictions and the speculations about the causes and consequences of witchcraft in this period.

Towards the middle of the sixteenth century it emerged that British sorcery had more to do with an unease that it might be heresy. A witch, for example, might be prosecuted under canon law, *de haeretico comburendo*. Statute law existed to prosecute a witch, but there is no detailed evidence that many were thus prosecuted. It was also difficult to know who would bring the prosecution. The two Acts of Parliament which concern us suggest a growing mystification of what to do about sorcery and whether it was something that should be dealt with by the justices or the church courts. In March 1563 the the Act against Conjururacions Inchantments and Witchecraftes was passed. This Act lasted more than thirty years. It was expected to be replaced with a more stringent Act in 1603, but the constitutional and social events of that year meant that Elizabeth was not inclined to call Parliament during the first few weeks of the year, and James had other things on his mind.

The 1563 Act could mean death for a witch. If anyone could be proved to have used sorcery to destroy or kill, then they were likely to be put to death. James had no more enlightened view of the practice, and when he did call Parliament, one of the first Acts went into some detail to condemn magical practices and was considerably harsher than the law it replaced. For example, it was now against that law to consult or consort with those who claimed they were witches. It was thought necessary to make it illegal for bodies to be removed from tombs. Whereas until 1603 a person might be imprisoned for an offence, they could now be executed and much was made of the punishment of people who *intended* to use sorcery – as well as those actually doing so. A person could now be put to death for: causing injury and certainly death by witchcraft, grave-robbing, and calling up so-called evil spirits. It was also against the law to try to cast a spell that would make a person unlawfully love another. If a witch were caught casting love potions like that he or she would be sent to prison for a year. If they were caught again then they would be executed. In 1603 many of the witches sent to prison never served their full sentence. They were not reprieved; they simply died in the dreadful conditions of the gaols.

Not all witches were women (the popular concept), although taking one set of surviving records, only 23 of the 291 people accused of witchcraft during the seventeenth century were men. It might be assumed that often a male witch was married to a female witch, and there is some evidence to show that between 1560 and 1679 the Home Circuit of assizes put to death 219 witches, 116 of whom were women. Equally, about 80 per cent of those accused of witchcraft in northern England were women; 90 per cent in Essex; and overall some 40 per cent were widows.

The nearest we can get to establishing the state of witchcraft in 1603 is perhaps a statement in the previous year by the Lord Chief Justice of the Common Pleas, Sir Edmund Anderson, one of the most celebrated judges of the period. Anderson was addressing the court in the case of the bewitching of Mary Glover, one of the famous trials for witchcraft because, quite unusually, medical evidence was introduced. This is what he had to say.

The land is full of witches, they abound in all places, I have hanged five or six and twenty of them. There is no man here, can speak more of them than myself; few of them would confess it, some of them did; against whom the proofs were nothing so manifest, as against those that denied it. They have on their bodies divers strange marks at which (as some of them have confessed) the Devil sucks their blood, for they have forsaken God, renounced their baptism, and vowed their service to the Devil: and so the sacrifice which they offer him is their blood. This woman [Elizabeth Jackson, accused of bewitching Mary Glover] hath the like marks on sundry places of her body, as you see testified under the hands of the women, that were appointed to search her. The Devil is a spirit of darkness, he deals closely and cunningly, you shall hardly find any direct proofs in such a case, but by many presumptions and circumstances, you may gather it. When they are full of cursing, use their tongue to speak ingenuously and it falls out accordingly, what greater presumption can you have of a witch? This woman hath that property: She is full of cursing, she threatens and prophesies, and still it takes effect: she must of necessity be a prophet or a witch. Their malice is great, their practises devilish, and if we shall not convict them, without their own confession or direct proofs, where the presumptions are so great, and the circumstances so apparent, they will, in short time, overrun the whole land. The maid now afflicted I have seen, and you have beheld. [Here he related the trial he had himself made. Turning to the physicians] You talk of the mother [hysteria],* I pray you have you ever seen or heard of the mother, that kept its course unchangeably, every second day, and never missed and yet that changeth his course upon the presence of some one person, as this doth, at the presence of this woman? Divines, Physicians, I know they are learned and wise, but to say this is natural and tell me neither the cause, nor the cure of it, I care not for your judgment; give me a natural reason or a natural remedy, or a rush for your physic.'†

Dealing with witchcraft and the apparent exorcism of demons was not considered likely by the legal process. Here was no mock Puritan belief that anyone with a cauldron, a black cat and of some stoic nature should be ducked until dead. In 1602 and into 1603 the lawyers on one particular case, that of Elizabeth Jackson, were very careful to seek medical evidence.

There was, after all, an obvious legal difficulty with condemning someone as a witch. If a court found a person guilty of witchcraft then that court had *de facto* declared that witchcraft existed and had real powers, not fictitious ones. Therefore, it was not simply a case of protecting the accused by exercising the law and bringing proper witnesses. Heresy could be condemned for its untruth. By condemning a witch in a court of law, heresy was set aside and the sorcerer's claims of mystical powers were thus recognised. So when, in our period, a girl was apparently bewitched by an alleged sorcerer, Elizabeth Jackson, the College of Physicians was called in

* In pre-modern physiology the womb ('mother') was thought to rise in a woman's body, occasioning hysteria. Thus 'mother' was used to mean a fit of hysteria.
† British Library Sloane MS 831, pp. 38–9.

to examine the girl. The interesting point here is that the witch was not examined medically. After all, how could a physician (in those days an enormously exalted position within a closed shop) determine whether a witch's claims were true or false? Only by examining the object of the sorcery. Hence the girl was quizzed and tested to see, first, if her demonic symptoms were genuine and, second, the causes of them.

The doctors could not say the girl's symptoms were caused by witchcraft, but they could say if the mind and the personality had been affected by any other condition, such as acute illness elsewhere in the body. Also of interest was that the physicians were called in not by the court, but by the Bishop of London. In the Church's mind, the heresy of witchcraft could be punished even when the sorcery was disproved. Simulating witchcraft was, to the Church – although not in law – just as evil a crime.

There is a further confusion easily accepted as fact. Even in the twenty-first century there is a small part of us that would like to believe in mysticism. Imagine then the feelings in a year such as 1603. It would be so much easier and likely to accept mystical reasons for ordinary happenings. For example, in 1603 there would not be an irrefutable scientific explanation for many natural occurrences. Where pathology in the twenty-first century can tell us a cause of death or we can reasonably believe there is an explanation for the unexplained, in 1603 there were no such convincing explanations. For example, how would one have explained an apparently healthy baby dying when there was no way of recognising illness in the first place other than that accompanied by fever and blotches? When in the twenty-first century we blame global warming for extremes of weather patterns and the floods and curious harvests that follow, someone in 1603 was far more likely to agree with the general opinion that there was some unscientific reason. Also, the position of the Church had changed.

A bishop could condemn witchcraft as heresy. But this straight-forward expression of authority could not be extended any longer to apparently natural phenomena whether it be manifested as the death of a child or a harvest-wrecking storm. When these islands were unequivocally Catholic, then all the saints' names could be called on for explanation or retribution, or malcontents could be whisked into the confessional and their sins accounted for. Under the reformed Church of England, and especially with the trend towards Nonconformism and Puritanism, none of this Church mysticism was officially accepted, even though a large part of the population still held Catholic beliefs. The wizards of the Roman Church had been banished. It was not surprising, therefore, that the clean-cut orthodoxy of the reformed Church stripped of its Catholic protection could but point at things it did not understand and brand them as heresies.

This disturbed the physicians, who as we have seen might have been looking for medical rather than mystic reasons, for the girl's condition pointed to epilepsy. They were uncertain in their judgement because the girl also displayed the symptoms of attention-seeking and therefore pretending to be bewitched. Mary Glover seemed under the influence of Elizabeth Jackson.* Given the status of Sir Edmund Anderson, one senses the importance of the issues in the case. One of the physicians thought that whatever the cause of the apparent epilepsy, it would be wrong to set aside a supernatural reason. The distinction between supernatural and unnatural cause and effect was a difficult one to argue and almost inevitably a discussion would be inconclusive. Two doctors, Spencer and Hering, thought the symptoms abnormal. This diagnosis was largely based on their observation that no one had seen before this condition brought on naturally. For example, Mary Glover was said to make grunting noises through her nose as part of her epilepsy only when Elizabeth Jackson was present. When Jackson left the grunting ceased. Mary Glover, seemingly in a trance, would react to the closing words 'deliver us from evil' in the Lord's Prayer by convulsing. Anderson had clearly made up his mind when he observed that no matter how

* H.M.C., App. 8th Report, p. 228b.

clever the doctors, they could not convince him that there was any natural cause or cure for Mary Glover's condition.

Much might be made of the quackery and lack of medical knowledge of physicians at this time. Yet some were deeply disturbed that such an authority as Anderson in his Court of Common Pleas could insinuate that sorcery was a real and not a bogus power. There was, even in 1603, a basic knowledge if not understanding of hereditary disease and medical excitement. Some doctors, including Edward Jorden, observed that although one should not ignore the possibility that a person might be possessed by the Devil, it had to be accepted that, for example, hysteria might be an inherited condition. Jorden was thus touching on genetic medicine. Not all his colleagues within the College of Physicians agreed. Stephen Bradwell thought Jorden's view 'sly . . . scandalous impugnations'. Another doctor, John Cotta, wrote *The Triall of Witch-craft, Shewing the true and right Methode of the Discovery; with a Confutation of erroneous wayes*. Cotta could not bring himself to deny there might be darker forces abroad and thought his fellow physicians should be wary of how they made a discrimination between a 'true worke of the devill and the strange likenesse which phantasmes . . . strongly worke in their opinion and conceit'.

King James has acquired a common fame that has made him a sinister figure in the history of English witchcraft. One school of thought had it that witch-hunting had waned during the latter years of Elizabeth's reign; James's accession coincided with the beginning of a violent and long-continued outburst of witch-hunting, for which he was personally responsible.* James came to the throne with a little-observed lust for witch-hunting, and his interest in sorcery started well before 1603.

In Scotland, there had been a series of prosecutions of witches between 1590 and 1597. It was in December 1590 that John Fiene

---

* George Lyman Kittredge in *Studies in the History of Religions* (Macmillan, New York, 1912).

was sent to trial and James is said to have attended the hearings. Fiene (sometimes Feane) was terribly tortured to extract his confession, for what it was worth. Why did James attend? Thrill? Curiosity? Probably the latter. James appears to have regarded many of the confessions of witches as downright lies. He saw the reasoning that someone indulging (he thought it an indulgence) in this black art was hardly of normal mental balance and simple personality. Therefore, a confession could be bravado, even if the consequences were terrifying. The Scots were only too willing to see supernatural influences at every level. No play, no verse, was without its spirit. In true life, had not Agnes Sampson accused Bothwell of using witchcraft to take the King's life? On 27 January 1591 (1590 Old Style) Sampson was tried for sorcery.

> Nether Keith January 27. Trial of Agnes Sampsoune in Nether Keythe, for conspiring the king's death, witchcraft, sorcery, incantation, etc. Strangled and burnt on the Castle-hill of Edinburgh. She confessed that at the great witch gathering on All-Hallow-even Geilis Duncan played the dance tune Gyllatripes on the Jews-harp. This confession so pleased king James VI that he sent for Geillis to play the tune before him, which he did to his great pleasure and amazement.*

Yet, to James's mind, the matter of witch-hunting was out of hand in Scotland. There were so many indictments that few, if any, could be treated seriously and examined clinically. He saw most of the claims as being fraudulent. In 1597 the courts were being overwhelmed with what was perhaps the biggest witch-hunt in the sixteenth century in these lands. James VI saw the stupidity of the situation and revoked all the outstanding indictments. This did not mean he thought the

* Robert Pitcairn, *Criminal Trials Compiled from the Original Records and Manuscripts with his Notes and Illustrations*, vol. VI, pp. 230–41 (R. Pitcairn, Edinburgh, 1833).

subject nonsense, only the method and means of prosecution. Trials continued but there were fewer, and the methods of investigation were refined – as much as they could be. By the time James reached London, the English discourses on witchcraft and the sense that a law should be found to replace the Tudor Act were well founded.

In Scotland there was a decline in the number being brought to trial. The records of trials in Scotland suggest that in 1603, for example, only three trials took place.

Musselburgh, July 21. James Reid sumtyme serveand to George Anderoun. Strangled and burnt on the Castle-hill of Edinburgh.

Shetland, August 7. Nicole in Culyeastter.

Inverness, December 2. Donald Moir, miller charmed Robert Steuart by cutting four nickis of his coit and casting them in the myln burn; and charming Robert Steuarts childe with vater [water] and nyn stanis [nine stones]. To be burned on the Haouche Hill.

In England, there was a deep suspicion growing that the superstitious nature of the common people led to injustice and an increasing credibility for witches which none deserved.

The Cambridge theologian William Perkins had died in 1602 without publishing his *Discourse of the Damned Art of Witchcraft*. It was a masterpiece in describing the views of the learned of 1603 on his subject. James warmed to Perkins's work. He agreed with the old don's view that all claims of special powers should be treated with utmost scepticism. As for scratching a witch to loosen her powers (see below), or thatch-burning her cottage, or trial by drowning, Perkins had no time for any of it. But had not James himself in his *Dæmonologie* (1597; published in England 1603) contradicted this? 'It appears that God hath appointed for a supernaturall signe of the monstrous impietie of Witches that the water shall refuse to receive them in her bosome that have shaken off them the sacred Water of Baptisme and wifully refused the benefite thereof.' James was not prepared to argue. He rarely did; he simply explained.

Perkins's view was unequivocal. To him, the basis of all sorcery was a covenant with the Devil – real or unreal. Yet that did not mean the witch really had supernatural powers. It did mean that he or she had an imagined pact with the Devil and that he or she tried to cast spells in some black and devilish way. It did not mean that those powers (persuasion, conjuring, psychological authority over others) were anything other than natural talents. The Perkins view was that an imagined league with the Devil primarily gave confidence and ability to the witch in exercising some natural talents. That is, the witch performed with Satan's aid, using existing powers. The learned of England in 1603 followed the Perkins philosophy.

> By the lawes of England the thiefe is executed for stealing and we think it just and profitable: but if it were a thousand times better for the land, if all Witches, but specially the blessing Witch might suffer death. For the thiefe by his stealing, and the hurtfull Inchanter by charming, bring hinderance and hurt to the bodies and goods of men; but these are the right hand of the divell, by which he taketh and destroieth the soules of men. Men doe commonly hate and spit at the damnifying Sorcerer, as unworthie to live among them, that they hold themselves and their countrey blessed that have him among them, they flie unto him in necessitie, they depend upon him as their god; and by this means, thousands are carried away to their finall confusion. Death therefore is the just and deserved portion of the good Witch.*

Also in 1603 there was a new publication of George Giffard's *Dialogue concerning Witches and Witchcraftes*. Giffard was an

* William Perkins, *A Discourse of the Damned Act of Witchcraft* (Cambridge, 1608).

Oxford scholar and preacher from Maldon in Essex. He made the point that someone with an illness, say, epilepsy, might easily be thought to be bewitched. Therefore, said Giffard, the interrogation of anyone accused of sorcery should be thorough and based on good scholarship. That did not, of course, mean than Giffard was a liberal where broomsticks were concerned. In his *Dialogue* he gives his views through the words of Daniel. He is quizzed by a schoolmaster, called M.B.

Daniel. A witch by the word of God ought to die the death, not because she killeth men, for that she cannot (unless it be those witches which kill by poyson, which either they receive from the divell, or hee teecheth them to make) but because she dealeth with divells. And so if a Jurie doe finde proofe that she hath dealt with divels, they may and ought to finde them guiltie of witchcraft.

M.B. If they finde them guiltie to have dealt with divels, and cannot say they have murdered men, the law doth not put them to death.

Daniel. It were to be wished, that the law were more perfect in that respect, even to cut off all such abominations. These cunning mean dew omen [*sic*] which deale with spirites and charmes seeming to doe good, and draw the people into manifold impieties, with all other which have familiarity with devels or use conjurations, ought to bee rooted out, that others might see and feare.

So this was the code of the well meaning and well read. In the countryside and towns, the beliefs were simpler to interpret. Little wonder that one of the first moments of James's reign was spent in arranging that when Parliament was called (only the King could summon Parliament) measures would be taken to strengthen the old Elizabethan Act. Daniel would have his way.

Witchcraft was believed because the so-called witches were often feared. They could inspire fear by appearance but mostly by their deeds and trappings: no broomsticks, but bowls and spoons, potions and darkness. Johane Harrison and her daughter had all the appearances and acts of witchcraft, and in Royston in 1603 practised the passing of fear from one superstitious soul to another. The more they succeeded in casting this fear, the more the story ran of their success, although there is little on record to show that they achieved anything other than criminal and heretical misdemeanour. The law said it was bad to practise the art and denied that conviction gave authority to the witch's claims of supernatural powers. To the victims and the fearful, conviction did just that. In the Harrison case, there is an interesting illustration of how a victim would indeed believe that he had been bewitched, and there is evidence of country superstition when we see, the physician having failed to find a cure, the victim resorting to folklore for relief. If blood may be drawn from the witch herself, then a cure may be found. The melodramatic horror films of the latter half of the twentieth century had some historical merit in their scripts after all. The evidence at the trial of the Harrisons was damning enough and it gives us an immediate insight into the utensils kept by a practising witch in his or her mysterious box of tricks.

This chest being opened, there was first taken out . . . all the bones due to the Anatomy of man and woman and under them haire of all colours that is customarily worne, in the bottom was found a parchment lapt up in a compass no bigger than a groat but being open was in breadth every way two spans, in ye midst of this parchment was coloured a heart proportioned to the heart of a man and round about fitting even to the very brim of the parchment were coloured in severall colours very curiously divided braunches on which hung dangling things like Keys and at the end of them in some places figured and other proportioned a mouth, in briefe the whole joynts and artries of a man. This Johane Harrison being upon her examination and finding such apparent witness induct against her severall felonies and murthers neglected not to confess her utmost secret therein that she had power (by the help of that parchment, man and womans bones and man and womans haire) to inflicte by the help of her spirits, which she reported to have two attending on her, one for men another for cattell, in any joynt synnew or place of the body by only pricking the point of a needle in that place of the parchment where in his or her body she would have them tortured, which torture of hers once beggun in them their paine should continue so restless that a present death had been more happier than so lingering a calamity and those whome she intended to kill had the same effect, if she gave a prick in the middle of the parchment where she had place the heart. Which relation of her may be beleeved by the several consequents that she was condemned upon, first a good country Yeoman (a neighbour of hers) and she falling at some words together he calling her Old Hagge, she made him this answer:-

'I will say little to thee, but thou shalte feele more from me hereafter.'

The honest man had scarce departed from her halfe an hour but he felt himsel as if he had been set into your Scotche Boote or Spannish Strappes or your Morbus Gallicus* was nothing to it sometimes in a pestiferous heat, at others a chill cold, but in all times in continuus aches and wracking of his limbs as if the Divell had set him on his Lentors [sic]† to make broad cloth of him. In this perplexitie he continued consuming himselfe

---

* The Scotch boots and Spanish straps (also known as the strappado) were methods of torture used to extract confessions. The former were used in Scotland to crush the legs of victims. The latter was a pulley-and-strap system by which the victim was hoisted into the air with his hands pinioned behind him and then dropped, dislocating his shoulders and arms. The Morbus Gallicus was the venereal disease also known by its English name of the French pox.

† 'Lentors' is an error for 'tentors'; a tenter (or tentor) was the framework on which a cloth was stretched out to dry as part of the manufacturing process. Hence the victim felt aches in his limbs as if he had been stretched out on a tenter. (Cf. the expression 'on tenterhooks'.)

not being able to goe nor stand. No Physicke could help him nor no means he had to ease him. When one of his neighbours coming in to visit him he began to open his mind to him that he persuaded himselfe by such a one she was bewitched and he was as faithfully persuaded that if he could but have two or three good scratches at her face whereby he might draw blood of her he should recover presently. His neighbour advised him by some will to send for her home, yet between them both held inconvenient for that, either suspecting herself of for not being friends, she would not come, that in the night following his neighbours would have this fickle man carried in a chaire lodged in his house, and in the morning his wife who knew she was good friends withal, should by some will draw her thither, what if he of himselfe were not strong enough to scratch her he as he held charily would help him. This the next morning was done accordingly the Witch comes, and is well Scratcht upon which within three or foure daies (as fast as the man could recover strength) he is up and goes abroad which this Johane Harrison perceiving arrests him by a tryall in law for the battery had 5s damages and her costs of suit given her, the man acording as he was condemned paid her which no sooner by her received, but the honest man fell into his former passion languishing a while and died. In the same she served another two who meeting her out of the towne in a lane took the like revenge upon her and recovered. Both which blowne over, only a little murmured againste by a neighbour of hers a young woman being washing clothes in an outer roome near the Streete where in a cradle lay a child asleep when Anne Harrison the daughter chanced to come by just in the instant that she was throwing out a little wrinsing water and by chance some of which unawares sprinkled upon her which the wench seeming moved at, called to her with these words:-

'Do you throw your water upon me gossip, before it be long I'll be revenged for it.'

The woman sorry for the offence she had done followed her business and thought no further of it, but when she stept but into the next roome to hang up some clothes the cradle wherein her child lay was throwne over, shattered all to pieces, the child upon the face whelmed under it and killed. Thus we see the Divell hath such power on these his damnable servants that neither men nor infants are to be pitied by them. Not long after she had bewitched a wealthy mans daughter in the towne who having a good substantial yeoman for her brother in pitie of his sisters griefe rode to Cambridge and their acquainting a friend of his with his sisters affliction the scholler told him she was bewitched, yet in regard the two had beene of an ancient friendship and that himselfe had some acquaintance with his sister in spite of lunibi [sic],* her spirits and the Divell, offered help which according to promise he performed and by that time her brother was returned his sister was recovered. In revenge of (for her sorcery was crost, and the mayd returned to helth by her brothers carefulnesse) she caused such a plague upon all his cattell that they all perished and consumed.†

On 4 August Johane Harrison and her daughter were strangled then burned to death, the common execution of those convicted of witchcraft. Burning, of course, saved a fee for one of the oldest officers of justice, the man whose task it was to determine the cause or causes of death – the coroner.

* 'lunibi' is a misprint for 'Incubi', the demons believed to have sexual intercourse with women.
† *The Severall Practices of Johane Harrison and her daughter, condemned and executed at Hartford for witchcraft, the 4th August Last* (1606). British Library shelfmark 010882.g.34.

12

THE CORONER'S TALE

HE COMPLEXITIES OF COURT POLITICS AND THE CURIOSITIES OF STYLE IF NOT SUBSTANCE AT THE FRINGES OF THE NEW MONARCHY DID NOT MUCH IMPINGE UPON THE DAILY DOINGS OF ENGLISH SOCIETY. The bonfires may have burned through and the mourning was over, but the festival of the new monarch would not distract a person from his or her daily life. Not all of the doings of 1603 were bleached by the arrival of the new majesty and pomp. The swineherd's motives were as uncomplicated as they had been under Elizabeth. So too were those who thieved and committed violence. So too was the law that committed them to English justice. Many of them died in the custody of that law. Suspicious circumstances, but most of all wretched conditions, proved cruel cellmates. The sadness of their deaths was no less than the endings of many on remand in our own century but the circumstances of incarceration were quite different. For those who believe modern gaols to be miserable places, then the houses of penitents in 1603 would properly seem ghastly, even hellish. Little wonder that prisoners often perished either by their own hands or simply from utter destitution. The lot of the villain is rarely described as happy. The characters and circumstances of the Elizabethan and early Stuart offender were unenviable. Death came slowly but surely from common starvation and consumption in a prison, more often than it did through the direction of a court. Now, as then, it is the coroner's task to hear the evidence and decide the circumstance of that death as well as those who perished, curiously, on the outside of the prisons. The coroner's was, and is, perhaps the most independently powerful of the ancient courts. The coroner's personal view and decision decided matters of life and death and began, ominously, with the latter. This office, which dates from the 1100s, may be restricted, but a coroner's decision is crucial to the basis of criminal and civil law.

Examples of the coroner's court cases in that coronation year for one county alone, Sussex, give a good picture of the sadnesses and the seriousness of crimes as viewed through his office.

On 22 January 1603 at Henfield, John Aylwyn brought his coroner's court to order. The jury was Thomas Francke, described as a gentleman, Nicholas and John Godsemarcke, Thomas Chapman, Edward Parson, Richard Langford, William Whitbreade, John Parson, Richard Weller, Peter Coffe, Thomas Dunstall and Nicholas Backshall. Before them was the case of James Goble. On 9 January, Goble at about six hours after sunset, apparently with the intention of breaking and entering the home of Henry Gratwike at West Grinstead, climbed a pear tree. He either fell or jumped from its very top and broke his right shin. Goble languished with his wound until 18 January and died of it. Now, Goble had indeed died through an act instigated by himself. That is, he had appeared intent on entering Gratwike's house and had fallen from the tree. However, Gratwike was suspected of doing grievous bodily harm to Goble which hastened his death and may even have caused it. Witnesses were called to give evidence at the next assizes against Gratwike, who stood accused of causing the death of Goble. On 25 February 1603 a jury heard evidence from Sussex yeomen, and Henry Gratwike was faced with the charge of feloniously killing Goble at

West Grinstead with a hedging bill 'worth tuppence which he held in both hands, giving him a wound . . . one inch deep of which he languished until 18 January and then died'. Gratwike pleaded not guilty. He got off, probably because it was decided that it was Goble's own act of falling from the pear tree that was the principal cause of his death.

On 16 March 1603 at Ancton, George Ardern, the Avisford hundred coroner, heard that at about 2 p.m. on 14 March, one Richard Leach was alone in his tenement. That night he 'feloniously hanged himself with a halter worth tuppence which he held in both hands, putting one end round his neck and tying the other round a beam of the tenement'.

On 3 April 1603 John Aylwyn examined the death of Thomas Barker, who had died that day in Horsham gaol. No one saw him die. During the hearing it came out that Barker had been committed to gaol by one Richard Blount, the local justice of the peace at East Grinstead. Evidence offered against Barker alleged that he had stolen a grey gelding from a London merchant by the name of John Challenor. At the Horsham assizes the previous July Barker (who apparently was a glover by trade from Billingshurst) was indeed charged with 'taking and carrying away a dark grey gelding worth £7'. He pleaded not guilty. The jury did not believe him. He could be imprisoned but not fined because he had no goods or chattels. So he was on remand. Just as in the twenty-first century, the stress and lack of fortune for remand prisoners in the early seventeenth century were considerable, and Barker, as do some of the twenty-first-century prisoners, hanged himself.

On the same day that Barker died in Horsham gaol, so too did Thomas Burchall. As with Barker, no one saw Burchall's death. Also, as with Barker, Burchall was on remand. The previous year the grand jury at East Grinstead assizes (the same court that had committed Barker) presented an indictment charging Burchall (also from Billingshurst, as it happens) with feloniously taking and driving away an ox worth £4 belonging to someone called Haler. Another man was charged with Burchall. He was John Wastlen, who had been hiding him. So Wastlen was aiding and abetting. They were both found guilty. Burchall at some time shortly after his conviction was allowed out and then rearrested. Almost immediately he died of 'natural causes'.

Clearly Horsham gaol was an unhealthy place because yet another prisoner died there on 3 April and, again, no one saw him die. All we know about him was his name, John Umfry.

We do, however, know more about William Harvie, another inmate of Horsham who died there on 30 September 1603. 'No one else was privy to his death to the jurors' knowledge.' So what was he doing in Horsham? Fourteen months earlier at Horsham assizes Harvie was indicted with taking and carrying away two pewter porringers worth 12d., four saucers worth 16d. and a pair of shoes worth 22d., all belonging to Thomas Russell of Icklesham. He was also accused of stealing a pair of stockings worth 12d. and a cambric band worth 12d. belonging to Edward Russell, as well as a silver spoon worth 8s. belonging to Deborah Russell. The Russells lived in Icklesham, and Harvie was a labourer from that village. Harvie said he was not guilty, but the Horsham court did not believe him and he was remanded. They left him in the gaol at East Grinstead because they had other charges against him. On 25 February 1603 the East Grinstead grand jury charged him with stealing from another Sussex man, George Tyler, of Ardingly. He apparently stole two doublets worth 6s., a coat worth 2d., two pairs of breeches worth 1s., three pairs of stockings worth 1s., a hat worth 6d., a pair of belts worth 1d., three silk girdles worth 1s., a linen sheet worth 6d. (and quite handy to carry away swag), a tuppenny shirt, a pair of pillows worth 10d., fourteen neckbands and two pairs of shoes. Not guilty, pleaded Harvie. Yes you are, said the court. He then successfully pleaded 'benefit of clergy'. This suggests that Harvie was either in holy orders – and given the character and alternative occupations of some priests this is not unlikely – or, as the original text suggests, he was looked after by the parish in the

care of the parson. This did not mean that he got off without some
penalty for his offences. The punishment was the source of a phrase
still used today: Harvie was branded – thus, 'branded a thief'. He
was, however, not let out. He was remanded in gaol as there was
yet another charge to be brought against him, one of breaking and
entering in daytime. Harvie was sent to Horsham gaol, probably for
his offence to be heard before the October assizes, due to sit on 3
October 1603. On 30 September 1603 Harvie gave up the ghost in
Horsham.

At a distance one may see comical consequences of a coroner's
court without too much disrespect towards the deceased. On 13
May 1603 Henry Peckham, the coroner of the Bishop of Chichester's
liberty, heard that a Ferring labourer called John Robinut had been
getting water in a watercart at Weres Bridge when the horse jerked
the cart and Robinut fell off. He broke his neck and died. The court
solemnly noted that the horse and cart 'are worth 46s. 8d. [£2.33]
and are sold by Anthony, bishop of Chichester'.

And just to show that a coroner's work is never done, on Boxing
Day 1603 Richard Lyfe, the Hastings coroner (at the time he was
also the mayor), called together a jury to hear the sad circumstances
of the death of a young lad. At about nine o'clock on Christmas
morning a fourteen-year-old boy called William Emes, who seems
to have been apprenticed to a Hastings weaver, left the house of
his master, Richard Dyer, and made his way towards the priory
in Hastings (the priory fields were until recently one of England's
most famous cricket grounds and now, as Priory Meadow, house a
shopping centre). To cross the bourn, he mounted the bridge called
Le Clappers. It was indeed a crisp and even morning, and Emes
slipped and fell from the bridge and was drowned. Richard Lyfe
and his jurors recorded 'Accidental Death'.

Public death, sometimes official public death, was common
enough in 1603. The spectacle of a man swinging from a rope
was hardly a phenomenon. Sometimes the stretched or hacked
necks were famous, sometimes infamous. In 1603 the public missed

what might have been the most famous execution of the decade. The decline of Sir Walter Ralegh was confirmed within days of Elizabeth's death. The agony of his disgrace was prolonged for the rest of the year.

13

RALEGH AND PLOTS GALORE

WITH THE ARRIVAL OF JAMES VI IN ENGLAND, WALTER RALEGH'S FORTUNES CHANGED. Ralegh's London home was Durham House in Strand. It was called that because it was owned by the see of Durham. Ralegh had been at Oxford with the then Bishop of Durham, Tobie Matthew. When James arrived in Durham he immediately got on with the Bishop, who mentioned that he felt that he should have back Durham House. James agreed – but at this time he seemed to agree with everything. The lawyers drew up an eviction notice on Ralegh, who was not there anyway. He had been in the West Country when Elizabeth died. Many saw the chance of getting back more than Durham House from Sir Walter. A rumour was spread that Ralegh was planning a *coup d'état*. To get in with the new King many knights announced their intention to challenge Ralegh. Ralegh decided to pre-empt the rumours and bad faith and so hurried north to meet the King before he could be overwhelmed by the whisper-mongering of London. Ralegh was hardly alone in his pilgrimage. So many had tried to travel north to gather royal favour that the council of courtiers had banned petitioners and well-wishers (they were usually one and the same) unless they had official business. Ralegh claimed that he needed to get the King's signature on letters to do with the Duchy of Cornwall. This was a paper-thin excuse and did him no good. It was the seventeenth-century biographer John Aubrey who claimed that when Ralegh was introduced to the King, James took one look at him and said, 'O my soul, mon, I have heard rawly of thee.'

Sir Walter did not linger and hurried back to London for Elizabeth's funeral. He was still captain of Her Late Majesty's guard. Shortly after the funeral, while James was still at Cecil's Hertfordshire home, Theobalds, much preparation was made to throw out Elizabeth's hangers-on and greedy possessors of royal sinecures. This was especially true of many of the business arrangements she had allowed. Effectively James was establishing the first Monopolies Commission. For example, Ralegh had quite a decent income from an exclusive licence to import wine and cloth. That he lost. The next day he was stripped of his captaincy of the guard and replaced by one of James's Scottish knights, Thomas Erskine, who by all accounts was so lice-ridden that it was freely commented 'that there was already Scottish innovation at Court'.* So he had lost his honourable position, many of his business interests and his London house in which he had lived for twenty years.

It was pretty rough justice from those who advised the King, and Ralegh was moved to write in June of 1603 to the Attorney General among others,

> I am of the opinion that if the kings Majesty had recovered this house, or the like, from the meanest gentleman and servant he had in England, that his Majesty would have given six months time for the avoidance, and I do not know but that the poorest

---

* Norman Lloyd Williams, *Sir Walter Raleigh* (Eyre & Spottiswoode, London, 1962).

artificer in London hath a quarters warning given him by his landlord.*

Worse was to come for Ralegh. Within a month of that letter in June, Ralegh was in the Tower. There was talk of a plot. James took plots quite seriously. After all, the whole history of Scottish monarchy was a succession of murder plots. Ralegh was accused. He denied the accusations. We have to remember that England was still at war with Spain. James had not earlier minded that conflict because the Spanish had some claim on the English throne and fear of Spain might lead English waverers to look to James as the preferred candidate. But now that James had got the throne for himself he saw no great need for the war which, apart from anything else, was very expensive and he declared that all attacks on Spanish ships, especially by the royally sanctioned privateers, should cease immediately.

The case against Ralegh was founded on the evidence of Lord Cobham, a close friend of Ralegh but a man not well trusted at Court. At the centre of the so-called plot was Cobham's brother, George Brooke. With them was the young, apparently high-minded Lord Grey de Wilton, a hopeful gentleman blasted in the bud. Grey was a Puritan and of that persuasion described by King James as 'Protestants flayed out of their wits'. Cobham was never much liked, even by his friends. One writer in the nineteenth century said he was 'condemned and detested by every reader of history capable of feeling virtuous indignation. To his natural imbecility there was an accompaniment not very unusual, a degree of stupid and remorseless assurance, which enabled him to tell a lie with as much ease and confidence as a fact.'† Also supposedly involved were two priests, William Watson and William Clarke, as well as Sir Edward Parham, Bartholomew Brooksby, Anthony Copley and Sir Griffin Markham.

* J. Payne Collier (ed.), *Egerton Papers*, Camden Society (1840/1842).
† A. T. Thomson, *Memoirs of Sir Walter Ralegh* (Longman, Rees, Orme, Brown, and Green, London, 1830).

The three most likely to be involved with plotters were George Brooke, who seems to have been a very ambitious and dangerously clever man, Lord Cobham, for the reasons stated above, and Lord Grey, partly because he was well in with the other two and a plot of this nature would simply appeal to his sense of devilment.

So what brought about the trial of these men, including Ralegh, in 1603? A series of events and seemingly everyday occurrences was later to be built into a package of evidence against Sir Walter. For example, the accused had at the beginning of that year considerable influence. The Queen was still alive. When James I came to the throne we know that that influence was gradually stripped away. Yet before that happened and before some were to realise what was happening, Ralegh worked hard at capitalising on his reputation, inside knowledge and influence. It is a style which is still seen every day, for example when former government ministers or senior civil servants are taken on as directors or consultants in businesses not only because of what they know and whom they know, but on account of who knows them. In 1603 with the uncertainties of the succession there were quite a few foreign ambassadors who would probably pay people like Ralegh for his ability to introduce them to the right people and, in today's jargon, 'to make things happen for them'.

More serious accusations concerned the diplomatic efforts of Spain to persuade England to give up her close relations with France and the Low Countries. A crucial player in this was the dark figure of the Count of Aremberg, who was the Archduke Albert of Austria's ambassador. Any dealings with Aremberg, whose interests were far more akin to Spain's than to England's, were likely to be treacherous.

We have seen that James, once he had secured the throne, was inclined towards peace with Spain. This did not mean betraying the security of his nation and therefore his throne, nor making any compromises. It may not therefore be surprising that in May 1603, supposedly to protect the interests of England and to warn against the deviousness of Spain, Ralegh had presented a pamphlet to James which appears to have laid out the reasons not to rush towards a peace treaty with the Spanish. There was some good argument that it was much better to be in league with the Flemish, who feared the Spanish, than with the Spanish, who could commit international robbery among England's neighbours in the Low Countries.

In June, Aremberg arrived in England. Cobham appears to have been in contact with him at this time. One version suggests that Cobham was told by Aremberg to offer Ralegh a bribe. The purpose of the bribe was to persuade Ralegh not to push the case against Spain and a peace treaty. Here is the connection between Aremberg's influence and the paper Ralegh had presented to James. It was not the first time that Aremberg or his agents tried to get at Ralegh. It is tempting to believe that such a wonderful character in history as Ralegh could be beyond bribery. This would be a naive view. After all, if Ralegh had a reputation of such political and diplomatic piety why would anyone have tried to bribe him in the first place? Moreover, bribes were commonplace at that time. Courtiers made their fortunes, sometimes their only incomes, from 'commissions'.

At the beginning of July Robert Cecil, who had a first-class intelligence system, received a visit from Anthony Copley, who told Cecil that there was a plot, of which he was unwittingly a part, to topple the monarch. At that stage Copley only implicated Grey and George Brooke as well as, to a lesser extent, himself. Cecil, who was as astute as his father had been at Elizabeth's court, knew exactly who was in league with whom. But it would not take a wizard to work out that if George Brooke was somehow involved then so might his brother – Lord Cobham – be. If Cobham was implicated, then so might be Ralegh, under whose influence the not overly bright Cobham operated. Cecil was not one to toy with treason. Later that month he persuaded Ralegh to remain at Windsor after a gathering. Unsuspectingly, Ralegh imagined he was to be brought into the confidence of the Privy Council at a meeting at the castle. Instead he was interrogated. Ralegh talked himself out of the accusation. Cobham was easier meat. He was summoned to Richmond and the lord commissioners of the Privy Council. It did not take much to persuade Cobham that Ralegh was accusing him of treason. This was not true, but then Cobham was a peer of very little brain. He then made up, using part truth and part lie, the story which would soon be used as the pretext to arrest Ralegh and for him to be tried. He claimed that Ralegh had forced him to go to see Philip III of Spain to borrow gold to pay for the army that had to be raised to overthrow James. That is the background to Ralegh's arrest and his trial and his insistence that Cobham should be brought to the court to face him with his evidence. Ralegh confidently believed that Cobham would crumble before him.

Cobham found himself accused by Ralegh and through Robert Cecil of knowing about the plot. Cobham was cornered. Yes, he had been in discussion with Aremberg. Yet who was the instigator of the plotting? According to Cobham, it was Ralegh. So there was Ralegh in the Tower, and on 27 July 1603, a week on from Cobham's claim, Ralegh stabbed himself in the chest with a table knife. He struck a rib and no vital organ. Interpretation of the state of Ralegh's mind has centred on the contents of a letter to his wife written just before the suicide attempt – if that's what it was. The letter, a copy of which is in All Souls, suggests despair and the neglect of his family.*

A motley group of gentlemen was now involved in the apparent treason, including Anthony Copley, Sir Griffin Markham and Cobham's brother, George Brooke. By now we had two plots. One was called the Main Plot and the mini-one was known as the Bye Plot. They may have sounded unlikely and petty, but they were good enough for the executioner.

While all of this Court intrigue was going on, the plague was sweeping London. People were dying in their thousands. The courts

* Agnes Latham, *Sir Walter Ralegh's Farewell Letter, Essays and Letters* (English Association, London, 1939), offers a discussion of the letter and its contents.

of justice abandoned Westminster for Winchester. On 10 November 1603 Ralegh was taken under escort to Winchester to be set before Lord Chief Justice Sir John Popham and the examining commissioners, who included Lord Thomas Howard, the Earl of Devonshire, Robert Cecil and Sir William Wade. Wade observed,

> I thanke God we brought all our prisoners safely hither yesterday night in good tyme; and yet I protest to your Lordship, it was hab or nab whether Sir Walter Rawley should have bin brought a live thorow such multitudes of unruly people as did exclaym against him. He that had seen it would not think there had bin any sicknes in London, we toke the best order we could, in setting watches thorow all the streets, both in London and in the suburbs: if one hair brain fellow amongst so great multitudes had begunn to set upon him, as they were verry nere to do it, no nit-watch or meanns could have prevayled, the fury and tumult of the people was so great.*

On 17 November 1603 Ralegh sat on a stool before the lords commissioners as a clerk of the Crown Office read the charge: 'that he did conspire, and go about to deprive the king of his government; to raise up sedition within the realm; to alter religion, to bring in the Roman superstition, and to procure foreign enemies to invade the kingdom'. The nervousness and ambitions of his accusers had already been demonstrated. Other than Sir Edward Parham, the rest of the so-called plotters had already been tried and found guilty. More often than not prisoners on treason charges were found guilty. The circumstances of being charged, either being caught red-handed or finding themselves victims of political scores, meant that the accused were presumed guilty and remained that way until they could prove otherwise. Moreover, the commissioners and courtiers were determined to show the new King, on whom they relied almost

* S. P. Dom. IV. 76 PRO; also Williams, *Sir Walter Raleigh*.

exclusively for their patronage, how well they were looking after his interests.

The indictment also gives us a pretty good flavour of the times and anxieties. For example, nothing is left to chance in the accusation against Sir Walter Ralegh. He is accused of attempting to deprive the King of his government, in other words of his authority to be king. Also here we have an expression of the fear of so many in the seventeenth century, a fear even greater than the plague that had caused such disaster in London that year. Ralegh is accused of trying to replace the Protestant Church of England with the Church of Rome. The indictment does not talk about religion; it talks about superstition. The cruellest definition of Catholicism was that it was akin to witchcraft.

Ralegh was only fifty-one years old, but he was not at all well. He was also depressed to the point that he had apparently attempted suicide. He had lost office, privilege and income. He had no friends that could relieve his difficulties. He sensed also that none in that court at Winchester would show clemency. He was philosophical about his chances. He observed that the jury were all Christian and honest gentlemen.

Of course, Ralegh pleaded not guilty. The Attorney General, Sir Edward Coke, was a determined and uncompromising prosecutor. He set about delivering his evidence like an incisive don or politician, sweeping up innuendo and circumstantial evidence to link Ralegh with the general mood of insurrection, even though he was not charged with any of the other conspiracies, including the lesser but very real Bye Plot. (A priest, William Watson, planned to kidnap James and force him to accept religious toleration. A Jesuit who knew of the plan betrayed Watson and his supporters. Watson was topped. The Bye Plot was supposedly part of the Main Plot, hence its title. This is unlikely.)

Coke tried to show the enormity of what he claimed was royalist ambition by going into detail about the murder of Edward II at Berkeley Castle (21 September 1327) and the admittedly ineffectual treasons of Perkin Warbeck against Henry VII.* If the nation and the Court had imagined the severity of those treasons then they should prepare themselves to accept that Ralegh's plotting was even more dastardly. Here, Coke believed Ralegh intended *crimen laesae majestatis* and *extirpatae majestatis et totius progeniei suae*. In other words the plot was to destroy majesty and its progeny. The expression used that year was that there would be no 'safety in England until the fox and his cubs were taken away'. Majesty destroyed. Coke then faced the seated Ralegh. 'I will prove you the notoriest traitor that ever came to the Bar [Bar of the King's Bench]'. Ralegh professed bewilderment. 'Prove one of these things wherewith you have charged me and I will confess the whole indictment and that I am the horriblest traitor that ever lived and worthy to be crucified with a thousand thousand torments.'†

Coke was not going to let Ralegh get away with such an outburst. He told the court that not only would he prove all his accusations, he would show that Ralegh was what he called 'a monster'. And then came a damning line which today seems innocent enough, but then was hardly that. 'Thou hast an English face, but a Spanish heart.' Could there ever be in early seventeenth-century England a stronger invitation to damnation? He then accused Ralegh of inciting Lord Cobham to plot with the Count of Aremberg to raise funds for the coup. Ralegh wanted to answer this accusation immediately. Coke would not let him. Because the law of the day did not let a

---

* Perkin Warbeck (c. 1474–99), said by some to be a bastard of Edward IV, was an impersonator of prominent people, including Edward IV's nephew, the Earl of Warwick, and Prince Richard, the younger of the two princes in the Tower. Involved in plots against Henry VII, he was imprisoned in the Tower, escaped, was recaptured and executed.

† Sir Thomas Overbury, *The arraignment and conviction of Sir Walter Ralegh at the King's Bench Bar at Winchester on 17 Nov 1603* (1648), in William Cobbett (ed.), *Complete State Trials and Proceedings from High Treason and other Crimes and Misdemeanours*, vol. II, col. I *et seq.* (Longman, London, 1809–26).

defendant have counsel, Ralegh had to try to intervene himself. He did not get far.

Coke was in a triumphant mood, especially when he tried to show that he had proof that Aremberg had agreed to pass on money (presumably from Spanish bankers); that he had evidence of Cobham and Ralegh plotting at Durham House that the former should go to Spain and come back via Jersey to meet Ralegh, who was captain (governor) of the island; and particularly that Ralegh intended that James's first cousin, Lady Arabella Stuart, should replace him on the throne.

Arabella Stuart was a particularly hapless member of the Stuart line, which, considering that family's many flirtations with misfortune, is saying something. She was the daughter of the Earl of Lenox, the King's uncle, whose elder brother had been the sad Darnley. Lady Arabella was certainly not averse to the idea of becoming monarch and she was supported by Pope Clement VIII. He appears to have believed that she was inclined to the Catholic faith and there was even some thought that the Pope wanted to marry her off into the family of the Duke of Parma. Whether or not this was hearsay hardly mattered. There were enough people who might have believed it. Certainly, Lady Arabella that year was not inclined to involve herself in any plotting. She could hardly afford to. She was almost totally dependent for her social and, more importantly, her financial position on the King, and so it is very unlikely that she would have allowed herself to be involved in any plot, and equally unlikely that Ralegh would have attempted to involve her. Yet such was the stupidity of some of those accused, anything might be believed.

Coke was trying to make Cobham credible – a difficult task inasmuch as Cobham was supposed to be part of the scheme. He said that everyone knew that Cobham was never either politician or swordsman. He said it was Ralegh who was both politician and soldier and that he had involved Cobham. Indeed, it was Cobham who was persuaded to make the accusations against Ralegh, whose reaction had been that it was nothing to do with him and that the evidence did not incriminate him: 'Here is no treason of mine done. If my Lord Cobham be a traitor, what is that to me?' Coke pounced. 'All that he did was by thy instigation, thou viper, . . . thou traitor. I will prove thee the rankest traitor in all England.' The Lord Chief Justice, although perfectly understanding the way the case would eventually go and that the verdict was preordained, felt moved to tell both Ralegh and Coke to control themselves. Coke was speaking out of zeal for his service to the King; Ralegh out of zeal for his life.

Exactly what had Ralegh known of Cobham's claims that under Ralegh's instigation he had instructions to treat with the King of Spain and that he was trying to raise money for a plot? Also, did Ralegh really believe or even suspect that Arabella Stuart could be put on the thrones of England and Scotland? Would he really have been so mad as to make himself, as he put it, a Robin Hood, a Wat Tyler, a Robert Ket or a Jack Cade? He faced the court and his foe, Sir Edward Coke, full on.

At Windsor [in July 1603], my Lords asked me what I knew of Cobham's practice with Aremberg. I answered negatively . . . concerning Arabella I protest before God I never heard one word of it . . . true I suspected that the Lord Cobham kept intelligence with Aremberg. For I knew that long since . . . he held that course with him in the Low Countries as was well known to my Lord Treasurer and to my Lord Cecil . . . I told my Lord Cecil that I thought my Lord Cobham had conference with Aremberg . . . but I was willed by my Lord Cecil not to speak of this, because the king, at the first coming of Aremberg, would not give him occasion of suspicion . . . Master Attorney, whether to favour or to disable my Lord Cobham you speak as you will of him, yet he is not such a babe as you make him. He hath dispositions of such violence which his best friends would never temper.

Ralegh then went on to dismiss the idea that the King of Spain could be bribed into plotting against James I. At this time the Spanish were broke, or close to it. Their navy, once the proudest and fiercest fleet on the Spanish Main, was decimated. The Spanish monarch's poverty was said to be so great that the Jesuits, his imps, begged at his church doors. And what was Spain doing about this? Desperately trying to agree peace with James I. The Spanish were in no position to finance a coup – they simply did not have that sort of money (estimated at some six hundred thousand gold crowns) and needed the stability of, at the very least, a truce with England. Moreover, where was the surety for any loan to come from? When monarchs financed the wars of others they expected towns and territory in return. There was nothing that Ralegh could have pawned for the favour of the Spanish King. So what was the basis for Cobham's accusation? There was always the truth that Cobham had been found out or at least legally implicated and therefore was determined that Ralegh should fall with him. Ralegh said that Cobham accused him in a fit of passion. Again, today we'd like to think that Cobham would not be believed. After all, it was he who had told his brother, George Brooke, 'we mean to take away the fox and his cubs'.

Ralegh stood to defend himself. He demanded that Cobham be brought to the court so that they could face each other. He had the law on his side. The statute of Edward VI was clear, 'no man shall be condemned of treason unless he be accused by two lawful accusers' and that those accusers 'must be brought in person before the party accused, at his arraignment, if they be living'. Cobham was very much alive. For good measure Ralegh then quoted the Old Testament – always a sensitive reference – that seemed that day crammed with examples and exhortations that none should be accused without his accuser being present. Was not, after all, this the fundamental belief of the Christian Gospel? Was not the same confirmed by Jesus Christ, by St Paul and by the whole consent of the Scriptures? Ralegh thought so and hoped sincerely that the court would confirm his legal and theological case law. The court really did not want Cobham to appear. Cecil observed that it was up to the judges. In a contorted judgement, the Lord Chief Justice said, 'you plead hard for yourself, but the law pleas as hard for the safety of the king'. Justice Gawdy was a little more analytical.

Sir Walter Ralegh, for the statutes you have mentioned, none of them helped you. The statutes you speak of in cases of treason were found to be inconvenient and were taken away by another law . . . all is now . . . put to the common law. And by the common law, one witness is sufficient and the accusation of confederates or the confession of others is foolproof.

Justice Warburton thought the whole thing ludicrous. He felt that if defendants could demand witnesses be brought to court, then all the horse-stealers in England would get off: 'By law, a man may be condemned upon presumption in circumstances without any witness to the main fact.'

Here was a test of not simply the law of the land, but how it might be interpreted. Ralegh believed that his case had been strengthened because common law demanded trial by jury and witnesses. The Lord Chief Justice thought that unnecessary. He made the extremely important constitutional point that the judges did not concede the law, they simply knew it. Therefore, equity might come from the King. Only justice could come from the judges.

Cobham had said that his task was to raise money and that that money would be used to finance a coup. How it would be distributed was never understood. The difficulty with Cobham's testimony was that he was in effect a co-conspirator. In fact, three of the other conspirators – already tried and found guilty – Copley, Watson and Brooke (Cobham's brother), claimed that Cobham and Ralegh 'stood for the Spanish faction'. Ralegh never denied that money gained surreptitiously was to hand. In his statement to the court he claimed that

Lord Cobham offered me 10,000 crowns of the money, for the

furthering the peace between England and Spain; and he said that I should have it within three days. I told him 'when I see the money, I shall make an answer' for I thought it one of his ordinary idle conceits and therefore made no account thereof.

The Attorney General believed Ralegh had condemned himself with this statement because the amount of money hardly mattered. The fact that he had been willing to take it made him a traitor. Ralegh dismissed Coke's assumption.

Master Attorney, you have seemed to say much but in truth nothing that applies to me. You conclude that I must know of the plots, because I was to have part in the money. But all you have said concerning this I make void, by distinguishing the time when it was spoken. It is true my Lord Cobham had speech with me about the money, and made me an offer. But how? And when? Voluntarily, one day at dinner, some time before Count Arembergs coming over. For he and I, being at his own board, arguing and speaking violently – he for the peace, I against the peace – the Lord Cobham told me that when Count Aremberg came he would yield such strong arguments for the peace as would satisfy any man. And withal he told – as his fashion is to utter things easily – what great sums of money would be given to some Councillors for making the peace and named my Lord Cecil and the Earl of Mar. I answering bade him make no such offer unto them for they would hate him if he did offer it.

Coke was determined that none should doubt Ralegh's guilt. It was clear from the day the trial started that Ralegh would be found guilty. It was Coke, as chief prosecutor, who had the task of convincing everyone that the evidence against Ralegh was so overwhelming that there should be no question of clemency. A lot of the evidence would have been in a recognisable form today: who knew what and when did they know it? Furthermore, the existing law was being examined by this trial and the justice of the form of examination questioned. The circumstances suggested that Cobham had got quite a lot of money together and that this was to be used, as Ralegh suggested, to bring about a truce between Spain and England – a paradox of a war chest for peace. Ralegh's point to the court was that Cobham, having got the money to spend on encouraging a peaceful settlement between Spain and England, then decided to try to finance a *coup d'état*. That was Cobham's problem, not Walter Ralegh's. All the way through he insisted that it was ludicrous to believe that he of all people could contemplate an attempt to topple a monarch from the throne. He told the court that he had spent forty thousand pounds of his own money 'against the Spanish faction for the good of my country'. Coke was not impressed. He repeated his claim that Ralegh had a Spanish heart. He called him a spider of hell because 'thou confessest the king to be a most sweet and gracious Prince and yet hast conspired against him'. Much of Coke's evidence was necessarily based on Cobham's confession, but Cobham by now, November, had been imprisoned for nearly five months and was encouraged to confess (and therefore to shift the blame on to Ralegh) by a promise that he would be stretched on the rack to help his memory. The King himself had made it clear that he wanted no one tortured. Ralegh did not believe that the other prisoners had not been threatened with torture sufficiently for them to produce almost any confession the commissioners wanted to hear.

The trial staggered on, sometimes on seemingly nonsensical evidence. There was a claim that Ralegh had a book that was written against the King or, as the seventeenth-century phrase would have it, 'against the king's title'. This was a silly point, but it was going to be pursued. The fact that it was written twenty-six years before the event made it an almost laughable piece of evidence. What was more, the book was written to justify Queen Elizabeth's proceedings against Mary Queen of Scots. Moreover, this was not subversive literature produced by Ralegh himself. He had actually found the book in the library of the late Lord Treasurer, Lord Burghley, whose son, Robert Cecil, was the King's most trusted courtier. Cecil found himself having to partly defend Ralegh, which is not what he was there to do at all.

Sir Walter used me a little unkindly to take the book away without my knowledge . . . nevertheless, I need make no apology in [sic] behalf of my father considering how useful and necessary it is for Privy Councillors and those in his place to intercept and keep such kind of writings; for whosoever should search his study may in all likelihood found all the notorious libels that were writ against the late Queen and whosoever should rummage my study . . . may found several against the king, our Sovereign Lord, since his accession to the throne.

Why did Ralegh have the book anyway? According to him it was in a bundle of odds and ends that Cecil had let him have to plan a future expedition. The trial was becoming farcical. If Ralegh had really been plotting he hardly needed a book like this to help him plan a do-it-yourself *coup d'état*. Cecil must have been a little sad. After all, he had not been an enemy of Ralegh. Yet he felt moved to interrupt the great adventurer as he made his final declaration of innocence before the hostile court.

I am accused concerning Arabella [Stuart] and concerning money out of Spain . . . Cobham is guilty of many things . . . let him be brought being alive and in the house hard by, let him avow any of these speeches and I will confess the whole indictment and renounce the king's mercy.

Now came the first of Cecil's interruptions. It was to defend Arabella Stuart who, after all, was kinswoman to the King. She was, declared Cecil, utterly innocent of any plotting to have the throne. The

Attorney General quickly agreed that Arabella had known nothing of a plot. With some difficulty, because of all the interruptions, Ralegh returned to the matter of Cobham's witness against his innocence: 'were it not for his accusations all this were nothing'. Coke then tried to stop Ralegh speaking. Ralegh fought back demanding that he be allowed to speak. After all, if found guilty the penalty would be execution. Cecil came to his defence: 'This is his last discourse. Give him leave, Master Attorney.'

Ralegh could see his hopes drifting away. Cobham would never be allowed into the court because Ralegh would destroy him as a witness. The jury, for what it was worth, would find it difficult to accept him as a credible witness. Moreover, the Lord Chief Justice himself was worried that Cobham might change his story and thus have Ralegh acquitted. Ralegh appealed to the jury.

You gentlemen of the jury mark this. He said I have been the cause of all his miseries and the destruction of his house; and that all the evil that happened to him by my wicked counsel. If this be truth, whom hath he cause to accuse and to be revenged on, but on me? And I know him to be as revengeful as any man on earth.

The Attorney General still would not have it. He said that it was against the law for a witness to be brought to court to give evidence. However, the recent case law of that year defied this opinion, but that did not bother the court, and there was no evidence that it disturbed the jury. Ralegh, this great figure from our history whose statues in London and elsewhere would survive the images of Coke, needed to make another strike at defending himself. None other would.

It is a toy to tell me of law. I defy law. I stand on the facts . . . there is no cause so weak nor title so bad but these men by wit or learning can maintain it for good and that against men of their own profession. I beseech you, therefore, consider their ability and my disability who never studied law til I came into the Tower of London. They prove nothing against me. Only they bring the accusation of my Lord Cobham, which he hath lamented and repented as heartily as if it had been a horrible murder. For he knew that all this sorrow which should come to me is by his means . . . Remember what Saint Austin sayeth *sic judicatis tanquam ab alio mox judicandi* [judge as you would be judged]. Now if you would be content on presumptions to be delivered to the slaughter, to have your wives and children turned into the streets to beg their bread, if you would be contented to be so judged, judge so of me.

Part of the trial that November afternoon could have been taken from Shakespeare. There could easily have been one of the playwright's fools splitting hairs and witticisms in Ralegh's place against the pomposity of one of the Bard's gentlemen dressed as the Attorney General. For example:

Ralegh. 'If truth be constant and constancy be in truth why hath he foresworn what he hath said? You have not proved any one thing by direct proofs but all by circumstances.'
Coke. 'Have you done? The king must have the last.'
Ralegh. 'Nay, Master Attorney, he which speaketh for his life must speak last.'
Coke. 'I protest I never knew a clearer treason. Go to! I will lay thee upon thy back for the confidentest traitor that ever came to a bar.'
Ralegh. 'I will prove myself to the end and in the end a true subject and an honest man and that Cobham is a base, poor, silly, perjured soul.'
Coke. 'Is my Lord poor?'
Ralegh. 'Yea, in spirit.'

There were even scenes of mechanical farce that surely Shakespeare could have written in his stage directions. For example, Coke, who by now was saying that he had never known a clearer treason and that Ralegh was an 'odious traitor', sprang up to tell the court,

> The Lord Cobham hath confessed that, about four days before his coming from the Tower, there passed intelligence between him and Ralegh. Ralegh had an apple and pinned a letter to it and threw it into my Lord Cobhams window. The content whereof was this 'it is doubtful whether we shall be proceeded with or no. Perhaps now you shall not be tried'. That was to get a retraction. It was Adam's apple whereby the devil did deceive him.

But the tenor of this dialogue would not end with the hero and the King's Men bowing to an admiring audience at the Globe or Rose. The executioner and not the critic waited to test his craft.

The jury of groundlings* retired to consider their verdict. Each knew his duty. Each knew what was expected and what could be expected if he failed to deliver. They stayed out just one-quarter of an hour. Guilty. It was now the turn of the court solemnly to observe the rites.

> Sir Walter Ralegh thou hast been indicted, arraigned, and pleaded not guilty for all these several treasons and for trial thereof hast put thyself upon thy country which country are these that have found thee guilty. What canst thou say for

---

* The first literary reference to groundlings is in *Hamlet*, probably performed first in 1602 and first published in 1603. The ground is the low point in front of the stage, sometimes known as the pit, and the groundling was often the ill-educated theatregoer to be found there. *Hamlet*, Act III, Scene. II: 'O it offends me to the soul to hear a robustious periwig-pated fellow tear a passion to tatters, to very rags, to split the ears of the groundlings, who, for the most part, are capable of nothing but inexplicable dumb shows and noise.'

thyself why judgement and execution of death should not pass against thee?

They never imagined Ralegh was going to break down and confess all. Nor did he.

> My Lord, the jury hath found me guilty. They must do as they are directed. I can say nothing why judgement should not proceed. You see whereof Cobham hath accused me. You remember his protestations that I was never guilty. I desire the king should know of the wrongs done unto me since I came hither . . . I desire my Lords to remember three things to the king. I was accused to be a practitioner with Spain. I never knew that my Lord Cobham meant to go thither, nor of his practice with Aremberg. Secondly, I never knew of the practices with Arabella. Thirdly, I never knew of the surprising treason . . . I submit myself to the king's mercy.

Again, let us remember exactly who it was who had stood trial and been found guilty. Sir Walter Ralegh was one of the greatest men of his time. His reputation was known throughout Europe and his historical place would survive into the twenty-first century. That he was one of the most prominent people of his day was reflected in the thoughts of Lord Chief Justice Popham.

> I thought I should never see this day to have stood in this place to give sentence of death against you because I thought it impossible that one of so great past should have fallen so grievously . . . you have been taken for a wise man and so have showed wit enough this day . . . two vices have lodged chiefly in you: one is an eager ambition the other corrupt covetness . . . let it not grieve you if I speak a little out of zeal and love to your good. You have been taxed by the world with the defence of the most heathenish and blasphemous opinions which I list not to

repeat because Christian ears cannot endure to hear them . . .
it resteth to pronounce their judgement which I wish you had
not been this day to have received of me . . . the judgement
of the Court is this: that you shall be had from hence to the
place whence you came [the Tower] there to remain until the
day of execution and thence you shall be drawn upon a hurdle
through the open streets to the place of execution there to be
hanged and cut down alive and your body shall be opened, your
heart and bowels plucked out and your privy members cut off
and thrown into the fire before your eyes; then your head shall
be stricken off from your body and your body shall be divided
into four quarters to be disposed of at the king's pleasure. And
God have mercy on your soul.

Ralegh was returned, as Lord Chief Justice Popham had directed, to
the Tower. The Earl of Devonshire agreed that he should lead those
who would beg James I to have mercy. James had probably never
believed that he should have Ralegh executed. That would have been
foolish. James was sometimes foolish, but not on this occasion. Many
people, including the Queen, tried to save Ralegh. There seems to
have been a general opinion that he was too great a person to be
treated as the court had decreed. The bizarre pantomime continued.
The lesser players in the so-called plot were executed. Brooke was
beheaded in Castle Yard in the Tower on Monday 6 December.
From his window Ralegh looked down on the execution. The court
sent the Bishop of Winchester to extract from him a confession.
Probably only a confession would satisfy the people that he should
die. The Bishop reported that Ralegh had accepted that he was
to die and that he would do so not as a feared Catholic, but
as a Protestant. However, there could be no confession. Ralegh
would say only that he was innocent as charged. On Friday 10
December Cobham and the two other senior conspirators, Grey
and Markham, were to be beheaded beneath Ralegh's window.
The following Monday, 13 December 1603, was the date set for

Ralegh's terrible ordeal. Could saving grace have been so cruelly enacted? Markham was brought to the block and moments before the executioner would swing his axe he was lifted to his feet and led away. Now Lord Grey was brought to the scaffold. He knelt about his devotions. Once again the executioner was denied. Grey was returned to his cell. Next came Lord Cobham. He too stood before the block, apparently composed, and Markham and Grey were brought out into the yard to see justice performed. But not by the executioner. A pronouncement was made that the King had not pardoned them, but had spared their lives. Ralegh immediately wrote to the commissioners, to Cecil, to everyone who might have influence with James I. If they could be spared that wet Friday, why not him on Monday? The executioner was instructed to keep the scaffold intact.

There remains a fine description of the cruel melodrama of that Friday afternoon in November.*

Dudley Carleton, Esq., to John Chamberlain Esq.,

Salisbury, December 11, 1603

The two priests that led the way to the execution were very bloodily handled; for they were cut down alive; and Clarke, to whom more favour was intended, had the worse luck; for he both strove to help himself, and spake after he was cut down. They died boldly, both, and Watson (as he would have it seem) willing; wishing he had more lives to spend, and one to lose, for every man he had by his treachery drawn into this treason. Clarke stood somewhat upon his justification, and thought he had hard measure; but imputed it to his function, and therefore

* Dudley Carleton, *Dudley Carleton to John Chamberlain (1603–1624), Jacobean Letters*, edited with an introduction by Maurice Lee (Rutgers University Press, 1972).

he thought his death meritorious, as a kind of martyrdom. Their quarters were set on Winchester gates, and their heads on the first tower of the castle. Brooke was beheaded in the castle-yard, on Monday last; and to double his griefe, had St Croftes in his sight, from the scaffold, which drove him first to discontent. There was no greater assembly than I have seen at ordinary executions; nor no man of quality more than the Lord of Arundel and young Somerset; only the Bishop of Chichester, who was sent from the court two days before, to prepare him to his end, could not get loose from him; but by Brookes earnest entreaty was fain to accompany him to the scaffold, and serve for his ghostly father . . . the bishop went from him to the Lord Cobham, and at the same time the Bishop of Winchester was with Ralegh both from express order from the king, as well to prepare them for their ends, as likewise to bring them to liberal confessions and by that means reconcile the contradictions of the ones open accusation and the others peremptory denial. The Bishop of Chichester had soon done what he came for, finding in Cobham a willingness to die, and readiness to die well, with purpose at his death to affirm as much as he had said against Ralegh; but the other bishop had more to do with his charge; for though for his conscience he found him well settled and resolved to die a Christian and a good Protestant; for the point of confession he found him so strait-laced, that he would yield to no part of Cobhams accusation; only the pension he said was once mentioned, but never proceeded in. Grey in the mean time with his minister, Field, having had the like summons for death, spent his time in great devotions; but with that careless regard of that with which he was threatened, that he was observed neither to eat or sleep the worse, or by any ways be distracted from his accustomed fashions. Markham was told that he should likewise die; but, by secret message from some friends, at court, had still such hope given him that he would not believe the worst news until the last day; and though he could be content to talk with the preacher which was assigned him, it was rather to pass time, than for any good purpose, for he was catholicly disposed; to think of death no way disposed.

The Court of King James did not sit idle in these moments. Some argued for clemency, suggesting that the King might find it pleasing to be known as Clemens Rex as well as Justus R. Others, including the court cleric, Patrick Galloway, preached hotly against remissness and moderation of justice. The King could give little ground. Carleton's letter continued:

Warrants were signed and sent to Sir Benjamin Tichborne, on Wednesday last, at night, for Markham, Grey and Cobham, who in this order were to take their turns, as yesterday being Friday at about ten o'clock. A fouler day could hardly have been picked out, or fitter for such a tragedy. Markham being brought to the scaffold, was much dismayed and complained much of his hard hap, to be deluded with hopes, and brought to that place unprepared. One might see in his face the very picture of sorrow; but he seemed not to want resolution; for a napkin being offered by a friend that stood by to cover his face, he threw it away, saying he could look upon death without blushing. He took leave of some friends that stood near, and betook himself of his devotions, after his manner; and those ended, prepared himself to the block. The sheriff in the mean time was secretly withdrawn by one John Gill, a Scotch groom of the bedchamber; whereupon the execution was stayed and Markham left upon the scaffold, to entertain his own thoughts, which no doubt, were as melancholy as his countenance was sad and heavy. The sheriff at his return told him that since he was so ill prepared, he should have two hours respite . . . The Lord Grey, whose turn was next was led to the scaffold by a troop of young courtiers, and was supported on both sides by two of his best friends; and coming in this equipage had such gaiety and cheer in his countenance that he seemed a dapper young bridegroom. At his first coming on the scaffold, he fell on his knees, and his preacher made a long prayer to the present purpose, which he seconded himself with one of his own making . . . and thereupon entered into a long prayer for the kings good estate which held us in the rain more than half an hour; but being come to a full point, the sheriff stayed him and said that he had received orders from the king to change the order of the execution and that the Lord Cobham was to go before him; where he was likewise led into Prince Arthur's hall [where Markham had previously been led].

This left Cobham, who made his prayers and then denounced Ralegh, although he hoped that he would receive forgiveness in the next world. He too was about to be executed when the sheriff stepped forward to continue with the cruel but proper game of staying these doings, and Grey and Markham, each not knowing what had gone on with the others, were returned to the scaffold. A mass hanging? No, said the sheriff. They must see the mercy of their prince. He had reprieved them. Ralegh had been watching this bit of black theatre from a window overlooking the execution yard. He was to be executed on the following Monday, but it transpired that his death sentence had been commuted to life imprisonment. He would remain in the Tower with Cobham and Grey. Markham, Brooksby and Copley were 'banished the realm'. Ralegh was spared because to have executed him would have been a supreme act of misadventure which would have done few any good. He remained in prison with his wife and son (also Walter) in reasonably comfortable surroundings – the dungeons and racks were for a much lower caste. Perhaps they pondered on the consequences of the death of his last patron, the suspicions of the new monarch, the politics of Cecil, the malice of Lord Henry Howard, too few friends, too many enemies.

Ralegh in 1603 could not expect to retain many friends. A Court society where the great (and even some of the good) jostled for position was hardly the place to expect anyone to cry injustice. That was not the way to catch the King's attention nor Cecil's eye.

In the following March (1604) Ralegh, his wife and son were sent to Marshalsea prison because King James's household had grown so much that they needed somewhere to live and lodge. Ralegh remained imprisoned until 1616. He had by then convinced the King that he would find the treasures of Eldorado and he was allowed to mount an expedition to search for gold along the mighty Orinoco River. This was the occasion when the Spanish town there – truly no more than a settlement in modern terms – was laid waste. Of course, there was no gold. Ralegh returned to London penniless and gaunt-eyed. The King was waiting. So was the Spanish ambassador. The Spanish saw the chance of vengeance they had sought for two decades against Ralegh. He was arrested, or rather rearrested. He had never been reprieved nor pardoned, so he was only 'out on bail'. On 28 October 1618 at the King's Bench Bar in Westminster Hall the attorney, Henry Yelverton, pronounced,

My Lords, Sir Walter Ralegh, the prisoner at the bar, was fifteen years since convicted of high treason, by him committed against the person of His Majesty and the State of this kingdom and then received the judgement of death to be hanged, drawn, and quartered. His Majesty of his abundant grace hath been pleased to show mercy upon him til now that justice calls unto him for execution . . . He hath been as a star at which the world gazed but stars may fall, nay they must fall when they trouble this sphere wherein they abide. It is therefore His Majesty's pleasure now to call for execution of the former judgement and I now require order for the same.

Ralegh was given the time to make his peace and put his affairs in order, but no time had been lost to prepare the scaffold in Old Palace Guard so that he could be executed the following morning. It took two blows to remove his head.

As a footnote, the fear of plots and counterplots continued to haunt the reign of James I. Each August, a prayer was said in all churches for his protection against such vile ambitions. It was the Gowrie conspiracy that caused this anxiety – the Gowries with their long history of treasonable acts.

Prayer to be used every 5 August in thanksgiving for deliverance of the king from the Gowrie conspiracy 1603.

O Almightie and most mercifull God, which doest pitch thy tents about thy people, to deliver them from the handes of their enemies: wee thy humble servants which have ever of olde seene thy salvation, doe fall downe and prostrate ourselves with prayer and thanksgiving to thy glorious Name, who hast in thy tender mercies from time to time saved and defended thy servant James our most gracious king and espccially as this day diddest make frustrate their bloody and most barbarous treason, who being his naturall subjects, most unnaturally violating thy Divine ordinance did secretly seeke to shed his blood. But through thy mercy, O Lord, their snare was hewen in pieces, and upon thy servant's head doeth the Crowne flourish. The wicked and bloodthirstie men thought to devoure Jacob, and to lay waste his dwelling place: But thou, O God, which ruleth in Jacob, and unto the ends of the world, doest daily teach us still to trust in thee for all thy great mercies, and not to forget thy mercifull kindnesse shewed to him that feareth thy Name. O Lord, we confesse to thy glory and prayse, that thou onely hast thereby saved us from destruction, because thou hast not given him over for a praye to the wicked: his soule is delivered and we are escaped. Heare us now we pray thee, O most mercifull Father, and continue forth thy loving kindnesse towards thy servant our Soveraigne Lord, towards our most vertuous Queene, and all their Princely children, and evermore to thy glory and our comfort, keepe them in health with long life and prosperitie whose rest and onely refuge is in thee, O God of their salvation. Preserve them as thou art wont, preserve them from the snare of the enemie from the gathering together of the froward [*sic*], from the insurrection of wicked doers and from all the trayterous conspiracies of those which privily lay waite for their lives.

14

POETS

RALEGH'S POPULAR IMAGE OF COURTIER, EXPLORER AND SEA-DOG SHOULD NOT OBSCURE HIS CONSIDERABLE LITERARY MERIT. It was he who, in the opening weeks of 1603, formed the Poets Club. The bards and mini-bards would meet on the first Friday of each month at the Mermaid Tavern in Bread Street. It continued after the club's chairman reluctantly took up his quarters in the Tower. Their patron's imprisonment may have cast an inspirational poet's gloom over Bread Street, but, for an entirely different reason, there was not much jollying in the Mermaid Tavern that summer. The Mermaid, like many houses of whatever repute, were deserted by all but the unfortunate. Instead of the landlord being called upon to bring another flagon of ale, the eagerly sought tipple was mithridatum. This mithridate was a herbal powder mixed with honey. It was taken in enormous quantities as an antidote to the cruel plague that would kill nigh on one-fifth of the population of the capital that year.

Ralegh, having been sent first to the Tower and then to Winchester, survived. So did his sense of poetry, admired in the new but temporary club. We do not know very much about his texts because only thirty or so pieces of his verse have been found. Even then, not all are complete. For example, his show of desperate devotion to Elizabeth I is incomplete today, but enough of it survives in *Cynthia, The Lady of the Sea** to lead us to believe that this was the expression of a poet rather than a casual verse-maker. For example, in prison, Ralegh wrote 'The Lie'.

> Go, Soul, the body's guest,
>> Upon a thankless arrant:
> Fear not to touch the best;
>> The truth shall be thy warrant:
> Go, since I needs must die,
>> And give the world the lie.

Certainly this verse, written at Westminster and left in his Bible on the eve of his execution, is as solemn as one might expect, but, as so often with poetry, is capable of offering hidden meanings the more it is read.

> Even such is time, which takes in trust
>> Our youth, our joys, and all we have,
> And pays us but with age and dust,
>> Who in the dark and silent grave,
> When we have wandered all our ways,
>> Shuts up the story of our days.
> And from which earth, and grave, and dust,
>> The Lord shall raise me up, I trust.

Watching at a safe distance, the other poets and writers stepped about the doomed Ralegh as well as the rotting form of London

* Also known as *The Book of the Ocean to Cynthia*.

and continued to write. It was this year that the sometime bricklayer Ben Jonson wrote his first surviving tragedy. Jonson would then have been in his early thirties and came from the Scottish Borders, although born in London. As a playwright, Jonson had learned his craft under Philip Henslowe, one of the sharp and practical breed of theatrical managers in the late sixteenth and early seventeenth centuries. Jonson had joined the school that produced the likes of Henry Chettle, Samuel Rowley and Michael Drayton (like Shakespeare, a son of Warwickshire). In 1603 Philip Henslowe was still running the famous Rose playhouse on Bankside which he had rebuilt. Chettle had written such thrillers as *The Blind Beggar of Bednal-Green* with John Day, another of Henslowe's in-house writers. Day was now writing with Thomas Dekker. Ben Jonson did not think much of Dekker, although the two collaborated, largely thanks to Henslowe's influence and insistence.

In 1603 Dekker was hard at work on one of his famous pamphlets, *The Wonderful Yeare 1603*, which gives us a literate description of the stricken capital. Chettle, meanwhile, was publishing his elegy to the late Queen, *Englandes Mourning Garment* . . . By now, Henslowe's power was waning and when Jonson's tragedy *Sejanus* was performed for the first time in 1603, it was not in Henslowe's Rose theatre. Instead, Shakespeare's own company put it on at the Globe and Shakespeare himself acted in it. This was far from being a masque for the living or an elegy for the late reign. It was all about Sejanus who had the ear of the Roman Emperor Tiberius. It was a text observed wryly by Ralegh, for it is the story of an intimate courtier's rise, fall and execution. Incidentally, another actor in *Sejanus* was a close friend of Shakespeare and Jonson, and one of the most celebrated theatrical men of his day. He was Richard Burbage, who was considered a great tragic actor. He had just that year moved into his house in Halliwell Street in Shoreditch which, although vulnerable to the wafted plague, was not, as it is now, in the very centre of London's life. Burbage had a financial share in Shakespeare's Globe that year and made something of a living from it as well as his interest in the other theatre on the opposite bank, the Blackfriars.

This was a rich year for theatre and prose. Thomas Heywood produced his *A Woman Kilde With Kindnesse* and Dekker was writing *The Magnificent Entertainment Given to King James*. Shakespeare, on the other hand, is said to have been in a sour mood at this time, and some fancifully believe it was because of this that he embarked upon writing his tragedies. He certainly seems to have stopped acting, and Jonson's *Sejanus* was perhaps his last appearance as a performer.

Society expects its writers and poets to reflect its misgivings even when they are little understood or recognised. In 1603 there was a rich garret of pen men. The cities and naturally, more particularly, London were crammed with pamphleteers, story-tellers, wits and writers of almost every artistic, political and religious persuasion. There was no need for a poet laureate to scribble verses in memoriam nor welcome. In fact, it was now that the notion of a poet laureate was thought of. The first person to have this office was John Dryden, who was not born until 1631 (d. 1700). It was, however, Ben Jonson who would become the first unofficial holder of this title when James I granted him a pension. 'Rare Ben Jonson' was in fine form with the arrival of James.* Jonson was a fearless intellectual who often lost control of his passions (in 1598 he killed an actor in a duel) but never of his wit. Elizabeth had been a patron of the London players. Now James followed her example and seems to have been enthralled by this bubbling crowd of writers and poets which included George Chapman, Francis Beaumont and John Fletcher, all of whom were emerging in 1603, and the thirty-one-year-old John Donne, who had just lost his job as secretary to Sir Thomas Egerton, the Keeper of the Great Seal. (Donne had recently married Anne More, the niece of Egerton's wife, much to everyone's annoyance, except presumably Anne More's.)

---

* 'O rare Ben Jonson' is the wording on his gravestone.

Writers were just as much story-tellers and political satirists as they are today and often worked as a team, rather like modern scriptwriters. Take as examples Henry Chettle and John Day (sometimes Daye) who in May 1603 were writing *Jane Shore*. Day was, like most of his contemporaries, an out-churner of words. The appetite for plays, prose and verse appears to have been endless. They were produced by the hour and to order, with the Days, the Chettles, the Haughtons *et al.* working together. They were employed by a theatre manager to keep the company of actors moving from one production to another with barely a breath drawn. So we find, for example, in 1600 Day working with Henry Chettle on *The Blind Beggar of Bednal-Green* – a famous but unimaginative effort where scene follows scene with 'damnable iteration', as Philip Henslowe observed at the time. Then William Haughton replaced Chettle as collaborator in what today we would call a second series of *Thome Strowde*. Haughton and Day then worked on the third part of *Strowde* in 1601, and in the same year we find Day teaming up with Haughton again and a third writer, Wentworth Smith. Richard Hathaway then joins Day and Smith in 1602 in *Merry as May Be* and again in what we would call a revue, *The Boast of Billingsgate*. In 1603 the same scriptwriters are on the playbills for *The Unfortunate General*.

All the writers of the day expected to make small fortunes out of the death of Elizabeth and the coronation of James. Almost anything was bought and played. In 1603 Henry Chettle wrote one of the more survivable efforts. It had no great literary merit, but it did have an almost record book-long title: *Englandes Mourning Garment: worne here by plaine Shepheardes; in memorie of their sacred Mistresse, Elizabeth, Queene of Vertue while shee lived, and Theame of Sorrow being dead. To which is added the true manner of her Emperiall Funerall, After which foloweth the Shepherds Spring Song, for entertainment of king James our most potent Soveraigne.* Just to make sure everyone understood the balance and fortune of the work, it was *Dedicated to all that loved the deceased Queene and honour* *the living king.** The role of Philip Henslowe as theatre manager and the accounts he kept as diaries let us into the pounds, shillings and pence of the English theatre at that time, as it was Henslowe who employed the writers – or poets, as they were often called.

A good play, that is, one well received, could be worth ten pounds to the writer. Dekker got that amount for *Medicine for a Curst Wife* (1602). Sometimes, Henslowe had a bargain. He paid Chettle just six pounds for *Cardinal Wolsey's Life* in June 1601.

On 5 May 1603 Henslowe was doing his accounts:

Ther resteth dew unto me to this daye, beinge the v daye of Maye 1603, when we leafte of playe now at the Kynges cominge all Recknygnes abated, the some of a hundred fowerscore and seventene powndes and thirtene shellynges and fowerpence: I say dew . . . £197.13s.4d.

Apparently the Lord Chamberlain had ordered the theatres to close for the arrival of James at Charterhouse before his entry proper into London.

There is too a record of a conversation with a famous Shakespearean comedian of the day, Thomas Pope. It is a remarkable entry inasmuch as Pope was, according to some records, dead at least three years earlier.

25 June 1603
I talked with Mr Pope at the scryveners shope where he liffe, consernynge the tackynge of the Leace of the Littell Roose, and he showed me wrytynge betwext the pareshe and hime seallfe, which was to paye twenty pownd a yeare Rent, and to bestowe a hundred marckes upon billdinge, which I sayd I wold rather pulle downe the playhowse then I wold do so, and he beade me

* 'Printed in London by V.S. for Thomas Millington, and are to be solde at his shop under saint Peters Church in Cornhill'.

do, and sayd he gave me leave and wold beare me owt, for yt
wasse in hime to do yt.

The 'Littell Roose' is the Little Rose theatre. Pope was interested
in buying or taking over this as well as the Globe and Curtain
theatres.

The greater theatre of adventure and silliness was, of course, the
subject of much scripting and opportunity. Sometimes, the subjects
for the playwrights and poets were as controversial as they might be
today. All drama was political; theatre managers listened carefully
to fashionable talk and the chattering classes were noisiest at court.
A true drama was seized upon. Thus the writers grabbed at the tales
and woes of the Shirley brothers, Sir Thomas, Sir Anthony and Mr
Robert. A simple version of their story is that Sir Anthony and his
brother Robert, encouraged by their father to make their fortunes,
made their ways with considerable difficulty to Persia. It was said
they were trying to get the Shah – the Sophy, as he was known
at this time – to join with Christians against the Turks in another
crusade. Little wonder that Sir Anthony found himself imprisoned
in Constantinople (Istanbul). Robert Cecil, in a letter of 17 October
1600 to the English agent in Constantinople, a Mr Lello, explained
the distance he preferred to keep between Elizabeth and the whole
expedition and claims of the Shirley enterprise. In that letter we
see the new wiring diagrams of international trade from China to
Europe as well as the precarious balance England kept among kings
and emperors of continental Europe.

First you must know that he went out of this Countrey without
any manner of allowance from Her Majestie, nether was she
ever, since his departure consenting to any purpose or project
of his, onely on arrival in Persia he wrott many lettres to his
fathr and freends, what wonders were done by him there,
insinuating that the Princes amity might be of great use to the
Queene and that himselfe was of so great credytt with him, as

he could undertake to settle great security and commoditie to our merchants; Her Majestie considering first of the state of those Countries and the way for trafficqu which is propounded, to passe through Moscovy, dyd not onely thinck the matter in it selfe altogether inconvenient, but dyd also forsee how dangerous it might have ben to her Merchants trade with the Grand Signor yf and [sic] such fond practise should have been sett on fote. And therefore she dyd presently cause all his freends here to reproove him for his folly and vanity, notwithstanding, before such word could come unto him he hath taken upon him to be an Ambassador to all the Princes of Europe, to unite themselves in a League with the Persian for which purpose he cam through Muscovy and a Persian Embassadour joined with him, where he was long detayned, from thence he came by sea to Embden and took the audacity to write to the Queene for leave to come to her, assuring her that after he had ben with the Emperor he would bring her from the Persian a Grant of all Priviledges and Immunities for her subjects yf they would trade there, and to that ende desired libertie to come unto her. Hereupon her Majesty hath increased her former displeasure towards him so farr, in respect of this presumption as by no meanes she will suffer him to come into the kingdome: but wholly rejected any such offer: so as you may plainly answer yf you find any suspition conceaved or any sinister practises, because a Subject of her owne is joined in Commission with ye Persian, that her Majestie could not show more respect to any Prince in the world in such a case than she had done to him, to whom she accomps herself beholding for his juste usadge of her subjects: He is with the Emperor now, and from thence goes to the king of Spayne, the French king and the Pope as he gyveth out. The project is to convaye from China the commoditys through Persia to Astrakan over Mare Caspium, wherein yf it be considered how long a way it must passe through Muscovy, which must make it chardgeable, considering yet it shalbe at all tymes in his power to hinder it, there is no man of any sense that would imagine (yf it were true that the goods of China could passe such a long way thorow Muscovy) that there should be any great Comodity had by it.

Shirley had petitioned the Queen to be allowed to return to England. He was told that he was banished. As Cecil's letter shows, Shirley travelled from one European court to another petitioning for favours. His youngest brother, Robert, meanwhile, lived in Persia and became the court's master of the ordnance, or something similar. He had married a cousin of the Sophy and in or around 1603 was sent to England as the Persian envoy, where he was give all the honours of an ambassador. Anthony languished in Madrid with no hope of return, and never did as far as we know. Robert died in Persia in 1628.

The oldest brother, Thomas, became a buccaneer in the Mediterranean. In 1602 he was captured after his crew deserted him and he was imprisoned at Constantinople. In 1603 he petitioned Cecil to use his influence to have him freed. Cecil was in no mood to win favours for the Shirleys and the English agent was instructed to make no great effort to have Thomas Shirley set loose. He was let out in 1605 and apparently made it back to England and the safety of obscurity, much to Cecil's approval.

As might be imagined, the pamphleteers, the Fleet Street feature writers of their day, wrote much-exaggerated accounts of the Shirley brothers, and John Day, the celebrated playwright, produced a hasty and titillatingly inaccurate account in his play *The Travailes of the Three English Brothers*.

Far to the west of the Rose and the Globe, a further act in a longer-running drama was nearing its end.

15

KINSALE

IRELAND, EVER SINCE HENRY II, HAD BEEN A STORY WITH MORE ENDINGS THAN SOLUTIONS, AND WOULD CONTINUE IN THIS WAY FOR CENTURIES TO COME. The year 1603 was yet another moment in that tale. At the beginning of the year Elizabeth had hopes that the sometimes fearsome conflict in Ireland would be resolved, although there was too much history with Hugh O'Neill, Earl of Tyrone, and too much sadness in her heart for Elizabeth ever to have been happy with less than the utter destruction of him as a threat. His humiliation would have been a pleasant spectacle for Elizabeth to have observed. It was not to be. She had been told that O'Neill, the most consistent thorn in her Irish side, would finally submit. He had been defeated the year before, but Kinsale was no Bosworth Field. There was no naked corpse draped across a horse's back and Elizabeth would not live to see her thorn removed.

The eventual surrender of O'Neill was more important than the defeat of a mere Irish chieftain. For O'Neill's strength was twofold: his unremitting urge to revolt and the support that he was getting from Spain. We might well imagine Elizabeth's concern (probably too weak a description) for what she would see as the unrelenting Spanish ambition to cause mischief and worse against her throne using whatever agency or arm was most readily available.

The history of both Spanish and French help to the Irish by supplying troops and money was a feature in two centuries of Anglo-Irish history. It would not end until the routing of James II's forces at the Battle of the Boyne in 1690. Indeed, some might even argue that overseas aid to the Irish Republican Army in the twentieth century was a continuation of this tradition.

At the beginning of the 1600s O'Neill fought relentlessly against Elizabeth's rule. This was more than a campaign against the English. It was a means of asserting the authority of Tyrone over the rest of Ireland. For the final thrust the Spanish promised help. Like most Irish campaigns at the time, it was mismanaged. The Spanish landed at Kinsale on the southern coast of Ireland in 1601. The operation was something of a military farce, but its effect was considerable. The Spanish landing was a direct challenge to Elizabeth's authority, and the surrender of the Spanish force to the English in 1602 was a landmark in relations between Spain and England, if not between England and Ireland.

In July 1601 Elizabeth's general and Lord Lieutenant in Ireland was Charles Blount, Lord Mountjoy.* It was in that month that Mountjoy, having established outposts and fortresses to stop O'Neill raiding into the English Pale, was sent news that a Spanish fleet had put to sea. There was no telling for certain its destination, but it had to be assumed by Mountjoy that it was coming to Ireland. The vulnerable and unreliable county of Munster, the likeliest scene of conflict and the obvious choice for a landing by the Spanish, was in theory under English control. Cork had been defended and the fortress there improved. Moreover, many who could have led uprisings had been captured, including Florence McCarthy and James FitzThomas, who by that August had taken up lodgings in

---

* Charles Blount (1563–1606) was created Earl of Devonshire in July 1603.

the Tower of London. A tax had been ordered so that 5000 extra men from Munster could be raised for its defence. Two small vessels had been stationed on picket duty to watch for the arrival of Spanish ships. Here is a reminder of how, by our standards, much happened in slow motion. Mountjoy wanted more troops. He had to send a messenger to London even though his own authority allowed him to raise men, as the expenditure might be far more than he could authorise. It took until 29 September 1601 before the government in England wrote to the counties asking for a further levy to be made on the grounds that a Spanish fleet had been sighted. In fact, six days earlier the Spanish had already landed at Kinsale. Mountjoy and his commanders had been correct in supposing that Cork should be reinforced because that would be the target. However, the weather at sea plays havoc with the best-laid plans and a veering of the wind forced the Spanish to land, unopposed, at Kinsale.

Again, the news took a long time to reach London and it was not until two weeks later that the English gave orders for the supply of winter clothing for 5000 new troops and the victualling of a total of 8000 men until the end of the year. Here is another moment when we can see the structure of authority in England in the early seventeenth century. Mountjoy needed more cavalry. Where was he to get them? One answer was the Church. The clergy were called upon to provide a squadron (as many as sixty) of well-armed cavalry. The gentry throughout the whole of England provided two hundred more, many of whom turned out to be ancestors of famous aristocratic families of today.

The instructions were quite specific. The beast for a light-horse cavalryman should be 'a good horse or gelding with a Morocco saddle of buff or some other good leather and a good furniture to it, a sufficient man to serve on him furnished with a good cuirass and a casque, a northern staff, a good long pistol, a good sword and dagger and a horsemans coat of good cloth'. Not everyone followed the letter or even the spirit of the order. The Archdeacon of Colchester is said to have sent a horse that was a complete bone-bag, 'lean, old, having splint and spavin and wounded on the near leg behind'.

The Hatfield Papers, which contain letters of the Cecils, suggest that, as a reinforcement, 2000 Highlanders were to be paid for and brought to Ireland. By the end of November there were some 14,000 men in Munster, Ulster and Leinster, with ten ships blockading Kinsale. It was quite a task to raise soldiers. After all, in London Sir Robert Cecil was having to mastermind Britain's expeditionary forces elsewhere. There were 5000 men ordered to the defence of another English interest, Ostend, where the siege was not going well. And where was the money to be found for these soldiers? Raising a levy for each man on a community was a sensitive act. It would have cost about £3 10s. at seventeenth-century prices for each soldier to be clothed and provided with weapons. Each man's weapons alone would cost £1 10s. Finding the money was hard enough, finding the men equally difficult. Certainly many of them would have been press-ganged. Furthermore, not all the gentry raised forces and money. London and those counties close by raised most. Many counties distant from London had fewer resources and also felt less threatened. Yet some who did not provide levy and men were fined heavily.*

The story of what happened between the landing at Kinsale and 1603 is really the tale of the routing of the Spanish and O'Neill. But there is an aside that should not be ignored. Given the sensitivity over the value and the future of the pound sterling, modern readers might well understand the animosities that arose when the English decided to debase the Irish shilling. The Lord High Treasurer, Lord Buckhurst, sought and was given Elizabeth's permission to devalue the coin. The Irish shilling was, at its most valuable, worth only three-quarters of an English shilling. Buckhurst persuaded the Queen to let him

---

* The vexed question of raising forces led to the creation of a new hereditary title, the baronetcy, established by James I in 1611. It could be bought, and the money used to finance forces for Ulster.

mint a new Irish shilling which was worth only threepence; that is, one-quarter of the English coin. Apart from the act of devaluation, consider the management of such a transaction. Derry was chosen as the centre in the north of Ireland for the exchange of old for new (the city was founded by the City of London, hence the title Londonderry). The whole transaction was a farce. It also caused enormous distress to the English troops in Ireland, plus local opposition; their money was, as they saw it, worthless. The man tasked with resolving the difficulties in Ireland was the Irish treasurer, Sir George Carey. In 1603 he took over from Mountjoy as Lord Deputy of Ireland. One of his first decisions was to withdraw the debased coin from circulation.

The Spanish invasion was more than an aid to O'Neill. If it had succeeded – which arguably it did as a naval operation – it would have suggested to the English at least and probably the rest of Europe that the debacle of the scattered Spanish Armada of 1588 had not, as some suggested, stripped Spain of its naval capability. Furthermore, this was Spanish retaliation for the successful raids by the fleet of Elizabeth's privateer, the Earl of Cumberland, on Spanish towns in the Caribbean. Perhaps also it was a sign of Spain's annoyance at the way the English assisted Spain's opponents in continental Europe, particularly in the United Provinces. By going to the aid of Elizabeth's enemy in one of her own territories the Spanish were doing exactly what the British had done in the Caribbean and on the Continent. Spanish influence and aid had been reasonably successful. Eight years after the Armada, the Spanish had promised O'Neill that they would help him gain if not independence, then autonomy – that is, self-rule – from England. That promise alone gave O'Neill credibility in his island, and more than half or even as much as two-thirds of Ireland rallied to him in the belief that they could shake off the shackles of England.

Thus by 1598, two years after the initial Spanish interference (O'Neill would have called it intervention), Ireland was a very serious battlefield for England and its authority. Imagine the consequences if the island had been lost: disquiet at home and a notion abroad that Elizabeth was after all vulnerable. In 1599 she sent the Earl of Essex with orders to restore absolute rule. His campaign was a miserable and public failure. When Lord Mountjoy was sent in 1600 to replace Essex, much more than a military victory rested upon his shoulders. The Blount family had fallen on hard times, and Mountjoy, a professional soldier, saw his military calling as about the only way to save what was left of the family estates. Like most soldiers of his generation he had served in continental Europe, particularly in the Netherlands, and in 1597 he had fought as far south in the Atlantic as the Azores. He was just thirty-seven years old, yet an experienced campaigner, when he was sent by Elizabeth to Ireland to undo the nonsense left by Essex. Mountjoy was good at his job, and bit by bit he began to restore English authority. So in 1601, with the invasion and occupation of Kinsale by the Spanish, Mountjoy was determined that this should be the last exhibition of insurgency. Hugh O'Neill was equally determined that he should have the Spanish infantry at his command to roam Ireland picking off the English at will until they backed away to London, leaving him with authority and autonomy.

The simple rules of warfare were never really understood by O'Neill. He was a first-class marauder and raider, which was, up to a point, the best tactic to use against the English in Ireland. O'Neill failed to bring his own people into a sensibly structured force and had neither the wit nor the means to co-ordinate and command the Spanish attempt to help him. Considering the times, the terrain, the resources of O'Neill and the style of warfare, none of this military inefficiency should be surprising. His forces were split away from Kinsale. He did not hold the hinterland and so when the Spanish arrived they were not conquering heroes but immediately an army under siege. In 1602 the Spanish surrendered. O'Neill retreated (generously, we might say he withdrew) to his own territory of Ulster. The Battle of Kinsale thus marked the turning point in Ireland's history.

It depends on whose view – Spanish, Irish or English – we rely, but there are some basic facts which are worth setting out, including who else supported the Spanish and the Irish. For example, Pope Clement VIII had for some time been at odds with the Spanish. The Pope was quite capable of ignoring O'Neill's request for a new papal nuncio to be a Spaniard. His Holiness appointed an Italian Jesuit. O'Neill and the Spanish would have liked to have had the conflict declared a crusade, that is, a religious war against the English. The Pope said no. Thus there was no religious requirement, certainly not a directive, that Irish Catholics should take the side of O'Neill and the Spanish. True, the Pope said that Hugh O'Neill was the head of the Catholic army in Ireland and in that sense this was therefore a mini-crusade. But he could not bring himself to declare that what Irish Catholics generally should do was to support the rebellion. Clement VIII believed, or seems to have believed, that such a declaration would split the Irish Catholic community rather than unite it. An indicator of the importance of this point might be that some of the priests in Ireland were not preaching against the English, but against the Spanish.

And so in the autumn of 1601 the Spanish contingent around Kinsale was in a precarious position. They imagined that opposition might come from more sides than the English. The Spanish fleet could indeed harass the English Navy which might try to effect a landing to attack the Spanish forces. There were not too many men ashore anyway – certainly fewer than 3000 inexperienced Spanish soldiers. Reinforcements were supposed to be coming, as well as money to pay for them and supplies, but the logistical maritime train was far too vulnerable to rely upon outside supply. Mountjoy's troops did not have to launch a full-frontal attack. It was much simpler to skirmish and then withdraw to safety, whereas the Spanish were at action stations, if not actually fighting, twenty-four hours a day. They were becoming weak because they had only limited supplies. Moreover they had nowhere near the amount of warm clothing they needed for an Irish autumn and early winter. Where was O'Neill, the grandly titled captain-general of the Catholics? He was in the north. He had always said that it was pointless landing in the south because there was no way in which he could support the Spanish there. The Spanish commanders themselves were at loggerheads on tactics. Worse still, the Spanish were arguing at a lower level amongst themselves. Meanwhile in the north O'Neill had to get on with his own campaign in the vain hope that he would be so effectual that Mountjoy would give up the siege of Kinsale and rush back to defend Dublin. Mountjoy saw no great reason to do that, in spite of the pleas of some of his own people in the Dublin Pale. O'Neill's great hope was that as winter approached the Spanish could make themselves comfortable and secure in the walled town of Kinsale. They might even be more comfortable than Mountjoy's forces outside the town, who had only field shelter.

That November of 1601 the Spanish at Kinsale were forced to kill off stock grazing the Castle Park peninsula. Mountjoy's men had already fired the valuable cornfields. Starving soldiers made easy meat. Also, forces led by Sir John Barkley pressed the Spanish back and allowed Mountjoy's troops to tighten their siege. On 11 November, after bombardment from shore and from a small vessel, the *Pinnace Moon*, close inshore, the garrison surrendered. But this was not the end of it. Reinforcements for Mountjoy were on the way, and very few for the remaining Spanish. The Spanish did land more men, and O'Neill's force did march south along with that of Rory O'Donnell (the younger brother of Hugh O'Donnell, Lord of Tyrconnel, who had fought with O'Neill but had fled to Spain). But it was all too late. The core of Spanish resistance in Castle Park capitulated. There was only the town to fall. It was still a long struggle, and the resistance was vigorous if sometimes less than thoughtful.

For two weeks in gale-force winds and rain Mountjoy prepared for the final battle. The Spanish were off the coast; so was the English fleet. O'Neill was on hand with 6000 infantry. Mountjoy had 10,000 and 1000 cavalry. It should have been simple. War never is. The westerly gales meant that the logistic train could not get through, and Mountjoy's superior forces were in some areas literally up to their knees in mud. O'Neill's people fared no better. The Spanish and Irish hoped that they could continue the war through the bad weather into the spring. O'Neill had cut Mountjoy's supply line – on land anyway. The country, perhaps sensing a final victory, seemed in total support of O'Neill and the Spanish, and by the first week of January 1602 it did seem that a final push could destroy Mountjoy. The Spanish emerged, and O'Neill formed his reserve divisions into battle lines.

In its simplest form, the commentary might conclude that the Spanish and Irish efforts lacked co-ordination and elements of surprise. There was one point when the Irish cavalry might have downed the English hussars. They failed. On the second cavalry charge of the English, the Irish dragoons fell back and did so on their own infantry. The whole force scrambled away from the oncoming English cavalry who had set themselves the task of butchery.

By March 1602 Mountjoy had succeeded. The Spanish were left to hold a post-mortem on their own behaviour. They no longer had much interest in Ireland, which by now was being tidied up by Mountjoy. Although money was still sent to O'Neill, it was never expected to produce much of a return. In fact, the Spaniards were still trying to help O'Neill as late as the summer of 1603, but by then he, along with Rory O'Donnell, had bent his knee in submission, not to Elizabeth but to James I.

The coincidence of O'Neill's surrender and the death of Elizabeth was important. Mountjoy had received letters from Elizabeth, with their codicils from Cecil, as early as February. These were instructions that O'Neill was to be offered terms. So sensitive was the situation that Cecil's advice was that O'Neill might even surrender under another name. O'Neill was untrustworthy and quite possibly frightened – a dangerous combination in the circumstances. Mountjoy could command his surrender and offer him terms in the name of the Queen. If, however, O'Neill discovered that at the point of his surrender and hearing those terms the Queen was no more, then he was unlikely to offer himself or to accept the promises because they had no authority. Who could tell what James might do?

Mountjoy had not officially heard that the Queen had died. Letters written from Mellifont in County Louth to Cecil make this quite clear and show us something of the tension that must have surrounded the surrender of perhaps the greatest Irish rebel. On 25 March 1603 (New Year's Day Old Style) Mountjoy, not yet knowing of Elizabeth's death the previous day, wrote to Cecil.

Sir, I have received by my Captaine Hayes her Majesties letters of the sixth of February, wherein I am directed to send for Tyrone, with promise of securitie for his life onely, and upon his arrivall, without further assurance, to make stay of him, till her pleasure should bee further knowne and at the same time I received an other from her Majestie of the seventeenthe of February, wherein it please her to inlarge the authority given to me, to assure him of his life, liberty and pardon, upon some conditions remembered therein. And withall I received a letter from your selfe of the eighteenth of February, recommending to me your owne advice to fulfill (as far as I possibly could) the meaning of her Majesties first letter, and signifying her pleasure that I should seeke by all the best meanes I can, to promise him his pardon by some other name then Earle of Tyrone and rather by the name of Baron of Dungannon,* or if it needes must bee by the name of some other Earle. Secondly, to deliver him his Country in lesse quantity, and with lesse power then before he had it. And lastly to force him to cleare his paces and passages, made difficult by him againste any entrie into his Countrie.

Mountjoy would have had O'Neill killed if a face-to-face battle

---

* O'Neill's title since 1562, following the murder of his elder brother.

had followed. Now he was told to give Tyrone safe passage, but to disguise the Irishman's identity. Mountjoy would carry out his instructions, but he could not be expected to ignore his instincts and so gave Cecil clear warning of O'Neill's tendency to break his each and every word of honour. Yet there was another element to Mountjoy's thinking. Could it be that he thought O'Neill was tired? He was perhaps weary of constant battle and also feared for his own life at the hands of the English and of his Irish enemies.

> [T]o speake my opinion freely, I thinke that he, or any man in his case, would hardly adventure his liberty to preserve his onely life, which he knoweth how so well to secure by many other waies, for if he flies to Spaine, that is the least whereof he can be assured, and most men (but especially he) doe make little difference betweene the value of their life and liberty and to deceive him I think it will bee hard; for though wiser men then hee may be over-reached, yet he hath so many eyes of jealousie awake, that it will unpossible to charme them and I do (upon assured ground) beleeve that it is nothing but feare of his safety that of a long time (especially of late) hath kept him from conformity to the state and if anything doe keepe now from accepting the lowest condition and from setling himself and his hart to a constant serving of her Majestie, it will be feare of an absolute forgiveness, or the want of such an estate, as may in any measure content him.

Mountjoy was one of the first to be told of Elizabeth's death. It was important to make O'Neill believe the Queen still lived. It was her order of pardon that was the authority for Mountjoy and the safe passport for O'Neill. She died on 24 March. Mountjoy heard in the very early hours of 28 March, an astonishing speed of communication and a credit to Cecil's pre-planning. The Lord Deputy in Ireland was one of the most important people in the high-security world of Cecil's foreign policy-making. So it was not long before Mountjoy was once more writing to Cecil assuring him that the silence needed to fulfil the mission to secure O'Neill's surrender was intact. Mountjoy, not unnaturally, also reminded Cecil of his own record. He wanted honour in the new monarch's court. He was to get it, but from Dublin he could not be sure of that.

> Touching the receiving of Tyrone to mercy, no man shall take from me the reputation (such as it is) to have beene the instrumentall cause doing this honour to my deceased Soveraigne & my Nation, and of giving this disgraceful blow to the Arch-Traitor Tyrone, that he humbly submitted him selfe to Queene Elizabeth, finding mercy at her royall feet, whom he had proudly offended and whose sole power (in despite of his domesticall associates and forraigne support) had brought him on his knees, and that the victory was fully achieved by the sole Sword of the English Nation and well affected English-Irish, whose blood he had spilt; and that so the Arch-Traitor lost the meanes longer to subsist in rebellion, by the advantages of Englands unsettled estate or at least the advantage and the vaine-glory to fasten merit on the sacred Majestie of king James, the said Queenes happy successor, by submitting to his royall mercy, and so hiding the extreme misery in which he was plunged, to have made this his action seem altogether voluntary and every way noble in him, to which he was forced by the highest constraint, and in the most base manner that can be imagined.

One of Mountjoy's closest advisers, an ambitious man, had a servant who by chance got a passage to Dublin from Wales with the news of Elizabeth's death. The servant told the master, the master, seeing great advantage in becoming the messenger, told Mountjoy that what they expected had come to pass.

O'Neill did give his formal surrender in that April of 1603 and a few lines of his grovelling text (he thought he was writing to Elizabeth) indicate that this was no languid opponent who had seen sense and who probably surrendered to a kinsman, as was so often the case in skirmishes and even battles. Mountjoy's view that O'Neill probably did not deserve to escape with his life was perhaps reflected in the latter's writing, which suggests that he too thought he had probably safely escaped his enemies both within and without Ireland.

I Hugh Oneale by the Queene of England, France and Ireland, her most gracious favour created Earle of Tyrone, doe with all humble penitency prostrate my selfe at her royall feet and absolutely submit my selfe unto her mercy, most sorrowfully imploring her gracious commiseration and appealing only to her Princely clemency, without presuming to justifie my unloyall proceedings against her Sacred Majestie. Onely most sorrowfully and earnestly desiring that it may please her Majestie rather in some measure to mittigate her just indignation against me, in that I doe religiously vow, that the first motives of my unnaturall rebellion were neither practise, malice, nor ambition; but that I was induced first by feare of my life.

Tyrone was not told of the Queen's death until 5 April 1603. He wanted guarantees that his surrender to James would be on the same terms and have the same assurances as Elizabeth's offer. James was persuaded and three days later issued formal decree for the terms, making it very clear that if people thought him too lenient, then he was only carrying out the wishes of their beloved Elizabeth.

Although the offences committed against the Queene our sister deceased, and the honour of her Estate by the Earle of Tyrone, were such as al Princes ought to be very sensible of, and not by the impunitie of offendors in so high a nature, give way to others to attempt the like: Yet because we have understood that before the death of the Queene, the said Earle having expected and made known to Her, many tokens of an unfained repentance, had so farre mooved Her therewith as Shee hath given power to the L [Lord] Mountjoy her Deputie, and now our Lieutenant of that Kingdome, to receive him to mercie if he should seeke it, Which Her purpose, We cannot but commend, as being derived from the vertue of Clemencie, of no lesse ornament to Princely dignitie then is the rigor of Justice, And for that the said Earle hath not onely done none offence against Us since coming to this Crowne, but also, as we are certainely informed by our Lieutenant, hath both abandoned his adherence to all foreine Princes, and offered himselfe in his own person to doe service upon any other Rebels with the Realme of Ireland; wee could not thinke him worthy of lesse favour at Our handes, then he obtained at Hers, against whom his faults were committed. And therefore he being now admitted by our said Lieutenant, by vertue of the power first given by the Queene, and since confirmed by Us, into his State and condition of a good Subject, and in the rancke and dignitie of Earle, And being also come over into this Realme to cast himselfe at our feete, and to testifie by his owne wordes, his unfained sorrowe of his former Offences, and earnest desire of our Mercie and favour: We have thought goode to signifie to all men by these presents, that we have received him into Grace and favour, and do acknowledge him our Subject, and a Noble man of such rancke and lace as in that our Realme of Ireland hee is: And that therefore if any man shall by Wordes or deed, abuse the said Earle of Tyrone, or misbehave himselfe towards him, and not yeeld him such respect and usage, as belongeth to a person of his sort received into our favour and good opinion, Wee shall esteeme it an Offence, deserving such punishment, as the contempt of our pleasure to expressely signified doeth deserve.

Given at our Manor of Greenwich the eighth day of June, in the first yeere of our Reigne.

Given the anger and often sheer hatred O'Neill had attracted from the English who had been commanded to fight him, there were many who wondered how it could be that O'Neill was so forgiven. Some might wish to draw parallels with a later government's concessions to members and former members of the IRA.

When O'Neill surrendered to Mountjoy at Mellifont on 30 March 1603 he did not know that Elizabeth had died six days earlier. If he had known, he might have got better terms for his surrender because he would have been able to exploit the uncertainty of the interregnum and the keenness of Mountjoy to present his new master with a victory. Instead, O'Neill's submission was absolute. So too were the thanks of James I to Mountjoy. The King created him Earl of Devonshire and Master of the Ordnance; curiously, Mountjoy also picked up a modest pension from King Philip of Spain. Such were the ways of war and recompense in the early seventeenth century. Mountjoy also became a privy councillor on 7 June 1603, and two months later Sir George Carey was Lord Deputy of Ireland.

The neatness of the feckless O'Neill's submission can be seen in a decree issued on 30 August 1603. In it we have a complete turnaround of fortune and respect for him.

Whereas our very good Lord the Earl of Tyrone having here presented his most humble duty to his Majesty and attended his royal pleasure for the settling of his country is now returning into Ireland with his Majestyies licence and good favour, these are to pray and require you and in his Majestyies name straightly to command you not only to suffer him and his servants quietly and peaceably to pass by you without let or molestation, but also to see him from place to place provided of sufficient and able posthorses for himself and his train at prices reasonable and accustomed until he cometh to the sea side, where he meaneth to embark in his Majestyies ship called the Tramontane which hath direction to transport him, and we do further straightly charge and command in his Majestyies name both you the Sheriffs of the several counties and you the Mayors and chief officers of other cities and towns through which he is to pass to be very careful to preserve him from all manner of violence, injury and discourtesy, and for that purpose to appoint him a convenient guard to attend him in your several jurisdictions and liberties until his Lordship be embarked, his Majestyies express pleasure being that he shall not only in this sort be provided for but that the country have warning from you to afford him in his travel such usage and respect as belongeth to his estate and calling, forbearing to do any thing that may give him cause of grievance or offence, and thereof that no man fail as he will avoid his Majestyies high displeasure and answer at his extreme peril.

While Elizabeth was on the throne there could never be formal peace between Spain and England. Whatever James's desire to stop piracy (see next chapter) and to create some rapprochement with Philip III, this would have been impossible while Spain supported O'Neill and while Cumberland and his like plundered the Caribbean settlements of Spain. The end of the Irish campaign meant that the new King had control of his seemingly uncontrollable island territory and that a military line could be drawn under the confrontation between England and Spain during Elizabeth's reign. One aspect of this hope for truce and even peace was that James would order the return to port of one of England's most profitable and well-founded fleets; not the Royal Navy, but her pirates.

16

PIRACY

E SHOULD TEMPER OUR IMAGE OF THE END OF THE ELIZABETHAN ERA AND THE BEGINNING OF THE STUARTS' WITH A CERTAIN CAUTION. We are too early for swashbuckling, yet there is a vision and a necessary confusion of dates which suggests good-natured piracy, sturdy adventures into the New World, witticisms at court, stinging and critical observations in the lines of the likes of Shakespeare, the pageantry of great river occasions, processions and coronations, Venetian ambassadors and envoys from an archduke, painters and poets, beamed and inglenooked architecture, jigsaws of contented rural life.

So why spoil this image? Perhaps because England was a very corrupt society. Even the terminology here has to be tempered by understanding the times and what was acceptable, commonplace and unremarkable. For example, although we often think of England being at peace after the Spanish Armada was scattered in 1588, the spoils of the continuing war were eagerly stacked in the City and the counting houses of the late Elizabethan merchant venturers. Many of the famous merchants and explorers were privateers – pirates by another name. The war finally finished in the opening months of 1603, and with it came all sorts of minor disasters for traders. The war had damaged many traditional English trading patterns when, for example, the ports on the Iberian peninsula were no longer open in that period to the English. What else might be expected in wartime? The consequence was that these restrictions encouraged even further piracy. The war also identified shortages, and apart from stealing to make up the losses on the high seas, other industries boomed. Sugar, as an example, did very well during the war years and started to tail off as a business in 1603 when there was peace. The West Indian trade struggled to make a profit and did not do so for many years after 1603.

One of the most profitable trades was indeed piracy. It was not so much the booty, but its influence on the commercial progress of these islands. It had become a totally acceptable way of money-making in Elizabethan England. In its simplest form, a sea captain and his crew robbed another sea captain and his crew of the contents of their ship. This is the common image. What is sometimes forgotten is who these captains were and what support they had, including financial backing. There is an illusion of the great Royal Navy from 1588 onwards maintaining Britain's sovereignty over the sea lanes. The Navy itself was as corrupt as any other business and often the ships in a fleet were mostly privately owned, manned and out for their own profits in any engagement.

Merchants and country landowners, the peerage and even the monarch herself invested in privateering. It was helped by anti-Spanish feeling and the idea that any ship running from a Spanish colony or to a Spanish port was more than fair game: it was a corsair's duty to capture her as a prize. In a curious manner, this common cause against the Spanish and the mixing of different economic and social classes at sea to plunder galleons produced a community and a sense of pulling together that was often seen as a magical if not nostalgic moment in the lives of those who had taken part in it. It is a sentiment in sensation not unlike the talk of the

1950s when, in spite of its horrors, people in these islands would look back wistfully at the 1939–45 war and speak fondly (if sometimes inaccurately) of the spirit of the people and how everyone, whatever their station in life, mucked in together. Thus piracy might even be seen as a social phenomenon – the product of the co-existence of ambitious traders and predatory gentry.* So strong was the City in Britain's foreign trade, and with some of its members financing and taking part in all sorts of what we would call dubious practice, that the leaders in that place were instrumental in keeping going the corrupt practices of the late Elizabethan and early Stuart reigns.

The war with Spain between 1585 and 1603 was an expensive and wearing conflict. Elizabeth's subjects by and large lived in peace. They would not have done if England had been a continental European country. Continentals were used to having their lands criss-crossed by migrations and warriors. England was protected by the steep and less than predictable seas and winds of the Channel and North Sea. Protected they may have been, but the war cost a lot of money to fight. As in all wars, money is made, and in this war corruptions were found where before few had existed. The war at sea was not simply a defensive operation. Queen Elizabeth expected to run the Navy at a profit. So did the men in the Navy. The naval operation against Cádiz in 1596 was led by the Earl of Essex and the opportunist Lord Howard of Effingham. Elizabeth had been advised, certainly by Sir Anthony Ashley, her (what we would call) Secretary of State for Defence, that a considerable profit was to be made in this venture. She was very disappointed when in spite of the sacking of Cádiz, her return was negligible. Someone made money. There were, after all, 150 ships in that Cádiz fleet. No more than 18 of them, however, belonged to the Queen; 24 were Dutch. That left 108, and each one expected to show a profit from the war. Many of their captains were pirates. Essex, Howard

* For more on this, Kenneth Andrews, *Elizabethan Privateering* (Cambridge University Press, 1964).

and (let us not forget) Ralegh were their leaders and they took their profits first.

By 1603 and the end of the war, the pernicious influence of the Howards was a manifestation of the disease inherent in the system of patronage, a manifestation worse than most because the opportunities for private gain at public expense were greater here than any elsewhere and because the normal restraints of law and morality were more easily overborne where the proper business of all concerned was robbery with violence.* Elizabeth, more and more out of control of her kingdom, suffered as some of her closest advisers used state money to pay for their own financing of piracy. One result was that the war at sea against the Spanish drifted into becoming a business rather than a military operation, and although Elizabeth in her later years had a reputation for turning a blind eye to piracy, she never really made much of a profit from it.

By the time we get to James and 1603 we can see that the authority of the state was being brought down by people pursuing private rather than public interests and exploiting all the advantages of a system of Elizabethan government that was desperately in need of overhaul. Little wonder then that in February 1603, with the war coming to an end and Elizabeth's reign closing, the Crown's officers proposed the naval reserve of not the royal fleet, but of privately owned and manned ships to protect the sea lanes. What are we to make of this? Principally, that here was the state admitting that the Queen's Navy was incapable of fulfilling its longest and most immediate obligation: to protect the nation. It sounded very good on paper. Even booty landed was to be exempt from customs duties. But the scheme never left the harbour of the officials who had proposed it. However, the proposal of such a private enterprise showed that James faced huge difficulties in his governance of England. The country was now in the hands of the merchant classes. Little wonder

* Ibid.

that one of James's first thoughts on hearing the news of Elizabeth's death had been to write not to Cecil nor to his exchequer, but to the mayor and aldermen of the City of London. James knew where true power existed in his kingdom.

It has always been assumed that Britain, and before that England, had a superb navy dating from the time of Alfred the Great. Only up to a point. Under Henry VII, Henry VIII and Elizabeth I the structure of the monarch's fleets (as opposed to the privateers who took part in naval adventures) was refined during the transition from mediaeval administration, ship construction and stability. Certainly, Elizabethan administrators found money for new shipbuilding techniques and, particularly important in larger and deep-sea vessels, changes in rigging. The Navy Board had a dubious past, but its yoke was fresh and, for the times, efficient. What distinguished the English fleet from its fighting rivals – those of Spain and the Lowlands – was that it was the first to purpose-build ships as fighting vessels, as opposed to converting merchant ships. It was not until the latter years of Elizabeth's reign that the Spanish built dedicated men-of-war. When she died, Elizabeth left her successor a maritime legacy, but, more importantly, a fleet with a structure and proven systems capable of maintaining England's maritime supremacy. James did not understand naval matters nor the need to appoint specialists who did, but he was not stingy towards the Navy. He spent more than Elizabeth did. Sadly, for Britain's maritime interests, James's judgement of a sailor's worth was not as sound as his eye for horseflesh. It took time for the Navy to sag beneath the weight of incompetent and corrupt administration. However, it did lose its efficiency and its understanding of its role in maintaining that dominance of the sea lanes so essential to Britain's long-term survival. The quickest and cheapest way to resolve some of the financial difficulty in maintaining a fleet was to stop the war. That meant stopping the pirates who operated within the remit of that conflict.

Rightly, in 1603 James was desperate to agree a truce with Spain. For this he should be praised. What he did not understand was that no truce and certainly no treaty of peace could survive without some verification process and some guarantee that the agreements would be honoured and that others would not see a pact with Spain as a sign of weakness.

On 23 June 1603 a proclamation ordered all the English vessels that patrolled the high seas and practised piracy to be recalled. The proclamation certainly had the tone that all had changed and there were now new rules of friendship with Spain. Equally, the King's acknowledgement that piracy had been an honourable as well as a lucrative trade and had served the maritime industry well in times of shortage sets the official status of freebooting very much in perspective for a reader four hundred years on. There is too an excellent illustration of the limitations of early seventeenth-century communications. Part of the proclamation from King James read:

> We are not ignorant, that our late deare Sister the late Queene of England, had of long time warres with the king of Spaine, and during that time gave Licences and Commissions to divers of her, and our now Subjects, to let out and furnish to sea, at the charges, divers ships warlikely appointed, for the surprising and taking of the said Kings subjects goods and for the enjoying of the same, being taken and brought home as lawfull Prise. By vertue of which Licenses and Commissions, our said Subjects, in the zeale and affection which they bare to the good of their Countrey in the annoyance and spoyle of the publicke enemy of this State at that time, and in maintenance & employment of the Shipping and Mariners of England, otherwise scant of Traffique at that time, not sufficiently set on worke; Did furnish out to the Sea divers Ships warlike appointed, to the exceeding charge, upon confidence to enjoy what goods soever they should take during the said Voyage, belonging to the king of Spaine, or any of his Subjects, according to the tenor of their severall Commissions.

Piracy

This was clearly a delicate matter. As the proclamation carefully noted, English sailors had for many years enjoyed the spoils of piracy with the official blessing of the monarch. There was also the considerable matter of the shipbuilders and repairers as well as the many sailors who sailed with the masters and owners in the hope of a share in the prizes. In other words, James, in search of peace, was about to decimate, if not destroy, a whole industry. James and English piracy? Thatcher and the coalmines? Far-fetched comparison? Not entirely. Piracy had to stop if there was to be peace. The English sailors who were already at sea before the third week in April would not be prosecuted. At sea, they would probably not know of the end of the war with Spain. They might not know that Elizabeth had died and that James was now king. For these corsairs there would be a concession. Piracy was, however, to be illegal after that April date.

> Wee in our Princely condition, having (above all things) tender care of the good estate of our loving and dutifull Subjects, and willing to give encouragement to all others hereafter, in time of our Warres, to shewe like forwardnesse in venturing their lives and goods for the weakening of the publicke enemy, and benefitting of this their Countrey: have thought good to signifie to all men by these presents, that our Will and pleasure is, that all such as have set out, or furnished to the Seas, and Shippes of Warre, by vertue of any the said Commissions and not having notice of our entrance into this Kingdome, have at any time before the foure and twentieth day of Aprill last (which time Wee limit unto all men of Warre at Sea as sufficient space, within which they might have taken knowledge of the discontinuance of the said Warre) thereby taken any Ships, or Goods belonging to any the Subjects of the king of Spaine, and are already are returned into any of our Dominions, shall quietly enjoy the sayde Shippes and goods taken as aforesayd.

. . . and We further will and command, That . . . our men
of Warre, as be now at Sea, having no sufficient Commission
as aforesayd, and have taken, or shal go to Sea hereafter, and
shal take any the ships or goods of any subject of any Prince
in league, or amitie with us, shall be reputed and taken as
Pirates and both they and all their accessaries, maintainers,
comforters, abbettors, and partakers shall suffer death as
Pirates, and accessaries to piracie, With confiscation of all
their landes and goodes, according to the ancient Lawes of
this Realme . . .

Given at our Manour of Greenwich the 23. Day of June, in the
first yeere of our Reigne of England, France, and Ireland And
in the sixe and thirtieth of Scotland. God save the king.

God save the pirates. James would no longer do so. This official
piracy had angered the Spanish, of course. It had, too, kept that
English maritime edge that would soon be missed at sea. The
sailors that James would need to supply his fleets were losing
a lucrative way of life. For example, one of the last ships to
be captured by the monarch's official corsairs was a Portuguese
vessel, the *St Valentine*. The cargo was sold for not much less
than £30,000, a not inconsiderable amount in 1603. It may
have been true that the English sailors were better pirates than
anything else. There was a formality that does not quite fit with
the gold-toothed cut-throat image of the pirate. Church services
had to be held twice a day on deck when a ship was at sea. As
each watch changed on the four-hour bell, psalms were sung. But
it was a raggedy-looking mob that trailed in the wakes of Drake
and Frobisher in 1603. Ralegh thought the average sailor would
have the same enthusiasm for serving as a galley slave as he might
for being an able seaman in one of James's vessels. Rarely was
half a ship's company in good enough fettle to man her properly.
Flogging was an everyday experience, so much so that some old

hands believed that a fair wind would not fetch up until the Monday morning floggings had been carried out.* Punishments such as tongue-scraping and keel-hauling were commonplace. A sailor who had slept on watch would be flogged. Should he have fallen asleep four times he would be tied to the bowsprit and left to drown.

None of this much concerned Charles, Lord Howard of Effingham, who was James's Lord Admiral. He had much to celebrate. It was he who in 1594 had given to Trinity House the duty of laying and maintaining the buoyage system. The importance of this was not simply good management – as indeed it was; it marked the influence of the City of London, to whom Trinity House belonged. Through Trinity House buoyage and pilotage is maintained into the twenty-first century. Howard, later the Earl of Nottingham, was well respected as a fleet commander in that glorious English maritime year of 1588. Yet there is no evidence that he was anything more than a good practical admiral. He left the running of the Navy to his subordinates in such a way that he over-delegated. Hence corruption and sloppiness were rife. Also we have to remember that he was no longer a young man by 1603 and was losing his grip. If some argue that Elizabeth handed over a good navy, then it was a good navy on the wane.

Towards the end of 1603 James was encouraged to appoint not a new Lord Admiral – as he should have done – but another controller of systems and finances, a treasurer. The man he chose was Sir Robert Mansell. His appointment was hardly surprising considering his closeness to Howard. To have a corrupt administrator, as Mansell appears to have been, as treasurer was something of a disaster. Worse still, he survived until 1618, and so from the first year of James's rule the Navy's efficiency declined further and further. The government Pipe Office Accounts for 1603 suggest that it was costing something in the region of

* Flogging was not abolished in the Royal Navy until 1879.

£42,000 for that year to run the Navy.* There was an immediate cutback, partly because the war with Spain had ended. During the next few years the budget was cut by about 40 per cent which, in real terms and considering the truce with Spain, was probably still more than Elizabeth had given the Navy.

A consequence of reining in the remnants of Elizabeth's privateers was that those still seeking prize ships had to sail further afield. It was true also that the English were not the only criminals on the high sea. Indeed, the English themselves were targets as they always had been. It was commonplace for corsairs from the Mediterranean to raid English vessels, and certainly Dunkerque was considered the home port for many buccaneers who raided the English coast. We find French pirates regularly sailing into English ports and robbing vessels. Considering that theft from vessels is one of the most prevalent crimes along the south coast of England in the twenty-first century, perhaps we should not be surprised. Moreover, the concept of compensation in 1603 – an early seventeenth-century version of the modern Criminal Injuries Board payments – should not surprise. There is, for example, a petition recorded in 1603 to the Privy Council from 'Michael Bell, mariner of Great Yarmouth' for 'redress of robbery of 200 marks worth of goods from his ship by a French vessel, which borded him near Newhaven, and committed great cruelties to his men'. There is another from Ralph Woodhouse, 'merchant of Yarmouth ... for restitution of goods, value 160L [£160] taken forcibly from his ship, the *Trinity of Yarmouth* by George Vast of Boulogne'.

In the harsh fishing grounds of Newfoundland, there were also good catches to be had by maritime thieves. Another petition for compensation came from four English fishermen, two of them

---

* The Pipe Office produced the Pipe Rolls. These are exchequer accounts, literally kept rolled in pipes like modern posters. They are the records of the sheriffs and royal officials. They began in 1130 and were kept until 1832, thus becoming the longest unbroken public record in Britain.

brothers. Robert and Oliver Gregory, Henry Rogers and Barthol Allen claimed they were robbed and beaten by Frenchmen from seven ships. They feared that trying to prosecute the robbers in France would come to nothing and might even have been dangerous. This thought, that it would be dangerous to take the case to a French court, was repeated by others.

> Thos. Starkey, alderman, Rich. Offaly, Ant. Waltham, and John Joules, merchants of London, and 11 others, owners of cloths, kerseys, &c., value 3,000L., laden on the *Anne Frances* of London, to the Council. Complain of the taking away the whole lading of their vessel, by a man-of-war of Brittany, on May Day last. Know too well the danger and unreasonable charges of obtaining redress in France, so beg recompense by their Lordships means.

In England there is an idea that piracy was a West Country tradition. So it was. Certainly Dartmouth was a well-known home for these sailors, and the goods they landed were often bought by officials who then protected the pirates from prosecution. And for those who could not find sanctuary in the West Country, then it was but a short sail to the nursery school of piracy, Ireland.

James did not understand the need for a navy and so left it in the hands of the wrong people. In 1603 it was sometimes difficult to decide who indeed were the right people to run the country's institutions. Corruption may have been endemic in most seventeenth-century societies, but so too was ignorance among those whom society supposedly trusted and admired.

17

JAPAN

I T IS IMPORTANT TO REMIND OURSELVES THAT WHEN LATE
SIXTEENTH- AND EARLY SEVENTEENTH-CENTURY ADVENTURERS
LEFT THESE ISLAND SHORES, MUCH OF THE WORLD WAS INDEED A
MYSTERIOUS PLACE. *Here be dragons* still adorned some charts. The
legends were not mocked. Just as English society was evolving with
new thoughts, doctrines and, most obviously, with new monarchy, so
other lands were taking enormous strides along roads of irreversible
change.

In the year 1603 a remarkable man began to change the way
of government in one of the most mysterious societies in the East,
Japan. In 1598 Shogun Hideyoshi – a sort of prime minister rather
than an emperor – had died and was succeeded by Hideyori. At the
time of Hideyoshi's death the most powerful warlord was a man
called Tokugawa Ieyasu. The situation was really an east versus
west conflict because this was the way that Japan appeared divided
then. Ieyasu had promised that he would kow-tow to Hideyoshi's
successor but, having no respect for the old order, he could never
do this. In 1600 the two armies clashed: on one side, the ambitious

Ieyasu; on the other, Hideyori's warriors and others who realised that they would have to join with Hideyori even though they were not really his supporters if they were to avoid the dominance of Ieyasu. On 21 October the armies met in what became the greatest battle in Japanese history, the Battle of Sekigahara. One hundred and sixty thousand samurai of all loyalties began, at some time shortly after eight o'clock on a misty morning, the skirmishes that would last into the late afternoon. The western campaign was defeated that day. Ieyasu gave no quarter. The western commanders were caught one by one and executed one by one in Kyoto. Ieyasu was overwhelmingly victorious. There was no one in Japan who could prevent him ruling the islands. In 1603, recognising Ieyasu's unassailable power and wealth, Emperor Goyozei created him shogun, and Ieyasu posted for all to see his heritage, the apparent genealogy of the Minamoto dynasty. The Minamoto dynasty had ruled for centuries since quashing the power of the Taira dynasty, notably in a great battle of the Inland Sea. It was through this, sometimes challenged, dynastic line that authority was claimed. Ieyasu would be shogun only until 1605 when he would retire and hand the shogunate to his son, Hidetada, although he remained the most powerful man in Japan even in his so-called retirement, which lasted until his death in 1616.

In feudal Japan there were two leaders. The emperor existed by Divine Right. He was an object of awe and cultic worship. This would have appealed to James I's concept of the Divine Right to rule and the idea of being an almost godlike father figure – except that the people in the business of government would be kept at a great distance from the emperor. The shogun was the real ruler. An English translation might be commander-in-chief. The importance of the appointment was that it was hereditary. So by appointing Tokugawa Ieyasu as shogun, the Emperor had created the hereditary Tokugawa shogunate. And the Tokugawa shoguns would rule Japan for more than two hundred and fifty years.

Ieyasu followed a military path which seemed inevitably to lead to a new shogunate. For the previous thirty or forty years the Japanese clans had fought each other to keep their own lands rather than aiming for the whole of Japan. Ieyasu was a very intelligent general and a superb politician. He even changed his name to Tokugawa Ieyasu in the 1560s and designed a new family tree so that he could claim descent from the revered Fujiwara dynasty. (In 858 Fujiwara Yoshifusa installed his grandson as emperor and became regent – in theory until the boy reached his majority, but in fact, because the regent could be the most powerful man in Japan. Thus, until the middle of the eleventh century, the Fujiwara regents dominated government. Shortly after that, and certainly by the twelfth century, the growth of provincial warlords usurped the authority of the regent and the Fujiwara dynasty lost power.) In a society which respected family trees, Tokugawa Ieyasu left nothing to chance. But power would not simply come from manipulating the records of Japanese nobility. He could only survive by overcoming enemies and then making sure he was so powerful that whoever led the country needed him as an ally. So it was in 1598, when Toyotomi Hideyori was still a minor and therefore could not assume the title of shogun of his family, that Tokugawa Ieyasu became one of the regents who would rule Japan while swearing their loyalty to Hideyori. There were five regents, with Ieyasu clearly the most powerful. The other four were more loyal. Ieyasu cared little for their loyalty and immediately plotted against them, as indeed they plotted against him.

In 1603 there was a remarkable transition from a rice economy to a society that now judged its performance in terms of money. Ieyasu set up his shogunate in Edo (modern Tokyo). He would rule with the tightest fist as a demonstration of the competent use of power supported not only by his officials and generals, but by the *daimyo*, the local feudal powers who had been his loyal supporters before 1603. The Tokugawa shogunate would rule with more than a sword, although it had to spend the next decade or so clearing out the opposition that had survived after the Battle of Sekigahara, including the very powerful Toyotomi warriors who ruled from

Osaka. But from the start in 1603 Tokugawa Ieyasu understood that the samurai, his warriors, would fail him if they simply provided their swords. They had to be educated and sophisticated. And so from this point we can see the beginnings of the importance to the Tokugawa shogunate of new forms of Confucianism – not simply as a series of moral tracts, but ones which prepared and promoted the concept of hierarchy in government and society. So the five groups in the Japanese class system in 1603 were easily identified. At the head of the state and social hierarchy were the samurai. Then came the *daimyo*, the loyal vassals and peasants, then the artisans, then the merchants, and finally the *eta*, or outcasts. The *eta* were not necessarily desperately poor as, say, in India, but had jobs and professions that were not deemed ritually pure. This concept was totally alien to Western culture, but in Japan in 1603 were the beginnings of something at which travellers would marvel for centuries to come – the Japanese arts, the deeper concepts of the martial arts, the wisdom of Japanese philosophy, and even the inner beauty and meaning of seemingly ordinary moments. Here were the beginnings, for example, of the tea ceremonies. Within thirty years Iemitsu would become shogun and almost isolate Japan from the world, except in a few special circumstances. At a time when Europeans, led by the English, were expanding their commercial horizons, only the Dutch were allowed any contact with the Japanese and then only at one place, Nagasaki.

Japanese art portrays Tokugawa Ieyasu as a broad, fleshy, fat-faced character whose scabbard may be camouflaged by the pattern of his robes and the decorations of his throne of cushions, but whose left hand hovers always at the hilt of his sword. Once the Toyotomi had been routed and the Ishida Mitsumari captured and executed, they became serfs of the Tokugawa with very little land, perhaps no more than three provinces of their own. For Tokugawa Ieyasu this was of no consequence. It was as if a feudal lord had allowed his vassals dull scratchings and pickings from some distant allotments. However, by the autumn of 1603 it was clear that the three provinces which at first had seemed of little consequence were now strongholds for the Toyotomi. Ieyasu regarded it his solemn duty to guarantee that the hard-fought-for and -won power should not be short-lived for his family, that the Tokugawa shogunate should live on and become an era rather than a chapter in Japan's history. He could only guarantee the longevity of the shogunate by destroying the increasing power of the Toyotomi over the three unconquered provinces. This was to take more than a decade to plan; not until 1614 was the war against the Toyotomi family begun and it was not won until the power base of that family, Osaka, was burned to the ground around 1615. Thus the Tokugawa shogunate was guaranteed and Japan lived in peace for the next two hundred years under the one hundred laws of Ieyasu – although he probably never wrote them himself.*

Here then in 1603 in a land hardly heard of by the British islanders was the high point of Japanese feudalism. It is from this point that we can see the decline in feudal powers of the *kuge*, the Japanese nobility, and even of the emperor himself. They became constitutional recluses. The power lay with the shogun. The shogun and the influential *daimyo* actually owned all the towns (probably only Edo and Kyoto could be called cities) and all the land. Thus everyone from agricultural workers to artisans in the towns (who, incidentally, were considered lesser people than the farmers) had to rent from the shogun and the *daimyo*. The land was therefore ruled by fearless knights, the *buke*, whose code was known and remains known as *Bushido*. Its followers, the *bushi*, were from toddling age trained to be fearless, ruthless and impervious to pain. Above all, they were trained to express no emotion. So when the travellers of Europe reached Japan, it was little wonder they returned saying that these people were inscrutable. These knights and warriors, the samurai, were devoted to a deeply understood sense of sincerity and determination. For example, any public expression of trust for a samurai was considered a deep insult. As a further example, no samurai

* The famous laws were published by the eighth shogun, Yoshimune.

would ever make a written promise. His code was his promise. The ceremonial act of suicide known as *kappuku*, *seppuku* or, more commonly in Europe, *hara-kiri,* was so solemn a moment that it was reserved only for a samurai. There is, in 1603, an apocryphal account of such a suicide: 'he grasped his dagger with his left hand without the slightest sign of excitement, drove it in below the navel, on the left side, without changing a muscle of his face, drew it along to the right side, turned it in the wound and made a cut upwards'.*

What was the great connection between this complex society under the first Tokugawa shogun and Britain in 1603? The answer: shipbuilding. The story of William Adams is one of the more remarkable tales of enforced exploration, although hardly unsurprising when one considers the limits of sailing knowledge, geography and navigation. What is particularly notable about Adams's adventure during the final years of Elizabeth's reign and for the first seventeen of James's, is the depth of awareness of other lands and their rough positions on the globe. So in terrible circumstances shortly before Elizabeth's end, we find Adams, a young man of little education from the Medway, rounding Cape Horn 'the wrong way' – that is, against the prevailing winds – and in desperation seeking Japan. To have found the Japanese islands from the eastern seaboard of South America was a feat of exceptional seamanship, in spite of the explorers who had gone before.

Adams had sailed as a senior navigator (pilot-major) aboard a 160-ton vessel called *The Charity*. She was one of five ships, probably under Dutch flags, heading for Brazil in 1598, under the command of Captain Jacob Mahu. In August of that year the fleet put into the Cape Verde islands to rest and recuperate the physically weakened crews – there were 110 aboard *The Charity*. Many died. It was another twelve months before the fleet approached the Strait of

* Hisho Saito, *A History of Japan*, translated by Elizabeth Lee (Kegan Paul, Trench, Trubner, London, 1912).

Magellan, and in September 1599, with the wind right on the nose of their vessels which had been rigged to sail with trade winds and not against them, they attempted to round the Horn. Two vessels never made it and turned back for Holland. Of the three that got through, one was attacked by Spanish vessels and the other two scattered. *The Charity* and one of the other ships, *The Hope*, met up on the Chilean coast. They were now running on skeleton crews, most of the other seamen having died from disease or been killed in skirmishes, including Thomas, Adams's brother. Towards the end of November 1599 the two surviving ships' companies decided to head for Japan. In a storm the *The Hope* disappeared. It was presumed to the bottom. On 19 April 1600, with Adams in command and only a handful of sailors left on their feet, *The Charity* stood off Kyushu island. The Japanese helped them as distressed seamen. Adams had arrived at a turning point in Japanese history. He was imprisoned for nearly two months by Tokugawa Ieyasu.

The period at the start of the seventeenth century represented the culmination of fifty years of violent struggling for power in Japan. As a later Oriental leader would note in the twentieth century, power came out of the barrel of a gun. For the first time this became so in Japan. In 1543 shipwrecked Portuguese sailors had introduced the Japanese to their first firearm – the harquebus, a recently invented long-barrelled gun which was rested on a vertical stick to be aimed and fired. In 1575 Oda Nobunaga (1534–84) was the first Japanese warlord to use a firearm in battle and so established his authority over most of the islands. It was this man who started the reunification of Japan, a dangerous ambition because many had much to lose if all worked together for a common good. Oda Nobunaga was assassinated at his own court. He was avenged by Toyotomi Hideyoshi, whose work continued until Japan was unified. However, Hideyoshi became too ambitious and invaded Korea. Overstretched, his resources as well as his health failed him. It was Tokugawa Ieyasu who, as a powerful young warrior, succeeded to the power over Japan. He spiked the peasant revolts and the opposition of the religious groupings and unified most of the warlords throughout the then sixty-eight provinces. This was the man who now inspected the talents of his English prisoner.

The Dutch and Portuguese had long been commercial rivals in the Far East. The Portuguese now demanded the death of Adams, who, because he sailed under the Dutch ensign, was considered an enemy. Ieyasu brushed aside the demand. He saw in Adams someone who could expand the authority of the shogunate. Here was a European shipbuilder and Adams starting building. The vessels became bigger, from 80 to 140 tonners. As they did, Ieyasu gave Adams honours – land, servants, authority, title: *aujin sama*, roughly, lord pilot. For all this, Adams was a prisoner. His reputation and whereabouts were known in England and various petitions for his release and return were made, unsuccessfully.

Adams was a pioneer. He built the Japanese Navy. He became an authority great enough for English commercial interests to establish in Japan. He remained an exile and shortly after he died in 1620 a street in Edo was named after him – *anjin cho*.

Tokugawa Ieyasu was, by now, also dead and the shogunate more and more isolationist. Religious efforts to spread the Christian Word were seen as intrusive and politically motivated. The Jesuits were ejected, and in 1623 the British were sent packing. But this is another story, better read perhaps in the beautifully told 1850 edition of Rundall's *Memorials of the Empire of Japan* published by the Hakluyt Society.

For now, 1603, the grand adventure of English mercantile investment was showing excellent profit. There was no need to attempt to trade with a watchful and suspicious Japan. Three years earlier, Elizabeth had given royal approval to a group of influential venture capitalists, and so the famed British East India Company had been formed.

18

THE EAST INDIA COMPANY

HE HISTORY OF THE EAST INDIA COMPANY IS OFTEN POR-
TRAYED AS THE STORY OF THE BRITISH IN INDIA. That
thought is misleading, certainly in respect of the state of affairs in
1603. The fuller purpose of the last and longest-surviving adventure
of Elizabethan profiteers was east of India, the East Indies. The
tale started in 1600, officially that is. It came in the form of a
royal charter.* There were in the first charter 214 petitioners'
names, including George Clifford, Earl of Cumberland, and Robert
Mildmay, the son of Elizabeth's chancellor, Sir Walter Mildmay.
The charter is a significant document. It is the parchment upon
which England etched its empire of two centuries later. It is, too,
a wonderful example of the language of late Tudor England, part
of what Shaw in *Pygmalion* hailed as the language of Milton,
Shakespeare and the Bible.

* *Charters relating to the East India Company from 1600 to 1761.* Reprinted
from a former collection with some additions and a preface by John Shaw, for
the Government of Madras, printed by R. Hill, at the Government Press, 1887.

Charter granted by Queen Elizabeth to the Governor and Company of the Merchants of London, Trading into the East Indies the 31st December, in the 43rd Year of Her Reign, Anno Domini 1600 Elizabeth, by the Grace of God, Queen of England, France and Ireland, Defender of the Faith, &c. To all our Officers, Ministers and Subjects, and all other People, as well within this our realm of England as elsewhere, under our Obedience and Jurisdiction, or otherwise, unto whom these our Letters Patents shall be seen, shewed or read, greeting. Whereas our most dear and loving Cousin, George, Earl of Cumberland, and our well-beloved Subjects, Sir John Hart of London, Knight, Sir John Spencer of London, Knight . . . William Starkey, William Smith, John Ellecot, Robert Bailey, and Roger Cotton, have of our certain Knowledge been Petitioners unto us, for our Royal Assent and Licence to be granted unto them, that they, at their own Adventures, Costs and Charges, as well as for the Honour of this our Realm of England, as for the Increase of our Navigation, and advancement of Trade of Merchandise, set forth one or more Voyages, with convenient Number of Ships and pannaces [pinnaces], by way of Traffick and Merchandise to the East-Indies, in the Countries and Parts of Asia and Africa, and to as many of the Islands, Ports and Cities, Towns and Places, thereabouts, as where Trade and Traffic may by all Likelihood be discovered, established or had; divers of which Countries, and many of the Islands, Cities and Ports thereof, have long been discovered by others of our Subjects, albeit not frequented in Trade or Merchandise.

The title was 'Merchants of London, Trading into the East-Indies'. There were twenty-four original directors, or members of the committee, as the style of the time had it. Goods shipped during the first four voyages home were to be 'free of Custom, Subsidy or Poundage, or any other Duties or Payments, to us or our Successors'. The charter covered the adventures for fifteen years, but made it clear that if the company could not make a profit then there would be a two-year warning period and the charter would be declared null and void. The company had just two years to show a profit to itself as well as the Crown. The venture was an enormous success and on 31 May 1609 James I would extend the charter.

In the sixteenth century Tudor explorers believed the wider world, much of it unseen, was theirs for the taking, even the plundering. The monarchs needed little convincing, yet had shallow coffers from which to buy into these ventures. The monarchy, often poor, was rarely willing to risk getting into this tenuous form of equity speculation – witness Columbus travelling about Europe trying to find a royal patron for his great voyages during the previous century. Now, at the start of the seventeenth century, navigators had proved there were sure ways to the Orient. Returning cargoes made it obvious that there were great riches to be had. Even the risk, while still great, seemed less than it had been just fifty years earlier. So, the merchants were willing to risk their considerable capital, becoming merchant venturers. Not all had honourable records, whatever the allusions (and probably illusions) in the title deeds of their companies. Claims were made as to methods and capabilities of payment that would equal any dubious deal on the stock exchange lists of the twenty-first century. Equally, these people were empire builders as well as fortune hunters, and it is from this stock that came the directors of the East India Company. It was they who sent vessels, not so much on voyages of exploration as in search of riches from the subcontinent of India. (Although the story of one of their most famous navigators, Francis Beaufort, two centuries later, began with exactly that, the need to chart waters until then rarely sailed by the East India Company. It was Beaufort who gave his name to the wind scale with which even today we measure wind speed.*) The wealth of those adventures began returning to England in 1603, but the voyages were rarely straightforward. The navigation was simple – the sextant as a sea-going instrument was not used until the eighteenth century – but with cross-staffs and back-staffs

* See Nicholas Courtney, *Gale Force 10* (Review, London, 2002).

navigators circumnavigated the world using currents, trade winds, coastlines and a reasonable estimation of latitude. By 1603 a captain could head north for the English Channel and with good chartwork, especially the use of soundings of the sea bed when closing the coast, make a successful landfall. Yet this Oriental adventure was not in uncharted waters.

Vasco da Gama (c. 1469–1524) had rounded the Cape of Good Hope more than a century earlier, in late 1497, and had landed in what became Calicut (modern Kozhikode) on the west coast of India on 22 May 1498. The first European settlement in India was founded at Calicut in 1500 by the Portuguese commanded by Pedro Alvarez Cabral (c.1467–c. 1520). Goa was captured by the Portuguese in 1510. They took Surat in 1530 and throughout the sixteenth century the biggest European trading influence in India was that of the Portuguese – all the more reason for the English traders to move further afield, as did the Dutch.

The Dutch and Portuguese fought over which should be the controlling influence in southeast Asia, and the Portuguese lost. Francis Drake (c. 1540–1596) refitted in Java during his unintentional (inasmuch as it did not start that way) circumnavigation between 1577 and 1580. In the 1580s Thomas Cavendish (c. 1555–c. 1592), the second English circumnavigator, also sailed through the Indonesian archipelago, and so, long before the East India Company was set up in the house of Alderman Goddard (known as Founders' Hall), English sailors had sailed and charted the Eastern seas.

The masters of the first East Indies Company voyage vessels and their navigators were experienced sailors in the Indian Ocean. Captain James Lancaster* (c. 1554–1618), who had served with Drake against the Spanish Armada in 1588, was the master of the

* Early seventeenth-century senior captains of flotillas were often called generals and their ships, admirals. So Captain Lancaster is styled in some records as 'the general'.

first trip. He had sailed in the first recorded trading flotilla to the East Indies ten years earlier. So too had Captain John Davis (1550–1605), the senior navigator, who was to be paid £100 salary for the trip, £200 of credit for any private business he came across, and bonuses of up to £2000 depending in the success of the adventure.* The cost of that first voyage was either £68,373 or £77,373 – the accounts vary. About half the capital was needed to buy and fit out four vessels. Whatever the figures, including the wages and bonuses of John Davis, there were not inconsiderable sums at the start of the seventeenth century.

Lancaster's 'flagship' for that voyage was called the *Dragon* or *Scourge*. She was 600 tons and had aboard 202 men. The second ship, the *Hector*, commanded by John Middleton, was half the tonnage with a ship's company of 108. Then came Captain William Brand's *Ascension* of 260 tons and 82 men, and the fourth vessel was the *Susan*, commanded by John Hayward with 84 men. There was a fifth vessel, a store ship, called the *Guest*.

The first voyage of the East India Company started from Woolwich on 13 February 1600 in Tudor dating (13 February 1601 New Style). That outward voyage was seen off with great cheer. The ships' masters might have wished the energy of the hurrahs be used to blow gusts into their sails. That winter tide was a balmy affair and it was not until 22 April 1601 that the wind was set fair for the south and the Canaries. It was an unpredictable voyage. A sailor will say that the only sure thing about weather forecasting is wind direction – and that may be variable. The long Atlantic swells were not helped by wind variations which set the vessels at odds with their charted courses. The men collapsed from long bouts of sea sickness, many died, stores ran perilously low, and it was not until 9 September that the mini fleet hove to in Saldanha Bay. We know quite a lot about that first voyage from the records published

* Annals of the Honourable East India Company.

in Samuel Purchas's four-volume collection of voyages and travels, known generally as *Purchas His Pilgrimes*.

> The people of this place are all of a tawny colour, of reasonable stature, swift of foot and much given to pick and steal. Their language is entirely uttered through their throats, and they cluck with their tongues in so strange a manner, that, in seven weeks which we remained here, the sharpest wit among us could not learn one word of their language, yet the natives soon understood every sign we made them. While we staid at this bay, we had such royal refreshing that all our men recovered their health and strength, except four or five. Including these, and before we came in, we lost out of all our ships 105 men.*

It should be remembered that the East India Company was a trader chartered to explore and trade with the whole of the East Indies – that is, southeast Asia. India, later the jewel of empire, was much less explored at this time than we might think, and the small ships of the East India Company went further to the east. In 1603, the year of the return of the cargoes to England, we find the ships as far east as what we call Malaysia and the islands in the Straits of Malacca. In November 1602, off the coast of Sumatra, the *Ascension* was ordered to depart the flotilla and set a course for the Cape of Good Hope and thence to England with letters for the City of London and Elizabeth. By 10 February 1603 the other ships were ready for the long voyage back to the English Channel and were about to weigh anchor when John Middleton, captain of the *Hector*, fell ill and died early the following morning. Eventually, all was ready for the triumphant return. It sounds a very tidy trip: barter, buying and good cargo loaded. However, a brief look at the logs of Purchas shows they would hardly roll home on the crest of the wave.

* Samuel Purchas, *Hakluytus Posthumus or Purchas His Pilgrimes*, 4 vols (London, 1625).

We all embarked on the 20th February, 1603 [New Style] shot off our ordnance, and set sail for England, giving thanks to God with joyful hearts for his merciful protection . . . On Sunday the 13th March we were past the tropic of Capricorn* [latitude 23 degrees 30 minutes South] holding our course mostly SW with a stiff gale at SE . . . we had a great and furious storm on the 28th, which forced us to take in all our sails. This storm continued a day and night, during which the sea so raged none of us expected our ships to live; but God, in his infinite mercy, calmed the violence of the storm, and gave us an opportunity to repair the losses and injuries we had received; but our ships were so shaken by the violence of the wind and waves, that they continued leaky all the rest of the voyage.

We had another great storm on the 3rd of May, which continued all night, and did so beat on the quarter [the left or right side of the ship's stern] of our ship that it shook all the iron work of our rudder, which broke clean off next morning from our stern, and instantly sunk. This misfortune filled our hearts with fear, so that the best and most experienced among us knew not what to do, especially seeing ourselves in so tempestuous a sea and a so stormy place, so that I think there be few worse in the world. Our ship now drove about at the mercy of the winds and waves like a wreck, so that we were sometimes within a few leagues of the Cape of Good Hope, when a contrary wind came and drove us almost into 40 degrees S among hail, snow and sleety cold weather. This was a great misery to us, and pinched sore with cold, having been long used to hot weather.

They had also long been used to having a rudder. It was the master

---

* Capricorn is the extreme southerly excursion of the sun in a year. The sun is vertically overhead Capricorn on 22 December each year. In the northern hemisphere, the Tropic of Cancer is latitude 23 degrees 30 minutes North and is the extreme northerly position of the sun on 21 June each year.

of the *Dragon*'s guard ship, the *Hector*, who suggested that they find a sheltered headland or haven and convert a spare mast to act as a steering oar. This was far less easy to do than the textbook might have suggested, yet they accomplished a jury rig and eventually the carpenters fashioned a new stock and rudder, only to have another storm make it useless. By now, James Lancaster had all but given up hope of surviving. Without telling anyone aboard his own ship, Lancaster wrote to London, his intention being to send the *Hector* on alone. The letter has survived.

Right Worshipful,
What hath passed this voyage and what trades I have settled for the company, and what other events hath befallen us, you shall understand by the bearers hereof, to whom (as occasion has fallen) I must refer to you. I shall strive with all diligence to save my ship and her goods as you may perceive by the course. I take in venturing my own life, and that of those who are with me I cannot tell where you should look for me, if you send any pinnace to seek me; because I live at the devotion of the winds and sea. And thus, fare you well, praying God to send us a merry meeting in this world, if it be his good will and pleasure.
The passage to the East India lieth in 62½ [degrees] by the north-west on the America side.

Your very loving friend
James Lancaster.

It was a close-run thing, but the *Dragon*, Lancaster and his ship's company survived, and on 16 June, having been swept far west of the Cape, they sighted an island. It was St Helena. The ships were refitted, the stores replenished, the men refreshed, and once more the tiny vessels (by today's standard) set a course for the North Atlantic and the English Channel. On by Ascension Island, at which ships rarely called, 'for it is altogether barren and without water', on then by Cape Verde, into August, and at last to the Azores. Then at the end of the first week in September, not land, but shallow water.

We had soundings of the 7th September, 1603, the coast of England being then 40 leagues from us by our reckoning; and we arrived at the Downs on the 11th of that month, where we came safe to anchor: For which we thanked the Almighty God, who hath delivered us from infinite perils, dangers, in this long and tedious navigation; having been from the 2nd April, 1601, when we sailed from Torbay, two years five months and nine days absent from England.

The *Hector*, the second ship in the fleet, might be remembered in British maritime and mercantile history as the most famous of the four. For it was five years later that *Hector*, commanded by Captain William Hawkins, arrived off Surat with letters of introduction from King James. This was the letter which asked the Mughal Emperor Jahangir for permission for the English to trade in India. Surat, therefore, and not Bombay or Calcutta, nor even Madras, was the toehold of the British Empire.

19

REFLECTIONS

T HE FEAST OF CHRIST'S MASS IN 1603 WAS MORE THAN A MOMENT FOR JOY AND RELIGIOUS FESTIVAL. For James, it must have been a time for reflection. The previous Christmas, he had been monarch of all the glens and King-of-England-in-waiting. He had been in the damp atmosphere of the ever-plotting Scottish court where he had long anticipated the death of Elizabeth. He had waited well, soothed and schooled for the accession by the wise Sir Robert Cecil.

Twelve months on, James sat unopposed as King of England and Scotland, Wales, Ireland and France, as was proclaimed. He liked to think he was King of Great Britain and was the first monarch to describe himself thus. He was supremely confident.

For more than twelve months he had known he could rely on Robert Cecil. Indeed, since that day in March when he had heard the news from the luckless Robert Carey, James had justifiably felt truly supremely confident that he was in safe hands – those of Cecil. Cecil would be rewarded handsomely for his bureaucratic pains. Elizabeth was gone and by many accounts not much missed.

Dead monarchs have their foibles and patronage buried with them. Petitioners and grovellers were no strangers to James. Even a Scottish king was supreme patron of his nation.

Now, as James reflected on the hundreds of new knights he had dubbed, the peerages he had offered and confirmed, and the rank and title of seemingly every stratum of civil life he had bestowed, surely he understood the fullness of his power as well as its frailty. He could indulge much of his capriciousness, but would do so under the unblinking eye of his senior bureaucrat, Cecil; it was he above all others who would choose when to stamp on the fingers of those who touched the hem of royal patronage. James now understood more than ever that he would do well to rely on Cecil. Might we not see Cecil as the supreme character in that year's drama? All power was in the name of the King. Cecil was the surest way to that power, seemingly for everyone from the most senior chancellor to the mole-catcher in the park.

26 December 1603. Warrant to Sir John Stanhope, Vice-Chamberlain and Treasurer of the Chamber, to pay to Rich. Hampton, appointed moletaker in St James's Park and the gardens and grounds at Westminster, Greenwich, Richmond, Hampton Court, &c., on resignation of Wm. Thornback, the fee of 4d. a day and 20s. yearly for livery. Altered from a like warrant by Queen Elizabeth for Wm. Thornback, on decease of David Chambers. With request by Will. Moys for the bill to be drawn from Lady Day last, or the poor man will lose his fee.

It is doubtful that Master Hampton, who set his traps for small tunnellers, wondered much at that greater picture of 1603. A job and a catch for life might well have left him more than content. Moreover, he too would have authority in his office that would allow him to patronise those beneath him – should their cause prove profitable. He would, of course, not forget to tip his moleskin cap to those in authority above him. The pecking order was distinct.

James was no stranger to the power that relied on far more than a sixpence here and a shilling there. It was more than leadership. Elizabeth had commanded absolute obedience from her people; James could not expect to, although he did not know this. Yet the official trappings of obedience had been presented to him each day of his reign that year. Carey had knelt before him – the first Englishman to do so. The abbot had secured Berwick in his name and was not questioned. The greatest houses in England had been thrown open as he journeyed south to take his throne. Coaches, jewels, fine clothes and money had met him on his way. He had feasted until satisfied. He had ordered dogs to fight lions and halberdiers to guard his ceremony. Only disease had mocked his authority. Maybe as many as forty thousand had perished and there was nothing that King, nor Cecil, nor the apothecaries and barber-surgeons and priests and mole-catchers he had indulged could do about it. His poets had strung together fine phrases and verses for his loyal subjects to dress up their flatteries. The hacks and the scribblers would have hacked and scribbled for any monarch; anyway, James thought himself more literate than they, and in many cases he was right.

Literacy, flattery and the gold lamé of privilege could not dissolve dissent. The Millenary petitioners had demanded far more than that he should simply notice their complaints. Their demands for the reform of the Established Church were awesome. He must have known that this expression of dissenting persuasion would not easily be satisfied. The one thousand ministers who supposedly signed the great document represented something far less dangerous to James's (and to Cecil's) mind than those of the militant Catholics. The Protestants could quarrel and express their indignation. The Catholic opposition was deeper and its potential consequences constitutionally sinister. The Jesuits would plot from their continental schools with the intellectual determination of what, in the twenty-first century, would be called revolutionary theology. James and Cecil brought no intellectual focus to this enemy. To them, it was fundamental opposition to the English way of life that the Cecils understood, that James inherited; simply, the Catholic opposition was the base from which sprang treason.

Had he not allowed Ralegh to go for trial? Could he have done otherwise? Certainly not. However contrived the evidence, the whiff of treason was in the air. So it was inevitable that, with old scores to be settled and foolishness to be unveiled, Ralegh would be arrested when James was not yet crowned in July 1603. That Ralegh was excused the executioner's attentions that November demonstrated the power of the monarch and more particularly the political nous of Cecil, who had no intention of allowing Ralegh's grave to be a rallying point. The very next month word from Paris had reached Cecil that the French King had recalled the banished and political Jesuits and offered to strengthen the authority of the Catholics. Did he do this to mount some assault on England? No. He did so because the French Protestants were gaining strength and the French King believed that they might just call on James to prove his Protestant credentials by challenging the French throne. After all, the British still claimed France, and James was titled King of France. Moreover, on 15 December, James had announced the suppression of popery. Few monarchs had regard for the motives of other kings and queens. Henry IV of France was no exception. There had been talk of James and Henry (before the former came to his English throne) joining forces. Nothing ever came of it. In truth, James's intellectual pretensions never made much impression beyond his own circle. Had not Henry IV called him the wisest fool in Christendom and a great king who scribbled small books, who, above everything else, was disloyal to his friends and allies? Kings had few hopes for their relations with the new ruler of England that year. Why then should Protestants and Catholics expect wisdom and understanding?

Shortly before Christmas 1603 the prominent English Catholic Sir Anthony Standen wrote to the leader of the exiled English Jesuits, Robert Parsons, that he was weary of this world and the way in which heresy had taken root in England and that there was nothing but dissension among the English clerics: *adieu paniers, vendangers sont faites* (it's all over). He was gloomy, yet he was correct. Catholics would never again have a hold over the English throne in the sense that they could change the constitutional form of these islands – which, however, would not mean that monarch after monarch would not fear Catholicism because of its political consequences. The shogun in far-off Kyoto was not alone in his suspicions.

James, now thirty-seven, the only son of Mary Queen of Scots, would rule for more than two decades. He would die on 27 March 1625, almost to the day the anniversary of Elizabeth's death. When he did, it would be said that Solomon slept. His acolytes recorded that his passing was peaceful. In truth, James was hopelessly and grossly ill and nearly choked on his own vomit. There was even talk that Buckingham,* once the royal favourite, had poisoned him. James would expire in filth and misery.[†]

His funeral on 7 May was said to have been the most magnificent and expensive ever seen for an English monarch. It was, however, considered confused and disorderly. Somehow, the way of James's first year would forecast such a reign and an end. That year was so often chaotic, a muddle of organisation and uncertainty, and expensive for everyone but James VI of Scotland, I of England. His kingdom in 1603 was pock-marked with poverty, intrigue and disease. It was perhaps a year best remembered for the obvious – the end of Elizabeth and the beginning of Stuart monarchy in England. Was it, however, the road to regicide?

It is difficult to prove that with the coming of James to the English throne the seed of revolution had been planted. Undoubtedly, the

---

* George Villiers (1592–1628) became a courtier to James I in 1614, was created earl in 1617, and Duke of Buckingham in 1623. It was Villiers who went on the madcap trip to Spain with the Prince of Wales (the future Charles I) to attempt to arrange marriage between Charles and the Infanta.

† David Harris Wilson, *King James VI and I* (Cape, London, 1956).

Millenary Petition left an impression. Conflict between religious persuasions was neither new nor abandoned. Puritanism and the protected Church of England could not easily coexist. The natures of Charles I and Archbishop Laud, and the harsh refusals of so many interested groups and parties to compromise, could never have been predicted in 1603. The nature of Stuart rule might have been utterly different had Prince Henry lived to reign. We simply do not know. Yet there is something in the nature of James I of England and the important transition in his civil service, for example, the going of Cecil, the rise of Robert Carr and of George Villiers, that suggests that this Stuart could never sire an ordinary English dynasty.

Was 1603 therefore so important? On reflection, yes it was. It is true that the Elizabethan Constitution would survive for four more decades. The people of James's green and pleasant land would prosper and breed as they might anyway have done. They would continue, in spite of that year's plague, to repopulate their sceptred isle that had been so devastated during the fourteenth-century pestilence that had swept through the whole of Europe. That year, the nation would not be at peace with itself. James would become a member of that collection of south German royalty that made up the Protestant Union. Here was a mini-alliance, each prince promising to help the other.

The pernicious government of these islands through Cecil's successors allows us to wonder if indeed 1603 was the beginning of a journey towards the constitutional crisis of the 1640s. On balance, therefore, what happened in 1603 cannot be ignored when we look for signs leading to the last time an English monarch was executed. That monarch, Charles I, was James's son. He was but three years old when 1603 closed, and none could have anticipated the irony that Charles would be beheaded at Inigo Jones's redesigned Banqueting House in Whitehall, commissioned by his father in his honour.

INDEX

Bacon, Francis 57, 151, 185, 202
Bacon, Nicholas 18
Bagshott Park 161
Baldwarden, Thomas 162
Bales, Peter 204
Bancroft, Richard, Bishop of London (later
  Archbishop of Canterbury) 7, 76–7,
  238–9, 240, 242, 243
Banqueting House 356
barber-surgeons 184–5
Barker, Robert 160, 180
Barker, Thomas 263
Barkley, John 312
baronetcy 308n
Basilikon Doron (King James) 147–50,
  239
bear-baiting 65
Beaton, David 20
Beaufort, Francis 343
Beaufort, Margaret 12
Beaumont, Francis 298
Bedford, Francis Russell, Earl of 80
Bedford, Lady 146
Bell, Michael 330
Bellarmine, Robert 220
Belvoir Castle 136
Bennet, Thomas 186
Berwick 122, 127–8, 137–8, 162, 353
Bèze, Théodore de 82–3, 226
Bible: Geneva Bible 234–5, 242, 243; King
  James Version 8, 231, 235, 242–3; on
  plagues 196–7; printing and translations
  of 22, 232–4, 242–3; quoted in tracts 54
Bilson, Thomas, Bishop of Winchester
  169–70, 287, 289
bishops 173; and Hampton Court
  Conference 241–2; and Millenary Petition
  238–9, 240
Black, James 44
Blackfriars theatre 298
Blande, George 162
blood sports 60–2, 64–7
Blount, Richard 263
Blower, Ralph 191
Boleyn, Anne 15, 17, 77, 225
Book of Common Prayer 16, 50, 164, 200,
  241, 242
Borders, Scottish 159–61
boroughs 209; see also towns

Bothwell, James Hepburn, Earl of 21, 79,
  80
bowling 64
Boyle, Richard 187
Boyne, Battle of the 306
Bradwell, Stephen 252
Brand, William 345
Breton, Nicholas 27–8
Brienne, Count of 80
Bristol 57
Brito, Jean 232
Brooke, George 269–70, 271, 272, 278,
  279, 287, 289
Brooke, Henry see Cobham, Lord
Brooksby, Bartholomew 269, 291
Brummell, Beau 67
Buchanan, George 81–2, 83–4, 85, 94
Buckhurst, Lord see Dorset, Thomas
  Sackville, Earl of
Buckingham, Duke of see Villiers, George
Burbage, Richard 297–8
Burchall, Thomas 263–4
Burghley, Lord see Cecil, William
Bushido 337
Bye plot 221, 272, 274

Cabral, Pedro Alvarez 344
Cádiz, sack of 323
Caernarvon Castle 162
Caesar, Sir Julius 204n
Calais 13, 20, 21
Calicut 344
Calvin, John 216–17
Calvinism 215, 216–17, 229, 230; Dutch
  19; Scottish 3, 20, 235
Cambridge Group for the History of
  Population and Social Structure 34, 35
Cambridge University 56, 139, 241; and
  Bible 233, 243; records of rents and
  prices 43, 44
Campion, Edmund 22
Canterbury, province of 206, 222
Cape Horn 338, 339
Cape of Good Hope 347, 348
Carberry Hill, Battle of 21, 80
Carey, George, Lord Hunsdon 105,
  309, 319
Carey, Robert 2, 102–7, 122, 126, 159, 353
Carey family 129

Gibb, John 141
Giffard, George 255–6
Globe Theatre 5, 297–8, 301
Gloucester 163–4
Glover, Mary 248–50, 251–2
Goble, James 262–3
gold standard 5–6
golf 83
government: corruption 206, 209, 210–11; five branches of 203–6; role of patronage 207, 209, 210, 212; *see also* local government
Gowrie, William Ruthven, Earl of 79, 87, 88, 151
Gowrie conspiracy 79n, 293–4
Goyozei, Emperor 334
Gratwike, Henry 262–3
grave-robbing 247
Gray, Ralph 128–9
Gray, Robert 44
Greenwich Palace: court 118–20, 158
Gregory, Robert and Oliver 331
Grey, Jane 16–17, 39
Grey, Lord, de Wilton 269–70, 271, 287, 288, 289, 290–1
groundlings 285
Guest (ship) 345
Guevara, Henry 162
Guildford, Henry 161
Guise, Duke of 24, 89
Gunpowder Plot 218, 224
Gutenberg, Johannes 232–3

Hampton, Richard 352
Hampton Court Conference 75, 76, 240–3
Hampton Court Palace 176, 181
handwriting 203–4
hara-kiri 338
Harrington, John 162
Harrison, Johane, and daughter 257–60
Harvie, William 264–5
Hastings 265
Hatfield Papers 308
Hathaway, Richard 299
Haughton, William 299
Hawkins, William 349
Hayward, John, captain 345
Hayward, Sir John (writer) 27
Hector (ship) 345, 346, 348, 349

Henry IV, king of France 74–5, 354
Henry VI, king of England 12
Henry VII, king of England 11, 12–13, 275, 325
Henry VIII, king of England 12, 13, 14–16, 112n, 216, 325; marriages 13, 14, 15
Henry, prince (son of James) 94–5, 146, 356; character and abilities 150–1; custody dispute over 125–6; death 151; education 204; James's gifts and advice to 147–50; popularity 151
Henslowe, Philip 65, 297, 299, 300
Hentzner, Paul 118–21
Hepburn, James *see* Bothwell, Earl of
Herbert, Philip *see* Pembroke, Earl of
Herring, Francis 192
Heywood, Thomas 298
Hideyori, shogun *see* Toyotomi Hideyori
Hideyoshi, shogun *see* Toyotomi Hideyoshi
highwaymen 46
holidays 164
Holyrood House 81, 122
Home, Alexander, Lord 107, 125, 126
Home, George 142
Hooke, Christopher 181, 186
Hope, The (ship) 339
horses 61
Horsham gaol 263–5
households 35
Howard, Catherine 15
Howard, Charles (Lord Howard of Effingham, later Earl of Nottingham) 100, 323–4, 329
Howard, Frances *see* Essex, Countess of
Howard, Henry (later Earl of Northampton) 8, 100, 101, 291
Howard, Thomas *see* Norfolk, Duke of
Howard, Thomas (Lord Howard de Walden) 100, 142, 143, 273
Howard family 202, 203
Howes, Edmund 173–4
Huguenots 19, 86
hundreds 208
Hunks, Harry 65
Hunsdon, Lord *see* Carey, George
Hunter-Blair, Oswald 175
hunting 31, 60–2
husbandmen 33
hygiene 145, 179

Index

Mint 5, 156, 163, 206
mole-catcher 352
monarchy, role of 180
Moray, James Stewart, Earl of 80
Morton, James Douglas, Earl of 23–4, 85
Moryson, Fynes 29–32
Moses, Miles 225–8, 230
Mountjoy, Charles Blount, Lord (later
    Earl of Devonshire): and Irish campaign
    306–7, 309, 310, 311, 312–17, 318, 319;
    and Ralegh's trial 273, 287
Muggins, William 191–2
Munster 306–7
Murray, William 84

Nagasaki 336
Nash(e), Thomas 41
navigation 343–4
Navy, Japanese 340
Navy, Royal 206, 323, 324, 325, 329–30,
    331; buoyage system 329; daily life at sea
    328–9; finances 329–30; and Ireland 311;
    prize money 108; purchase of supplies
    for 161
Neville family 23
Newark on Trent 137
Newcastle 129, 130
Newfoundland 45, 46, 330–1
Norden, John 27, 54–6
Norfolk, Thomas Howard, Duke of 22–3
Northampton, Earl of see Howard, Henry
Northampton, Marchioness of 139
northern England 6, 71, 206
Northumberland, Duke of see Warwick,
    Earl of
Northumberland, Henry Percy, Earl of
    95, 101
Norwich 34, 57, 225; diocese of 222
Nottingham, Earl of see Howard,
    Charles

Oda Nobunaga 339
O'Donnell, Rory 312, 313
Oldisworth, William 163
O'Neill, Hugh see Tyrone, Earl of
Ordnance Office 206
Osaka 337
Ostend, siege of 308
Overbury, Thomas 58–9

Oxford University 56, 241; and Bible 233,
    243; records of rents and prices 43, 44

Paiton, John 122–3
pamphleteers 47–51, 181, 298, 303
Parham, Edward 269, 273
Paris 234
parishes 208, 222; and church livings
    76; and plague 180; poor relief 44;
    records 34, 35
Parker, Matthew 19
Parkins, Francis 162
parliament 180, 211, 224, 240, 256;
    Catholic peers 223; Charles I and 200
Parr, Catherine 15
Parsons (Persons), Robert 22, 98, 354–5
Pass Notes 186–8
Patagonia 138
patronage 207, 209, 210, 212, 324
Pavyer, Thomas 183
peace commissioners 208
Peasants' Revolt (1381) 233
Peckham, Henry 265
Pembroke, Countess of see Clifford, Anne
Pembroke, Philip Herbert, Earl of
    109, 175
Pepys, Samuel 206
Percy family 23
Perkins, William 254–5
petty constables 208, 209
Philip II, king of Spain 13 14, 17, 22,
    86–7, 90
Philip III, king of Spain 14, 319, 320
physicians 184–5, 196, 250, 251–2
Pipe Office Accounts 329, 330n
piracy 154–5, 321–5; compensation 330–1;
    daily life at sea 328–9; foreign 330–1;
    George Clifford and 108; James opposes
    75, 76, 155, 320; James recalls all vessels
    326–8; Thomas Shirley and 303; West
    Country tradition 331
Pius V, pope 23
Pius IX, pope 217
plague 32, 46, 179–97, 272–3, 353; Church
    and 181, 185–8, 194–7; death rate 3–4,
    192; effect on coronation celebrations
    158, 164, 165–7, 176; Lodge's treatise on
    28; official measures against 179–82; Pass
    Notes 186–8; suggested causes 188–9,

385